The MILES DAVIS Companion

The MILES DAVIS Companion

Four Decades of Commentary

Edited by
GARY CARNER

OMNIBUS PRESS
LONDON · NEW YORK · SYDNEY

Exclusive Distributors
Book Sales Limited,
8/9 Frith Street,
London W1V 5TZ, UK.

To the Music Trade Only:
Music Sales Limited,
8/9 Frith Street,
London W1V 5TZ, UK.

A catalogue record for this book is available from the British Library.

Visit Omnibus Press at http://www.musicsales.co.uk

This paper meets the requirements of ANSI/NISO Z39.48-1992 (Permanence of Paper).

Contents

Acknowledgments

My deepest thanks go to Bill Kirchner, who so graciously helped me every step of the way. Don Luck at the Institute of Jazz Studies, Rutgers University, was enormously helpful too, as were the reference librarians at the Montclair, New Jersey, Public Library.

Thanks to everyone at Schirmer, especially Richard Carlin and Alicia Williamson. Thanks also to the staff of the Institute of Jazz Studies, David Pullman, Hilda Cosmo, Kelly Rogers, Francis Davis, Win Hinkle, Steven Lowy, Kweli Wright, Evelyn Bernal, Charlie Lourie, Warren Drabek, Pam Bendich, Laura Oblensky, Chris Calhoun, Toby Gleason, Kevin Maher, Eric Perret, Carol Christiansen, Bob Blumenthal, Dawad Philip, Rob Cohen, Theresa Weber, Amy Yellin, Christine Buckley, Julie Compton, Jane Feather, Peggy Walsh, Frank Alkyer, Laurie Lesher, Lewis Porter, Ira Berger, Katsuya Yoshida, Jeff Kent, Joy Matkowski, all the contributors to this collection, my wife, Nancy, my daughter, Erin, and all others who helped me along the way.

Introduction

On a sunny morning in late September, I received a call from Richard Carlin, my editor at Schirmer Books. "How would you like to do a Miles Davis reader?" he asked. "Well," I replied, "I'd love to do it but Bill Kirchner is already doing a Miles reader for the Smithsonian and he's been working on it for years." "There's room for two books on Miles Davis," Carlin said. "Our book is going to be aimed at a general audience, for the reader who doesn't know that much about jazz or Miles already."

I listened to Carlin's offer with burgeoning interest. I had admired Miles Davis and his music forever. Davis was a seminal jazz artist whose creative activity spanned four decades. He created several styles, constantly changing his musical outlook, often to the dismay of critics and fans. More than just an important jazz artist, he was one of the leading American artists of our time, one whose life as well as art had raised many provocative questions that many writers have addressed (and will continue to ponder for years to come). Carlin answered my questions about the scope of the project, the intended audience, the logistics of obtaining permissions, everything I could ask. Nevertheless, I remained skeptical. Carlin wanted the book done in three months and I wasn't sure that was possible.

I decided to talk to Bill first before accepting the job. I told Carlin, "It sounds good. I'd like to do the book and help you out. Let me call Bill and I'll get back to you." "O.K.," he said.

I told Bill that, if I were to take on the Miles Davis project, I would publish entirely different pieces. I viewed my project as a complement to his. After hearing his impressive list of contributors, I recalled other articles he wasn't using that I assumed I could. I told Bill I wanted to fill in gaps; to serve the jazz community, as I knew he had, by making a new set of pieces available for study. In short, I wanted to be collaborative, not competitive. I told Bill all my hopes for the Schirmer book and how I felt about it. "More power to you," Bill said, noting that he wouldn't object to my tackling the work. After a few minutes I told him that I had decided to do the project. He wished me good luck and we hung up.

I called Richard Carlin back and told him we should proceed. I knew that Bill had claimed many good pieces already but I moved ahead with cautious optimism. I spent the next few weeks reading anything on Miles Davis I could get my hands on. At home, at the bottom of a box I hadn't unpacked for years, I found a crumpled copy of Amiri Baraka's profile of Miles for the *New York Times*. In another box I found a yellowing copy of the *Village Voice* supplement, "Miles Davis at 60." I gathered all my Miles LPs and read the liner notes without getting a paper cut.

Then I went to the Institute of Jazz Studies. In their "Miles Davis" vertical file, amid scads of press releases and what seemed like a thousand clippings, I found new treasures: an interview conducted by Stephen Davis, an obituary written by Marc Crawford, even a reprinted letter by Davis's trumpet teacher. These were fascinating pieces I believed very few "jazz people" had seen. And who knew of the Benny Golson and Bob Brookmeyer record reviews I found later?

All those books with all those chapters on Miles! At last I knew I could assemble a dream team of 20–30 pieces that would convey the entire sweep of Miles Davis's career. None of them would be in Bill's book. But could I get them for the anthology? Could I get it done in three months? I remembered Bill's goodbye: he knew it was going to be a challenge. A few weeks later I called him for some phone numbers. I told him I had selected the pieces and it was time to go after permissions. "Ahhh, the fun's over," Bill said. "Now the real work begins!"

I started with a cover letter and a standard permission form. I faxed them to whomever I thought retained the copyright in question. Most of the faxes got there, some didn't. Some acknowledged my follow-up calls, some didn't. Some were the wrong addressees altogether. I learned as I went. I knew they had heard urgent pleas about deadlines but I really meant it. Most empathized and made me a priority.

I didn't get all the pieces I wanted. That didn't surprise me, actually. I had planned to follow Buchanan's opening letter with the first two chapters of *Miles: The Autobiography*. Couldn't I expect special treatment from Simon & Schuster, one of Schirmer's sister imprints? Sadly, the answer was "no." I also hoped to include Alex Haley's *Playboy* interview as a postlude to Dan Morgenstern's Prestige essay. However, I learned that

Ballantine had a three-year exclusive contract for it. From Oxford University Press, I requested "Talking with Miles" (a Francis Davis piece from his book *Outcats*), a musicological overview from Thomas Owens's book on bebop, and two pieces by Gene Santoro, one regarding Davis's work with Teo Macero; unfortunately, none of these pieces were available.

Like a baseball manager who's lost a marquee player, I reassessed my team and looked for replacements. I knew from the beginning that I couldn't choose the best pieces by the best writers that Bill didn't use. It was more important to select intelligent articles that spoke to each other and collectively traversed the whole terrain. I passed over many good pieces and banished them to the bibliography. Eventually, I found what I needed.

Looking back, I've learned a bit about Miles Davis after three months on the job but I won't pretend to be an expert. (If anyone wants to talk Pepper Adams, that's a different matter.) What I've tried to do, what I've had time to do, is to collect a panoply of interesting pieces from varying perspectives. Articles that capture Davis at important moments in his career. Articles that let him speak: Nat Hentoff with Davis after he'd vanquished his heroin addiction, Stephen Davis in Miles's townhouse after he's been busted, and Eric Nisenson's account of Davis's period of seclusion in the 1970s, to mention just three examples. I've tried to strike a balance between broad overviews and narrow accounts of particular bands, periods, or recordings. I've tried to give a sense of Miles Davis the man, not just Davis the trumpeter, bandleader, or recording artist. Hagiography doesn't interest me in the least.

I can't say I agree with everything the authors have written but that's intentional. I've structured the anthology to be as lively and wide-ranging as possible; one that reveals the breadth of thinking that Davis's life has inspired. For those put off by provocative commentary, may I offer you the words of Duke Ellington? A television interviewer once asked the maestro about critics who had dismissed his work. Ellington thought a moment, shook his head, and said, "Tolerance. Yes, that's what we need. What we need is more tolerance."

Hopefully, my own thoughts about jazz will be tolerated too. In the headnotes to each piece I've tried to express some of my views while highlighting major points for the curious or harried. For me, the more common approach of delineating the impressive credentials of each author is less useful than a concatenation of abstracts occasionally spiked with some old-fashioned subjectivity. (For those truly curious about the contributors, I've offered brief biographies of them at the back of the book.)

I have kept my own editorial amendments to a minimum, silently correcting obvious typos and misspellings. For years, it was believed Miles Davis's birthdate was May 25th; in his autobiography, Miles gives the date as May 26th, so I have changed this date in all of the contributions to the book.

This book is not meant to replace a biography of Davis. For the beginning reader who is not aware of Davis's life or times, I've concluded the book with a chronology, which will hopefully fill in the gaps. A bibliography of other articles and books is also included for further study.

Gary Carner
DECEMBER 1995

LETTER TO DAVID BRESKIN
ELWOOD BUCHANAN

The following letter, written by Miles Davis's first trumpet instructor, functioned as an epigraph to David Breskin's portrait of Davis for the September 29, 1983, issue of *Rolling Stone*. Throughout the years Elwood Buchanan was always graciously credited by Davis for having first shaped him as an instrumentalist. In *Miles: The Autobiography*, for example, Davis wrote, "My sound comes from my high school teacher." To his credit, Davis could use understatement in conversation just as surely as in a trumpet solo. But Davis wasn't suggesting that he merely copied Buchanan's tone. Rather, Buchanan's approach to the horn—his timbre, the way he held the instrument, his basic attitude while playing—was a template for Davis to personalize (as Buchanan urged him to do) into a highly original and influential style.

Judging from the letter, it would seem that Buchanan first recommended his prized student to audition for the job with Eddie Randall's Blue Devils. Davis, when recounting the event, simply maintained that Irene Birth, his high school sweetheart, "dared" him to phone Randall. Davis in turn made the call, went to the audition, and was hired for the gig. But Davis, like Count Basie, excelled at paring things down to their essentials, and his view of this episode is probably only part of the story. It is more likely that Birth challenged the ever-shy Davis to make that important call after Buchanan had first given Davis entrée.

Dear Sir:

I started Miles Davis out on trumpet in the sixth grade at the Corpus Attucks School about September 1937. He continued training with me at Lincoln Junior High School in 1938. He was playing good them. He remained with me through senior high school. He was one of my most progressive students in the Lincoln High School Band (and the instrumental program in Public School District 189 in East St. Louis, Illinois).

Miles Dewey Davis III was born on May 26th, 1926, in Alton Illinois. Miles' father was not only a respected citizen and dentist but a prosperous landowner. As the result of Miles' outstanding ability, I got his father to get him a trumpet of his own. After great success in the Lincoln High School Concert and Marching Band, he graduated about 1943. He was one of the best musicians I ever taught in instrumental music. He received all first awards with my band groups that competed in the Illinois State High School Music Association contests.

I had him try out with Eddie Randle's St. Louis "Blue Devils" Jazz Band. Miles gained recognition and received a scholarship to the Juilliard School of Music. His mother wanted him to go to Fisk University in Nashville, Tennessee. It took Miles almost a year to convince his father to allow him to go to New York, but he finally relented, much to the dismay of his mother, Mrs. Davis. When Miles was nineteen, still naive but strong-willed, he arrived in New York City.

Miles had mixed feelings about Juilliard. He really had gone to New York to try to hook up with Charlie Parker and his band. He met Charlie Parker in St. Louis at the Riviera Nite Club on Delmar at Taylor Avenue. (Big bands played there—Duke Ellington, Billy Eckstine, Jimmie Lunceford, Count Basie and others.) I think one semester was enough for Miles at Juilliard. He caught up with Charlie Parker and Dizzy Gillespie. After a while in New York, Miles lived with Parker one year. On Parker's first record as a leader he decided to take Miles. From then until present, Miles Dewey Davis III has been one of the top jazz musicians.

Sincerely,
Elwood C. Buchanan Sr.

THE COMPLETE PRESTIGE RECORDINGS
DAN MORGENSTERN

This biographical overview was published in 1980 as part of the highly ambitious twelve-record boxed set, *Miles Davis Chronicle: The Complete Prestige Recordings*. Very soon after its release Davis returned to the jazz scene with a new band and a new recording after a six-year layoff. The eighties would prove to be an active time for the trumpeter, capped by the 1989 publication of his autobiography. In it Davis would question the authenticity of the 1962 *Playboy* interview he did with writer Alex Haley. Nevertheless, that interview—the prototype for all *Playboy* interviews to follow—remains a powerful indictment of white America that should still be consulted.

Hopefully the republication of Morgenstern's piece will impel researchers to finally take note of the private recording that Davis's sister, Dorothy, claims Davis made in St. Louis in the summer of 1944 with an unknown rhythm-and-blues band. Although Morgenstern first alerted researchers to this session fifteen years ago, the recording has not surfaced despite voluminous research on Davis's career since then, particularly Jan Lohmann's fine Davis discography, *The Sound of Miles Davis*.

Those interested in the fascinating details of Davis's very early life, which were not available to Morgenstern at the time of his research, should read the first two chapters of *Miles: The Autobiography*.

Daring and style, or if you prefer, guts and grace, are two essential characteristics of the extraordinary trumpeter, leader, composer, and perpetual catalyst born Miles Dewey Davis, Jr. in Alton, Illinois, on May 26, 1926.

Alton lies about 25 miles upstream from St. Louis on the Mississippi, and Miles actually grew up even closer to that venerable ragtime and jazz center—in East St. Louis, right across the river. The town is notorious as the site of the First World War's ugliest race riot, on July 2, 1917. The trigger was employment of blacks in a factory holding government contracts. Six thousand blacks were driven from their homes; forty of them and eight whites were killed. The riot was followed by the NAACP's famous "silent parade" down New York's Fifth Avenue on July 28, an event that in its dignity and moral force was a direct precursor of civil rights actions to come.

By 1927, when the Davis family moved there, East St. Louis was once again a relatively peaceful industrial town of no particular distinction, with a sizable black population. The family was a solid and highly respectable one. Miles's father was a successful dentist and oral surgeon. A grandfather had held a large parcel of land in Arkansas, and Dr. Davis owned a 200-acre farm in nearby Millstadt, Illinois where he raised prize hogs and cattle. Mrs. Davis was socially active and later became a prominent Urban Leaguer in Chicago.

Miles's course in life was set on his thirteenth birthday, when his father presented him with a trumpet. Mrs. Davis had wanted the instrument to be a violin, but, as Miles quipped years later, "my father gave me the trumpet because he loved my mother so much." Actually, there was a less indirect reason for the choice. Dr. Davis had a patient, Elwood Buchanan, who taught trumpet in the St. Louis high school system and also came to the East St. Louis grade schools once a week. He strongly recommended that the dentist's son be given a trumpet.

St. Louis was a trumpet city, close enough to New Orleans to have heard Louis Armstrong early, when he played on the riverboats and made forays inland to jam. Charlie Creath, Ed Allen, Dewey Jackson and Louis Metcalfe were among the native sons who'd made musical names for themselves, locally and far afield, during the 1920's. During the next decade, it was the turn of Harold (Shorty) Baker, Irving (Mouse) Randolph, and golden-toned Joe Thomas from nearby Webster Groves. Baker, after playing with Andy Kirk, became a star in the Ellington firmament and later joined Johnny Hodges's little band when John Coltrane was a member; he was an early and lasting Davis favorite. Randolph played with Fletcher Henderson and Cab Calloway; Thomas was in the lead chair of Fletcher's great 1936 band. There were also such local favorites as Walter (Crack) Stanley, with the Jeter-Pillars Orchestra at the Coronado Hotel; George Hudson; and up-and-coming Clark Terry. Many of these trumpeters were notable for their purity of sound and sparing use of vibrato.

Vibrato was Mr. Buchanan's *bête noire*. He told his students, of whom Miles soon became one, to avoid a wide vibrato at all costs. He pointed to players like Baker and Bobby Hackett (another lasting Davis favorite) as models, and told the kids: "You're going to get old and start shaking anyway, so play without vibrato." Buchanan, who taught Miles for the remainder of his school days, was a strong influence. But Miles also made his own discoveries. A friend of his father's brought him a book about chromatic scales and showed him how to use it, and he stole a march on his schoolmates.

Competition was fierce, and there were all sorts of lessons to be learned. "In high school, I was the best in the music class on trumpet and all the rest knew it," Miles told a *Playboy* interviewer in 1962, "but all the contest prizes went to the boys with blue eyes. It made me so mad I made up my mind to outdo anybody white on my horn. If I hadn't met that prejudice, I probably wouldn't have had as much drive in my work. I have thought about that a lot. I have thought that prejudice and curiosity have been responsible for what I've done in music."

At age 15, still in high school, Miles got his first union card. Soon he was playing with Eddie Randall's Blues Devils (who patterned themselves on Harlem's noted Savoy Sultans, the swinging nine-piece outfit that was the house band at the Savoy Ballroom and took on all comers). Clark Terry, who is about five years older than Miles, heard him with this band, but it was not his first encounter with the youngster. As he told Stanley Dance (in an issue of *Metronome* magazine that has Miles's picture on its cover), Clark was with a band that had been hired for a picnic in Carbondale, Illinois. The day included high school sports events and there were several school bands playing in support of their teams. As Terry recalled, "One of the bandleaders was an old friend of mine. He wanted me to meet a little trumpet player he admired very much and brought the kid over to introduce us. The kid started right in asking questions—how did I do this, or that? We talked, but my mind was really on some girls dancing around a Maypole and I kind of fluffed the kid off."

About a year later, Terry went to the Elks Club in St. Louis, where he liked to jam. "As I was climbing the long flight of stairs, I heard a trumpet player flying about on his horn in a way I couldn't recognize. Eddie Randall had the band and I knew everyone in it but this little trumpet player. After I got over by the stand it dawned on me I'd seen the fellow before. As I said 'Aren't you . . .' he broke in with, 'Yeah, I'm the kid you fluffed off in Carbondale.' We've often laughed about that since."

The kid obviously already had something. At about the same time, in 1942, Sonny Stitt came through St. Louis with Tiny Bradshaw's big band and dropped by the Rhumboogie, where the Randall band was playing for the floor show. Stitt told Miles: "You look like a man named Charlie Parker and you play like him, too. C'mon with us." Stitt was serious, and Bradshaw offered Miles a job. As Miles recalled, "The fellows in the band had their hair slicked down, they wore tuxedos, and they offered me sixty whole dollars a week to play with them. I went home and asked my mother could I go, but she said no, I had to finish high school. I didn't talk to her for two weeks." Later, Illinois Jacquet also tried to take the young trumpeter on the road with him.

Miles graduated in June 1944. His first job as a full-fledged pro was with a band from New Orleans, fresh from a long run in Chicago, where a then-unknown singer named Joe Williams had worked with them. They were Adam Lambert's Brown Cats, and when they were booked for a date at the Club Belvedere in Springfield, Illinois, their trumpeter, Thomas Jefferson, returned to New Orleans. Miles was contacted and joined guitarist Lambert, pianist Phamous Lambert, bassist Duke Saunders, and drummer Stanley Williams for two weeks at no less than a hundred dollars per week. (The band, lest anyone should be misled, didn't play New Orleans style, but contemporary small-band swing.)

In July, Billy Eckstine's sensational band came to St. Louis. Miles and a friend were among the first to arrive at the Club Plantation on opening night. Miles had come from a rehearsal and had his trumpet case under his arm. A man he did not immediately recognize rushed over and asked, "Have you got a union card, kid?" It was the Eckstine band's musical director, Dizzy Gillespie. The band's third trumpet, Buddy Anderson, was ailing, and Miles was asked to take his chair. "I couldn't read a thing from listening to Diz and Bird," Miles recalled. He stayed in that chair for the band's two weeks in town. After this experience, no doubt whatsoever remained about wanting to be a musician.

His mother was insisting he go to Fisk University. But Miles had acquired a copy of the newly published *Esquire Jazz Book*, full of pictures of the jazz scene in New York. Mrs. Davis wasn't impressed, but Dr. Davis said the young man could go to New York, where he had a friend who was studying at Juilliard. He got his fare, tuition and a generous allowance. (Much later, as an adult, Miles discovered that his mother played the piano quite well and also knew the violin; things she'd never owned up to when she was trying to save her oldest son from becoming a jazz musician.)

Before taking leave of Miles's journeyman period, it is worth noting that his sister once told an interviewer that he had made a record in St. Louis with "some rhythm-and-blues outfit," adding that he sounded "terrible" on it and that it was still in some closet at home at the time. Discographers take heed!

Charlie Parker had left the Eckstine band not long after the St. Louis engagement, and Miles spent his first week in New York and his first month's allowance looking for the elusive genius of the new music. He did find Bird a bit later, at a jam session at the Heatwave in Harlem, and renewed the acquaintance. Meanwhile, he had been attending Juilliard in the daytime and hanging out in Harlem and on 52nd Street at night.

At Juilliard, in addition to theory and harmony, Miles studied piano. Dizzy, always the proselytizer, had told him that he had to know the keyboard in order to understand chords and learn how to build a solo. He also befriended Freddie Webster, a trumpeter with a beautiful tone and advanced conception. Webster wanted to know about some of the theoretical things Davis was learning at Juilliard, and in return gave pointers about tone production.

As any reader of Dizzy Gillespie's autobiography, *To Be or Not to Bop*, will know, the new music that was then taking shape had at least one important thing in common with the older jazz: a tradition of freely shared knowledge among musicians. If anything, that tradition became intensified. The newcomer got help from Tadd Dameron and Thelonious Monk, among others—and of course from Gillespie, who showed him how to shorten the trumpet mouthpiece shank ("to make a note faster") and who told him, when Miles wondered why he couldn't play as high as Dizzy: "You don't think up there; you think in the middle register."

And from Parker. "I roomed with Bird for a year and followed him around down to 52nd Street. Every night I'd write chords I heard on matchbook covers. Next day, I'd play those chords all day in the practice room at Juilliard instead of going to classes. Because everything at Juilliard, I knew." Parker kept trying to persuade his young friend (and no doubt benefactor; Miles hasn't said so, but it is likely he paid the rent) to get up and play, saying "Go ahead. Don't be afraid." But Miles wasn't ready to sit in with the masters yet. In early May of 1945, he made a record date (officially his first) with Herbie Fields, a tenor saxophonist and clarinetist then featured with Lionel Hampton. But as he confessed later, he was too nervous to take a solo on any of the four sides, just playing "in a mute" in the ensembles.

In that month, Coleman Hawkins, already a staunch supporter of the new sounds, opened at the Down Beat on 52nd Street with Joe Guy as the trumpeter in his group. Also on the bill was Billie Holiday, who had just married Guy. The trumpeter only showed up for work about half the time, and whenever he didn't, Miles would sit in. Otherwise, Miles would cross the street to the Spotlite and sit in with Eddie "Lockjaw" Davis and altoist Rudy Williams, and eventually Lockjaw hired him.

In the fall, Miles joined Charlie Parker at the Three Deuces. Parker was overpowering, but the young trumpeter found a solution of sorts. "I'd play under him all the time. When Bird would play a melody, I'd play just under him and let him lead the note, swing the note. The only thing I'd add would be a larger sound. I used to quit every night. I'd say, 'What do you need me for?'"

But Parker insisted. Another job, with Bird leading a different lineup including Dexter Gordon on tenor, followed. Then came another stint with Hawkins, this time for pay. In late November, Miles took part in Parker's first record date as a leader, for Savoy. This time he played solos, though Dizzy, who came by to listen, wound up handling the taxing ensemble passages on "Ko-Ko," Parker's masterpiece of the date. A most insensitive *Down Beat* review of the two tunes on which Miles soloed, "Now's the Time" and "Billie's Bounce," might be one reason for his long-standing low opinion of jazz critics. (He always spoke well of Ralph Gleason, however, and also likes Nat Hentoff.) In retrospect, the solos reveal a more-than-budding originality, a personal sound, and that rare thing, musical intelligence. And he sounds ever better on the then-unissued earlier takes.

When Parker left New York for his ill-starred journey to Los Angeles with Dizzy's group, Miles quit school and went home. In St. Louis, he found Benny Carter's band in residence at the Riviera. He joined the trumpet section and went west with Carter, winding up in L.A. and soon doubling into the Finale Club with Parker's group. When the union found out about the two gigs, Davis was severely fined; the choice of which job to keep could not have been a difficult one.

The Finale soon collapsed; California was not ready for bebop. But there was a date with Parker for Ross Russell's Dial label, and this time the reviews were better. Parker's breakdown came in July, and he was hospitalized at Camarillo for treatment. Miles found work with Lucky Thompson in a short-lived band also including a young bassist named Charles Mingus. In September, the Eckstine band, on its last legs as it turned out, hit town and Miles rejoined, staying until the singer dissolved his noble experiment in the spring of 1947. Miles then gigged around Chicago for a while, appearing at Jumptown with Gene Ammons and Sonny Stitt.

In April, Parker returned to New York to form the best regular group of his career: Miles; Duke Jordan, piano; Tommy Potter, bass; Max Roach, drums. As the records show, Miles had by now developed his own voice. Unlike most modern jazz trumpeters, he eschewed Gillespian runs and pyrotechnics. There was no need for flamboyance when playing with Parker. Instead, Davis offered contrast. It was an indication of the barely 21-year-old's sensibility and musicality that he could follow Parker's staggering solos on "Embraceable You" (both takes) with personal inventions of his own without, in the words of Martin Williams, "sounding a hopeless anti-climax." (It is well to bear in mind that these Parker solos easily rank among the greatest jazz works extant.)

To what extent Miles had become his own man was made even clearer by his first recording session as a leader, in August 1947. The group was actually Parker's, although, probably in deference, Bird played tenor. John Lewis had replaced Duke Jordan, and Nelson Boyd was the bassist. It's not just the sound of Parker's tenor that makes these sides different. The themes, all by Miles, are more structured than most of Bird's, the harmonic schemes more complex, and the general atmosphere more relaxed. The kid was no longer in awe of the master, in part perhaps because he had discovered the master's too-human weaknesses. (During his tenure with Bird, Miles often had to take charge when the leader was unwilling or unable.) But it goes almost without saying that Parker was the prime source of Davis's confidence. Some of his later comments on Bird have a tinge of ambiguity, but this one (quoted in Dizzy's autobiography) surely doesn't: "He used to do some shit, boy, you couldn't believe!"

In 1948, in his celebrated series of articles on bebop for the *Record Changer* magazine, Ross Russell could state: "Miles Davis may be said to belong to the new generation of musicians. There is now a mounting body of evidence that Davis is leading the way to, or even founding, the next school of trumpet playing."

As it turned out, it was not so much a new school of trumpet playing as a new school of *jazz* that Davis was about to found, with help from some new friends. During 1948, the last year in which he played regularly with Parker, Miles led his own groups at the Royal Roost on two occasions. One was with Parker, Allen Eager and Kai Winding. The other made history, though it only worked two weeks.

This was the celebrated "Birth of the Cool" nonet; a group with an unprecedented instrumentation of trumpet, trombone, French horn, tuba, alto and baritone saxophones, piano, bass and drums. The concept began in an unlikely place: pianist Claude Thornhill's big band. Since the early Forties, Thornhill, himself an arranger, had been refining a conception quite unlike that of the mainstream swing bands. Using a section of French horns, clarinets, and tuba (the latter as a melody rather than rhythm voice), he sought a lush, almost static climate of sound. But it was only when the brilliant Gil Evans joined the Thornhill arranging staff that the band's music began to acquire jazz content. "At first," Evans has said, "the sound of the band was almost a reduction to an inactivity of music, a stillness. . . . The sound hung like a cloud." Then the band acquired such gifted young soloists as altoist Lee Konitz and trumpeter Red Rodney. And when Evans, inspired by the discoveries of Parker and Gillespie, began to adapt such pieces as *Anthropology, Yardbird Suite* and *Robbins' Nest* to the band's sound, musicians took notice.

Among them was Miles Davis, who told a *Down Beat* staffer in 1950: "Thornhill had the greatest band, the one with Lee Konitz, during these modern times. The one exception was the Eckstine band with Bird." His friendship with Evans, a deep and lasting one ("We couldn't be much closer if he was my brother," said Miles in his famous September 1962 *Playboy* interview) began when the arranger approached Davis for permission to use his *Donna Lee* for the Thornhill band. The trumpeter agreed, but in return asked Evans to show him some things about chord structure and to let him study some of the Thornhill scores.

By mid-1948, the second recording ban called by the musicians' union (the first had stretched from mid-1942 to late 1944) was in effect, and musicians had time on their hands. Evans's one-room cellar apartment on West 55th Street became a hangout for a host of enterprising musical minds including Parker, Gerry Mulligan, John Lewis, George Russell, John Benson Brooks, and Johnny Carisi. "We all gravitated around Evans," Mulligan said years later.

The Thornhill band had temporarily disbanded, and Miles had done well enough during his first Royal Roost engagement to be offered another. It was decided to reduce the Thornhill sound to what Evans has called "the smallest number of instruments that could get that sound and still express all the harmonies (the band) used. Miles wanted to play his idiom with that kind of sound."

The two-week booking was as relief band opposite Count Basie. Miles broke precedent by insisting that the sign in front of the club (a forerunner of Birdland, a bit further down Broadway) read: "Miles Davis Band—Arrangements by Gerry Mulligan, Gil Evans and John Lewis." Never before had arrangers been so prominently credited. Basie was impressed: "Those slow things sounded strange and good. I didn't always know what they were doing, but I listened and liked it."

The band's personnel included Konitz, Mulligan, Lewis, and Roach, plus Junior Collins on French horn, Bill Barber on tuba, and bassist Al McKibbon, with Ted Kelly and Mike Zwerin alternating on trombone. There was even a singer, Kenny "Pancho" Hagood. When the recording ban was lifted in late 1948, Miles signed with Capitol Records, then on a bebop spree. The nonet's first session took place in January 1949, with Kai Winding on trombone, and Al Haig and Joe Shulman replacing Lewis and McKibbon, who were out of town with Dizzy's big band. Four sides were cut. A second session with some changes in personnel (notably J. J. Johnson and Kenny Clarke) was held in April, and this produced the band's acknowledged masterpieces, Carisi's *Israel* and Davis and Evans's *Boplicity*. The third and final session did not take place until March 1950, at which time the band also did a week at the Clique Club, a shortlived predecessor to Birdland. Roach and McKibbon were back for this, and the French horn player was Gunther Schuller. Some of the dozen sides by the nonet were not issued until considerably later, but those that appeared at the time made a deep and lasting impression on musicians. And contrary to generally held opinion they were also quite well received in the leading jazz publications, *Down Beat* and *Metronome*, if not as enthusiastically as hindsight might demand. (During 1950–51, Bill Russo and Lloyd Lifton devoted four of their *Down Beat* columns, "Jazz on Record," to analysis of solos from the sessions: Miles's *Israel, Move,* and *God-child,* and Konitz's *Move.*)

There can be little doubt that these records (which were reissued in 1957 on a Capitol LP that was titled "Birth of the Cool"), triggered the advent of a successor style to bebop (though bop, of course, did not fold up and steal away, but returned with a vengeance under the new guise of "hard bop" in the mid-Fifties). But they also remain classics—regardless of their influence—as *music* pure and simple. And while the arrangers' contributions to the success of the venture (artistic success; initially, the records did not sell very well) has rightly been stressed, it was Miles who was the catalyst and primary soloist. As Gerry Mulligan has written: "He took the initiative and put the theories to work. He called the rehearsals, hired the halls, called the players, and generally cracked the whip."

Thus, the leadership capabilities of Miles Davis became apparent while he was still in his early twenties. In May, 1949, in the midst of the "Birth of the Cool" period, came an invitation to the Paris Jazz Festival, the first international event of its kind. Parker and Sidney Bechet were the stars; but Davis was among the headliners: he and Tadd Dameron (the great arranger-composer-pianist who had helped Miles when he first came to New York) co-led a quintet that included James Moody and Kenny Clarke. Broadcast recordings from the concert, legitimately issued for the first time in 1977, reveal an interesting aspect of Miles, who plays as close to Gillespie's conception as on any records he ever made, including some uncharacteristic high-note forays, brilliantly adapting himself to the strict bebop format of the group. Presumably, appearing on the same bill as Parker but separately from him, plus the presence at the festival of Kenny Dorham as his replacement in the Parker quintet, represented both liberation and challenge to Miles, and he rose to the occasion—as he almost always would do throughout his career.

Ironically, however, this period of his first important impacts on the jazz scene coincided with perhaps the most difficult time in the young musician's life. As he told Marc Crawford in a candid interview for *Ebony* years later: "I got hooked. . . . I got bored and was around cats that were hung. So I wound up with a habit that took me over four years to break."

Those were listless years. During the year between the second and third nonet dates, there was no other commercial recording. And after that March 1950 date, Miles did not get back to the studios as a leader until his first session for Prestige, on January 17, 1951.

A year earlier, he was interviewed by *Down Beat's* Pat Harris during a Chicago gig. He attacked those who "say there's no music but bop," praised Sidney Bechet, had kind words for Dixieland jazz, cited Roy Eldridge and Harry James among his early influences ("You've got to have a foundation . . . before you can play bop") and took pride in his three-year-old son, Gregory, who already was playing a horn. But he ruefully described his current life as months of no work. "I've worked so little," he said, "I could probably tell you where I was playing any night in the last three years." And he attacked promoters and club owners for not treating musicians with respect, and said he would like to spend "eight months (of each year) in Paris and four months here. Eight months where you're accepted for what you can do, and four months here because—well, it's hard to leave all this."

The piece concludes: "During the last year, he worked a couple of weeks at Soldier Meyer's in Brooklyn, played the Paris Jazz Festival, four one-nighters around New York, and a month at the Hi-Note. When he closed here, nothing substantial was in sight."

And nothing much of substance did turn up while Miles was struggling with his demons. Having fallen into the same trap as so many (too many of them dead) of his contemporaries must have gone against Miles's basic nature. Handsome, proud, intelligent, competitive, and already fiercely individualistic, Miles was not psychologically predestined for the draining curse of addiction. We needn't dwell on this long-ago episode in the life of a man who went on to make so much of himself, but it does help to put into focus some of the music on these discs.

What is significant is that Miles came back, with relative speed, and that he did so without breast-beating, and by himself. As he told Marc Crawford: "I made up my mind . . . I was sick and tired of it. You know you can get tired of anything. You can even get tired of being scared. I laid down and stared at the ceiling for twelve days and I cursed everybody I didn't like. I was kicking it the hard way. . . . Then it was over."

During those days before it was over, Miles was sought out by Bob Weinstock, a bear of a man and a contemporary of Miles, who had begun his jazz involvement as a record collector. He had gone from collecting to selling, first through the pages of the *Record Changer* (we have mentioned this estimable magazine before; it was edited by one Orrin Keepnews), then in space rented at a jazz record shop, and finally in his own store, just a block west of the Royal Roost. Called The Jazz Corner, it began to issue records under that label name in 1948. (They were leased Australian masters featuring the revivalist Graeme Bell band. Weinstock's tastes were mainly in that direction then, but under the tutelage of Ross Russell he began to veer toward bebop, aided by the proximity of the Roost, then billing itself as "the Metropolitan Bopera House.")

By early 1949 Weinstock had issued his first modern jazz record, by Lee Konitz, on a label he called New Jazz. Subsequently, it became Prestige. He knew and liked Miles, personally and musically. As he told Joe Goldberg for "Jazz Masters of the Fifties": "Miles sort of disappeared from the scene, and I was on a business trip to St. Louis. . . . I made some calls (and reached his home). They told me he was in Chicago. . . . Finally, he got in touch with me, and he came back East. . . . At that time, though he still dug the cool music of Mulligan and Evans, some of the primitiveness in him started to come out. . . . On his first date, you can hear a very different Miles Davis than on the Capitols."

Sonny Rollins was present on that first date. He'd met Miles when he was 18 and just about to graduate from high school; they jammed together in the Bronx. "Miles was only four years older than I was," Sonny told Conrad Silvert, "but at that time, four years could be pretty big. . . . Miles was the first major player to hire me. I went on the road with him, I think in '49—to Boston, Philadelphia, Baltimore. That's when I first met Coltrane. We played with Miles at the same time, both on tenor." (And who wouldn't like to have heard that band?)

Record dates (there were six for Prestige and two for Blue Note during the grey period, 1951 through '53) must have meant sustenance for Miles, though nobody got rich making jazz dates for independent labels. In any case, he tried to get what money he could from Weinstock (and from Blue Note's Alfred Lion and Frank Wolff as well). The well-authenticated legend is that he and Weinstock would sometimes sit and stare at each other for as much as 20 minutes without exchanging a word after Miles had made a forceful request for more. Basically, more money meant more sides would be recorded, and most of these sessions did turn out to be quite productive.

But what a difference when 1954 came along! Five dates for Prestige and one for Blue Note, and what dates! This was the real comeback year for Miles—not the following one, when he appeared at the Newport Jazz Festival and the jazz press officially rediscovered him. Miles scorned the comeback talk. "You'd think I'd been on the moon," he quipped. "What are they talking about? I just played the way I always play."

Yet there was some truth to the resurgence theory, for reasons obvious and not so obvious. Clearly, the weight off his back was an enormous relief. But also, there were changes in approach. Tone had always been an essential aspect of Miles, but by 1954 he had found his own true sound. Musical logic and a splendid sense of balance and structure had also been evident, but now they all came together, as in that wonderful solo on *Bags' Groove*. Miles was telling a story now, and the world was ready to listen.

The mid-Fifties were among those recurring periods when the public (which is to say the media) rediscovers jazz. It was also the time when the long-playing record came fully into its own, both in terms of saleability and creative use. As Weinstock well knew, it was only a matter of time until a major label would become interested in Davis and make a contract offer he could not hope to match. It turned out to be Columbia, and a deal was struck: Miles, by now at the helm of his greatest band, would do a sufficient amount of recording to allow Prestige to release "new" material for the next few years. Immediately after recording he would be free to begin work for Columbia. Thus the marathon 1956 sessions that conclude this package.

What had transpired in the interim was that Miles had further refined his ability as a talent spotter, and his knowledge of what he wanted to do in music. The great quintet, which begins to take shape with the *quartet* session of June 7, 1955, had been fully formed by year's end, with a personnel of Red Garland, piano; Paul Chambers, bass; Philly Joe Jones, drums, and John Coltrane, tenor saxophone.

It is easy to forget that none of these players were at all well known at this stage of the game. Chambers, just 20, had come to New York that same year, played just a few gigs, and been hired on the spot when Miles heard him with George Wallington's group. Garland, three years Miles's senior, had kicked around on the periphery of jazz for years until he came to Davis's attention. (The fact that Garland had been a professional boxer, and that boxing had become Miles's favorite sport and pastime, would not have had any bearing on the matter if Miles hadn't liked his playing.) The remarkable Jones had first worked with Miles in 1952, not long after the drummer had settled in New York. Although known and appreciated among musicians, his was hardly a household name, and fans still got him mixed up with Jo Jones of Basie fame. And Coltrane, though he'd played with Dizzy's last big band and subsequent combo (as well as with Earl Bostic, and Johnny Hodges), was a near-unknown quantity.

But Davis knew what he was doing. He paid no attention to criticisms of Coltrane for his "harsh" (even "ugly") sound or "strained" style. In Coltrane's dense, vertical style, gritty sound and emotional ferocity Miles had found the perfect foil for his own sound and style. It was a bit like the contrast between himself and Parker—only this time, it was the trumpeter who played lead. And the rhythm section was perfectly suited to his aim: it could swing hard, it could listen, and it could leave the space he wanted without dropping a beat. It could simmer smoothly and also provide the accents and polyrhythms Miles loved.

At the time, Miles was profoundly influenced by an unlikely source, pianist Ahmad Jamal, who, whatever his other virtues or flaws, had a unique feeling for space and openness in his music. Miles instructed Garland to play as much like Jamal as he could, and it is not insignificant that the pianist's features with the quintet included *Ahmad's Blues*. (It should go without saying that there were decided stylistic affinities between the two pianists to begin with; Garland didn't just copy Jamal.)

As for Chambers, he was a marvel who had everything—tone, time, taste, technique—and also was an outstanding soloist and shaper of swinging counter-melodies in the ensemble. No wonder that within a year or so the trio was affectionately known in jazz circles as simply "The Rhythm

Section"—the first since the glorious "All American" rhythm quartet of the Count Basie band of the Thirties to earn a sobriquet of its own.

Certainly the quintet, which stayed together until the spring of 1957, and was basically reconstituted as a sextet (with the addition of Cannonball Adderley's alto sax and the substitution of Bill Evans on piano) early in 1958, was the most influential jazz group of its time, and one of the most memorable of all time. It marked, for Miles Davis, the distillation of the essence of his musical ideas up to that time—ideas related to yet different from those that had fueled the nonet. And it established him for the second time within a decade as one of the most influential figures in jazz.

What happened subsequently is part of basic contemporary jazz history. How Miles, with a single album ("Kind of Blue"), set in motion some of the major trends of the 1960s and his own third phase as a key influence. How these ideas and approaches were refined by the second great quintet, the one with Wayne Shorter, Herbie Hancock, Ron Carter and Tony Williams (the latter only 17 when he joined the band and possibly the trumpeter's single greatest outright discovery). How, intermittently, he resumed his collaborations with Gil Evans, yielding a series of masterful meldings of soloist's and arranger's arts. How, to the consternation of many dedicated fans (some musicians among them), he turned to so-called, mislabeled "jazz-rock fusion" with "Bitches Brew," the best-selling jazz album of all time. How he continued to bring to the fore new talent (Chick Corea, Keith Jarrett, Jack DeJohnette, Dave Liebman, Mtume, Airto, and others), while continuing to play a new kind of music that reached a new generation of listeners while alienating more than a few older ones. Then, basically due to illness and exhaustion, he disappeared from the active list, amid rumors of all sorts, in mid-1975. Since then, instant scuttlebutt news could be made by the merest whisper of his impending return to concert stage or recording studio.

Behind all that, the legend of Miles Davis, Prince of Darkness, Man Walking on Eggshells, Evil Genius of Jazz, etc., etc., began and kept building. At first, one might have theorized that the Davis mystique was the creation of the more-than-enterprising and imaginative Columbia Records publicity department, pouring forth pictures (excepting only Louis Armstrong, Miles must be the most photographed of jazz musicians), adjectives, and fancies. But the real story was the tension set up between the publicity drive and the actual character of its object.

So much that has been written and said about the man's personality and its seeming mysteries points up the wisdom of a choice once made by the late Ralph Gleason. When assigned yet another set of Miles Davis album-liner notes, Gleason (who had certainly written a great deal about Miles—and was credited by his subject as being the *only* jazz writer who knew what he was talking about) chose to turn out impressionistic prose-poems based on Davis album titles or to ring poetic-phonetic variations on the man's name (*Ma-ulz, My-ulz, My-ills*)! It was at least as good a solution as any, for the torrent of words—in the jazz press and the daily press, and then in magazines like *Playboy, Esquire, Nugget,* and *Cavalier,* and later in *Rolling Stone* and the *Real Paper* and the *Village Voice*—had rolled well past the saturation point. Every journalist within earshot of the artist seemed to have become a qualified psychologist and self-anointed mythmaker.

What chiefly fascinated writers, and obviously readers as well, was his seeming flamboyance—elegant, style-setting clothes, fast cars, exotic house and equally exotic paramours—and his contrasting surliness, profanity, and (or so it was assumed) outright rudeness.

It all started with the story of Miles turning his back on audiences and refusing to acknowledge applause. It mattered little that from the start he attempted, with impeccable logic, to explain these actions. He was—he pointed out—in a night club or concert hall only to play music; he didn't believe in distracting, or taking attention away from, the other performers when they were soloing and he had nothing to do. He saw no need to introduce players or compositions: the former were surely well known to audiences; the latter were often only decided on the spur of the moment and should be recognizable from recordings to those who really cared. He believed that his music was not an entertainment. But few cared to read between the lines of such statements to arrive at the realization that their hero was basically a shy man who didn't (indeed *couldn't*) go through the show business routines expected of popular performers.

Musicians and writers who knew him well often said so, but the mystique prevailed. It prevailed even though most of the articles, even those that made the most noise about the controversial aspects of the Davis image, wound up stating that there was a nice guy "behind the mask."

Dizzy Gillespie told me: "Miles talks rough—you hear him use all kinds of rough words. But when you hear the pathos in his music, that's a different story. His music reflects his true character. I once had a long conversation with his daughter, Cheryl. We talked about him—oh, did we talk about him! Seriously, I made a statement during that conversation. I said: 'Miles is shy. He is super shy.' A lot of people don't believe that, but I have known him for a long, long time."

And Sonny Rollins told Conrad Silvert: "I hate to use that word 'shy,' but he is a shy guy. Which is why he turned his back sometimes, and then people would say, 'Oh, gee, he's arrogant.' Miles wanted to hear the music, and he'd play something soft for us that he didn't want the public to hear because we were getting the music together. It was more the feeling of a workshop. . . . We were all experimenting and Miles encouraged it. It was music, music, music."

Indeed, it is because he takes the music so seriously that Miles refuses to dress it up with stage business, which is not to say that he, with the help of the aforementioned publicity, was not clever enough to turn his shyness to an advantage, to make a new kind of show business out of his anti-showbiz attitude. And there's no reason to be so naive as to ignore his studied sartorial flair, though it must be noted that he is as original and spectacular a dresser off stage as on.

In part, Miles's shyness is due to a handicap. In the mid-Fifties, he had a routine operation to remove some benign nodules on his vocal cords. While still recovering, he was infuriated by a club manager, raised his voice against doctor's orders, and suffered permanent damage, so that he speaks in a hoarse semi-whisper, not at all unappealing, but difficult to project. If he had chosen to make a practice of casual conversation with the customers in a noisy club, the resulting "what-did-you-say" would quickly have driven him up the wall. (I've actually seen this happen for, contrary to legend, Miles is basically friendly and on occasion has tried to oblige his fans.) Public address announcements obviously also became a problem under these circumstances.

Another contributing factor to the myth is his unsparing honesty in musical matters. His famous *Down Beat* "Blindfold Tests" bear witness to this, as do many of his quoted remarks. The fact is that Miles never curries favor or goes easy on his friends. If he doesn't like something, he says so, and *why,* usually with profanities added for emphasis. But actually the bulk of his publicly expressed opinions on music have been positive. When they're not, it's usually with good reason. Tastes may differ, but Miles has a broad and deep appreciation for all good music, and his critical opinions are based on a sharp and discerning—and certainly highly experienced—ear.

In any event, it seems impossible to dislike Miles Davis if one knows him at all, though, like all of us, he may have done some not-so-nice things during his lifetime. I cannot claim to know Miles well, but whenever I've had personal contact with him, I've come away with warm feelings. He is a kind, generous, witty, even considerate man. And for the past five years, and probably well before that, too, he has suffered some degree of physical discomfort and pain for most of his waking hours. First operated on for a hip-bone problem in 1965, he under went surgery again ten years later. A few years before that, he broke both ankles in a car accident. His preoccupation with physical fitness is in part due to these problems, and otherwise motivated by his firm belief that a black man in America, no matter how famous or well off, has to be ready to defend himself at any time.

Among the mass of interviews with Miles, the most personally revealing and touching was the one in *Playboy* in 1962. It ought to be required reading for all who carry with them a distorted image of the man, for it clearly shows his innate decency, as well as his just pride. At times, Miles has indulged himself in putting on (or putting off) interviewers. But in this instance, he clearly spoke straight from the shoulder and from the heart, about what motivates him as a man and an artist. And of the racism that gnaws "like a big sore inside your belly" at every black American—advances to the contrary notwithstanding, as surely in 1980 as in 1962.

What he said about trumpet players bears quoting. The interviewer, taking note of Miles's many poll victories, asks: "After yourself, how would you rate others?" and Miles explodes.

"*After* me! Hell, it's plenty great trumpet players don't come *after* me, or *after* nobody else! That's what I hate so about critics—how they are always *comparing* artists . . . always writing that one's better than another one. . . . That bugs the hell out of musicians. It's made some damn near mad enough to want to hang up their horns. . . . The thing to judge in any jazz artist is does the man project, and does he have ideas. You take Dizzy—he does, all the time, every time he picks up his horn. Some more cats—Clark Terry, Ray Nance, Kenny Dorham, Roy Eldridge, Harold Baker, Freddie Hubbard, Lee Morgan, Bobby Hackett—a lot of them. Hell, that cat down in New Orleans, Al Hirt, he blows his ass off, too!"

And then about Louis Armstrong: "I love Pops, I love the way he sings, the way he plays—everything he does, except when he says something against modern jazz music. . . . A long time ago, I was at Bop City, and he came in and told me he liked my playing. I don't know if he would even remember it, but I remember how good I felt to have him say it."

(A fond personal memory of Miles and Louis: some years back, I found myself seated next to Miles at Basin Street East when Louis was appearing there. Davis was accompanied by his then lawyer Harold Lovette, a loquacious man. Louis's set had begun, but Lovette was still talking. Without taking his eyes off Louis, Miles said: "Shut *up,* man! I want to hear Pops!" And from the way he reacted to that set, one confirmed Armstrong fan could tell he was in the company of another.)

While Miles has disavowed any direct influence from Louis, he has also said: "Nobody can play anything on a horn that Louis hasn't played already." And I agree with Martin Williams when he concludes his chapter on Miles in "The Jazz Tradition" with these words:

"More than any other player, Miles Davis echoes Louis Armstrong; one can hear it, I think, in his reading of almost any standard theme. And behind the jaded stance, behind the complaints, and behind the sometimes blasé sophistication, Miles Davis's horn also echoes something of Armstrong's exuberantly humorous, forcefully committed and self-determined joy."

If he should never pick up his horn again—an eventuality that anyone at all concerned about jazz abhors but nevertheless must (as of this writing in mid-1980) contemplate—Miles Davis will have left his indelible mark on jazz. The best of the music contained herein is among the reasons why.

PLAY THE RIGHT THING
STANLEY CROUCH

In his landmark essay, "Constructing the Jazz Tradition: Jazz Historiography," Scott DeVeaux has argued that the history of jazz writing is marked by a near century-old eagerness to advance the music's respectability. In order to make jazz cohere as one majestic entity, jazz writers, through the use of romance or tragedy, have habitually canonized their heroes, purchasing for their favorites a seat on "the jazz tradition" train in which each conflicting style is assigned its evolutionary place no matter how different or wide-ranging. The hushed reality of commercialism and other "corrupting" influences have been repeatedly swept under the rug. Better to look the other way, it's felt, than threaten the paradigm.

In some ways Stanley Crouch's piece follows precedent. For one thing, his account of Miles Davis's "sell-out"—in his view a fall from grace reminiscent of Adam's in the Bible—takes the form of a tragedy. Moreover, glorifying Davis's first twenty years of recorded work is an argument for that music's place in the canon and for Davis's enthronement in the pantheon.

But, in dramatic fashion, Crouch parts company with the jazz critical establishment. The author challenges long-accepted notions that comprise jazz tradition gospel: Davis's supremacy as a trumpeter and bandleader, Davis as innovator of modal jazz, even Davis as quintessential jazz fashion plate. And Crouch's denigration of Davis's post-1968 electric work as money-hungry, artistically wayward, and off the direct, acoustic path toward ecstasy—views shared by some older fans and something of a rallying cry among young, acoustic players, at least in the mid- to-late 1980s—deals head on with the issue of commercialism and is a de facto call for Davis's last twenty years of work to be expelled from jazz tradition paradise. Republished from the February 12, 1990, edition of *The New Republic,* this review of *Miles: The Autobiography* and the CD reissue of *Miles Davis Chronicle: The Complete Prestige Recordings* remains one of the most controversial jazz pieces of the last ten years.

The contemporary Miles Davis, when one hears his music or watches him perform, deserves the description that Nietzsche gave of Wagner: "the greatest example of self-violation in the history of art." Davis made much fine music for the first half of his professional life, and represented for many the uncompromising Afro-American artist contemptuous of Uncle Tom, but he has fallen from grace—and been celebrated for it. As usual, the fall from grace has been a form of success. Desperate to maintain his position at the forefront of modern music, to sustain his financial position, to be admired for the hipness of his purported innovations, Davis turned butt to the beautiful in order to genuflect before the commercial.

Once given to exquisite dress, Davis now comes on the bandstand draped in the expensive bad taste of rock 'n' roll. He walks about the stage, touches foreheads with the saxophonist as they play a duet, bends over and remains in that ridiculous position for long stretches as he blows at the floor, invites his white female percussionist to come, bare-midriffed, down a ramp and do a jungle-movie dance as she accompanies herself with a talking drum, sticks out his tongue at his photographers, leads the din of electronic clichés with arm signals, and trumpets the many fades of his own force with amplification that blurts forth a sound so decadent that it can no longer disguise the shriveling of its maker's soul.

Beyond the terrible performances and the terrible recordings, Davis has also become the most remarkable licker of moneyed boots in the music business, willing now to pimp himself as he once pimped women when he was a drug addict. He can be seen on television talking about the greatness of Prince, or claiming (in his new autobiography, *Miles*) that the Minneapolis vulgarian and borderline drag queen "can be the new Duke Ellington of our time if he just keeps at it." Once nicknamed Inky for his dark complexion, Davis now hides behind the murky fluid of his octopus fear of being old hat, and claims that he is now only doing what he has always done—move ahead, take the music forward, submit to the personal curse that is his need for change, the same need that brought him to New York from St. Louis in 1944, in search of Charlie Parker.

Before he was intimidated into mining the fool's gold of rock 'n' roll, Davis's achievement was large and complex, as a trumpet player and an improviser. Though he was never of the order of Armstrong, Young, Parker, or Monk, the sound that finally came to identify him was as original as any in the history of jazz. His technical limitations were never as great as commonly assumed, except when he was strung out on drugs and didn't practice. By January 1949, when he recorded "Overtime" with Dizzy Gillespie and Fats Navarro, he was taking a backseat to nobody in execution. By May 1949, when he traveled to France and was recorded in performance, he was muscling his way across the horn in molten homage to Navarro and Gillespie, the two leading technicians of the bebop era; he was three weeks short of his 23rd birthday and already had big band experience with Billy Eckstine and Gillespie, already had stood next to Charlie Parker night after night on bandstands and in studios.

The conventional idea that Davis discovered that he couldn't play like Gillespie, and proceeded to develop a style of stark, hesitant, even blushing lyricism that provided a contrast to Parker's flood of virtuosic executions, is only partly true. A methodical musician, Davis systematically worked through the things that were of interest to him. Eventually he personalized the levels of declamation, nuance, melodic fury, and pathos that are heard, for example, in Parker's "Bird of Paradise." But first he examined Gillespie's fleet approach and harmonic intricacy, which was the dominant approach to bebop trumpet. From Gillespie, he learned bebop harmony and was also encouraged to use the keyboard to solve problems; he even took from Gillespie an aspect of timbral piquancy that settled beneath the surface of his sound. But Davis rejected the basic nature of Gillespie's tone, which few found as rich or as attractive as the idiomatic achievements of the Negroid brass vocabulary that had preceded the innovations of bebop. Davis grasped the musical power that comes of having a sound that is itself a musical expression.

He moved in the direction of a refined *and* raw understanding of tonal manipulation based in the blues. His early problems with pitch demanded that he focus first on the quality, the weight, and the accuracy of his sound. Once he established control over his tone, Davis's work began to reflect his affection for the resources of color and nuance heard in Armstrong, Freddie Webster, Harry Edison, Buck Clayton, Rex Stewart, Navarro, Dud Bascomb, Ray Nance. But his extraordinary discipline led him to strip everything away, striving for a sound that was direct in its clarity, almost pristine in its removal from the world of Negro trumpet tone. On that clean slate, Davis later added dramatic timbres and attacks.

Next Davis chose to work out a style that was superficially simple, that was rarely given to upper-register explosions or to the rhythmic disruptions that the boppers had built upon the droll games that Lester Young played with the beat. On his first recording as a leader in May 1947, Davis already had the dark, warm sensuousness that he later extended and refined. By using Charlie Parker on tenor, rather than on his customary alto, Davis got a thicker texture, the sort of thickness that he favored in his later quintets; and a number of writers have heard premonitions of the tonal concerns, the phrasings, and the moods of "The Birth of the Cool," the highly celebrated but essentially lightweight nonet sessions that Davis steered a few years later.

But the essential influence on Davis's first recordings as a leader was still Parker. The saxophonist's 1946 recording of his "Yardbird Suite" with Davis as a sideman shows precisely the ease that characterizes the playing and the writing of the trumpeter's own session, especially "Half Nelson" and "Milestones." On that first date, Davis not only plays quite well himself, but uses the mood of the material to inspire Parker to reach for an emotional projection that the saxophonist rarely called upon. Davis resides comfortably in the middle register as he improvises through the difficult harmonies of his compositions, sailing and swinging in almost seamless legato eighth notes on "Little Willie Leaps" and inventing a meticulous thematic improvisation on "Half Nelson." Harmonically his notes say bebop, and he works toward the layered sound that has a top, a middle, and a bottom, all the while understating a thoroughly felt joy as he nearly swings the ink off his tail.

Equally important were a number of other recording dates under Parker's leadership. There are examples in the ballad sessions of the winter of 1947 of the softer approach to sound and ensemble, as when Parker plays delicate and soaring obbligatos behind Davis on "Embraceable You," "Out of Nowhere," and "My Old Flame." Even earlier, as the flutist and composer James Newton points out, the contrapuntal Parker writing of "A-Leu-Cha" and "Chasin' the Bird" brought to bebop qualities that Davis's "cool" nonet explored. By "Marmaduke" in 1948, Davis is much closer to the almost purely melodic style of quiet but calling intensity that became an important aspect of his musical signature.

Then came "The Birth of the Cool." Davis's nonet of 1948–50 played little in public and recorded only enough to fill an album, but it largely inspired what became known as "cool" or "West Coast" jazz, a light-sounding music, low-keyed and smooth, that disavowed the Afro-American approach to sound and rhythm. This style had little to do with blues and almost nothing to do with swing. That Davis, one of the most original improvisers, a man with a great feeling for blues, a swinger almost of the first magnitude, should have put "cool" in motion is telling. Indeed, it is the first, premonitory example of his dual position in jazz.

Heard now, the nonet recordings seem little more than primers for television writing. What the recordings show us, though, is that Davis, like many other jazzmen, was not above the academic temptation of Western music. Davis turns out to have been overly impressed by the lessons he received at Juilliard, when he arrived in New York in 1944. The pursuit of a soft sound, the uses of polyphony that were far from idiomatic, the nearly coy understatement, the lines that had little internal propulsion: all amount to another failed attempt to marry jazz to European devices. The overstated attribution of value to these recordings led the critical establishment to miss Ellington's "The Tattooed Bride," which was the high point of jazz composition of the late 1940s. Then, as now, jazz critics seemed unable to determine the difference between a popular but insignificant trend and a fresh contribution to the art.

Davis began making his truest contributions as a leader in the 1950s. The Prestige recordings from 1951 to 1956 have been reissued in a single package, and it constitutes one of the richest bodies of work in small-group jazz. One hears Davis consolidating influences, superbly cross-weaving improvisational styles and instrumental approaches, in his own playing and in that of the musicians he brought together. The quintet included John Coltrane and a rhythm section that was nearly as important to jazz of the '50s as Basie's was to that of the '30s.

In the early '50s, inspired by Monk, Armstrong, Young, and Holiday, Davis learned to strip away everything not essentially musical. He maintained the harmonic sophistication of the bebop school, but picked only the most telling notes for the construction of his melodic lines. He recognized that the smooth swing of Basie and the territory bands used pulsations that, for all their flirtations with the beat, were never jerky. In this work Davis sublimely combined the unsentimental detailings of tone, emotion, and attack of the blues; the joy and the surprise of Armstrong and Young that melodically rose up over the tempo and meter of ensembles in the '30s; and the idealistic but earthy sensuousness of the romantic balladeer.

One of the more interesting things about Davis during these years is that he brought together musicians with varied tastes in sound. As early as 1946, when he recorded "Yardbird Suite" and "Ornithology" with Parker, the smooth, vibratoless sound of Parker was contrasted with the heavier Coleman Hawkins-derived tone of Lucky Thompson's tenor. Davis himself had worked with Hawkins, and used tenor players rooted in Hawkins's work (such as Thompson and Sonny Rollins) until he hired Coltrane. But his alto choices were always Parker-derived, such as Jackie McLean and Davey Schildkraut. Just as he was interested in bringing together the essences of blues-based trumpet and ensemble swing with the lessons of the bebop movement, Davis also seemed to want to fuse the tones of those different schools in his ensembles.

Thus, in 1951, he brought McLean and Rollins together for a sextet recording, the instrumentation foreshadowing the six-piece group he later led with Cannonball Adderley and Coltrane. Davis played with confidence on the blues, gave poignance to the ballads, swung with very individual articulation on McLean's "Dig." But perhaps the high point of the session was Rollins's tenor on "It's Only A Paper Moon," where his gruff and ghostly sound reached startling levels of lyricism and fresh phrasing. For the next three years he was playing marvelously, with J.J. Johnson, Jackie McLean, Jimmy Heath, Horace Silver, Gil Coggins, Percy Heath, Kenny Clarke, and Art Blakey on Blue Note Records. And in 1954 Davis reached one of his first peaks as a bandleader and a player. In March he recorded a version of "Old Devil Moon" that had an arranged and recurring vamp that anticipated the sound of the Coltrane rhythm section of the 1960s.

In April he brought together trombonist J.J. Johnson, Lucky Thompson, pianist Horace Silver, bassist Percy Heath, and drummer Kenny Clarke. According to Silver, Thompson had written arrangements that didn't come off, and they did two blues numbers, a fast and a slow blues, "Walkin'" and "Blue and Boogie," to avoid a failed day in the studio. The results were signal achievements. The weight of the ensemble sound is perfectly balanced and darkened, Davis's and Johnson's broad brass tones melding in unison with Thompson's thick, breathy tenor; Silver's percussive attack and the ideal mesh of Heath's bass notes with

Clarke's cymbals and drums form perhaps Davis's first great rhythm section. On the swift "Blue and Boogie" the trumpeter moves over the horn with grace and pride, his last two choruses a response to the emerging challenge of Clifford Brown.

In December Davis used Heath and Clarke again, but instead of horns he brought Monk's piano and Milt Jackson's vibes. The overtones of Davis's trumpet and the ringing of Jackson's metal keys achieved another superior texture (this one foreshadowed the electric piano on *Filles de Kilimanjaro*, the trumpeter's last important jazz record some 14 years away). Davis's abstraction of the melody of "The Man I Love" reached back in conception, but not in execution, to Parker's classic transformation of "Embraceable You." Because of the trumpeter's problems with Monk's style—contrapuntal, icily voiced, given as much to ongoing improvised arrangement as to chordal statement—Davis asked the pianist to "stroll," or lay out, during his improvisations. The musical effect is systematically wonderful, however much Monk was irritated. Monk's improvisations are easily the highest expressions of originality and profundity in all of the Prestige sessions.

They are also the peak of piano playing on any Miles Davis recording. Monk brings a motivic brilliance, a command of inflection and timbre, and an idealistic lyricism that are unexpected in their purity. His playing is as far from European convention as bottleneck guitar work. His melodic response to Davis on "The Man I Love" is startling. And on "Swing Spring," Davis pulls off what must be one of his best spontaneous decisions. Featured first with just bass (Percy Heath) and drums (Kenny Clarke), he jumps back in after Jackson finishes his improvisation and Monk is about to play. Monk stops immediately, and Davis plays again with Heath and Clarke, choosing to use a patented Monk phrase for his last chorus. He builds upon it and finishes. Monk then picks up the phrase and invents one of his most masterful recorded performances. It is, quite simply, one of the high points of jazz.

As Davis developed into the next phase of his bandleading and his improvising, he continued to expand on blues, pop songs, Kansas City swing, and the conceptions he personalized from Parker, Monk, and Ahmad Jamal, whose 1955 arrangement of Ravel's "Pavane" provided the structure for Davis's 1959 "So What" and the melody for Coltrane's 1961 "Impressions." When he formed his first great quintet in 1955, with

Coltrane, pianist Red Garland, bassist Paul Chambers, and drummer Philly Joe Jones, Davis not only improvised marvelously eight times out of ten, but also wrote particularly imaginative arrangements. Much of the praise that this quintet has received is deserved. It was a unit that had invincible swing at any tempo, that utilized the possibilities of group color with consistent intelligence, that stoked fire as ably as it crooned. No small part of Davis's achievement was his rhythm section, an ongoing, spontaneously self-orchestrating unit of piano, bass, and drums that delineated the forms of the tunes, responded to the improvisation of the featured horns, loosened and tightened the beat, and swung with an almost peerlessly precise attention to color and the varied possibilities of harmonic-percussive drama. Still, what made this band so wonderful was Davis's breadth of emotional expression. His sensibility drew on the entire sweep of jazz feeling, from the playful to the tender to the pugnacious to the aloof to the gutbucket-greasy and the idealistically lyrical.

When he moved to Columbia Records in 1957 and *'Round About Midnight* was released with the same musicians, Davis was on the verge of becoming a star, a large influence, a matinee idol, and a man destined to sink down in a way no one—himself least of all—could have imagined. Columbia Records, with its distribution and promotion networks, its record club, the air play its products received, and the ink it could generate outside the jazz press, started the most significant leg of Davis's march to celebrity. The trumpeter soon saw his performances and his recordings become emblems of taste in contemporary art.

With Nat Cole and Sidney Poitier, moreover, Davis became part of an expanding vision of American glamour in which dark-hued Negroes were admitted into precincts of romance and elegance that had previously been almost the exclusive province of light-skinned Afro-Americans like Billy Eckstine. As Betty Carter observed of Davis's matinee-idol appeal, "Miles wasn't a power trumpet player, he was a stylist. He had a soft, melodic approach that made him very popular with women. Women really liked him the way they like Dexter Gordon, Gene Ammons, Ben Webster, Johnny Hodges, and all of those guys who knew how to play things that had some sweetness in them."

Davis also benefited from a shift in audience taste that harked back to the popularity of the glowering, sullen, even contemptuous 19th-century minstrel characters known as Jasper Jack and Zip Coon, who sassed and sometimes assaulted the plantation white folks. Davis's bandstand attitude originated in the bebop generation's rejection of Armstrong's mugging and joking, in a trend of aggression that opened part of the way to what became blaxploitation ten years later (and now causes whites who confuse their own masochism with sensitivity to celebrate Spike Lee). The result was superbly described by Ralph Ellison:

> a grim comedy of racial manners; with the musicians employing a calculated surliness and rudeness, treating the audience very much as many white merchants in poor Negro neighborhoods treat their customers, and the white audiences were shocked at first but learned quickly to accept such treatment as evidence of "artistic" temperament. Then comes a comic reversal. Today the white audience expects the rudeness as part of the entertainment.

A story about Davis from this period may be apocryphal, but it has poetic truth. It has been related that one night a European woman approached Davis at the bar in Birdland to tell him that she loved his music, that she bought all his records, even though they were quite expensive in her country. Davis is said to have replied, "So fucking what, bitch?" As the stunned woman walked away, the musician with Davis said, "Miles, you really are an evil little black sonofabitch, aren't you?" And the trumpeter replied, "Now the bitch will buy *two* of every one of my records. When you have stock in Con Edison and make all the money I make, you have to act the way people expect you to act—they want me to be their evil nigger, and that's what I'm ready to be."

These first developments in ugliness aside, Davis's achievement in those years was genuine. It drew not only on the detailed, idiomatic thought of his own musical conceptions, but also on his interaction with his musicians. Just as Davis had been deeply impressed by the spare side of Monk's decidedly Afro-American approach to instrumental technique, and by Monk's immaculate sense of thematic variation, so Coltrane, when he left Davis to work with Monk in the summer of 1957, was inspired to push beyond his superior bebop art; Monk remade Coltrane substantially, and even the 16th-note rhythms that the saxophonist worked on until the end of his career were introduced by the pianist's formidable "Trinkle Tinkle." Thus, when Coltrane returned to Davis's band in 1958, he brought materials that elevated the intellect, the surprise, and the fire of the group. In fact, as the 1960 Stockholm recording shows, the saxophonist was blowing the trumpeter off his own bandstand.

But Davis understood how to use Coltrane. By now he was fully his own man. The album *Milestones* shows how well he understood that a jazz recording should emulate a strong 40-minute set in a nightclub. Though the underrecorded piano greatly reduces the power of what is quite mighty swing, the recital shows just how much of a bopper Davis still was, and how strongly he believed in the blues as an organizing tool for the overall sound of a recording. Four of the six pieces are blues numbers; each is approached differently, utilizing varied tempos, big band effects, saxophone exchanges of entire choruses, drum breaks, harmonization, unisons, antiphony. With the title work, moreover, Davis began his exploration of modal materials—limited harmonic structures that relied on scales—and pointed toward *Kind of Blue,* perhaps his most influential album and certainly one of his finest achievements.

In the interest of accuracy, however, it is important to recognize that Davis's publicity, and the cult that has grown up around him, inflated his work out of proportion. As a trumpeter, Davis was constantly challenged by Clifford Brown, who died, at the age of 25, in an automobile accident in 1956. By 1953 Brown was being hailed as "the new Dizzy." His extraordinary technique, his large sound, his unlimited swing, and his heroic combination of melancholy and grandeur brought an Armstrong-like bravura to the bebop trumpet. Brown's recordings show that he possessed qualities of beauty that Davis would never equal. Had Brown lived, Davis would have had to deal with another force of unarguable potency. It is the influence of Brown, not Davis, that has dominated the instrument, from Donald Byrd and Lee Morgan through Freddie Hubbard and Booker Little, and now Wynton Marsalis.

Other strengths of Davis's have been overstated, too. His idea of the small group was, finally, no more sophisticated than John Lewis's, Charles Mingus's, or Horace Silver's, and he was rarely as imaginative in his arrangements. Though his fame grew, he had yet to explore the kinds of metric innovations that obsessed Max Roach. And as the Dizzy Gillespie–Sonny Rollins–Sonny Stitt sessions of December 1957 reveal, especially in the playing of Rollins and Gillespie on "Wheatleigh Hall" and of all three on the "The Eternal Triangle," the Davis group on *Milestones* was far from the last word in swing or fire.

As for formal innovations, both George Russell and Mingus examined modal forms before Davis, and each made use of pianist Bill Evans (who became important to the next stage of Davis's development). Rollins's *Freedom Suite,* from the summer of 1958, exhibits a much more provocative and successful conception of group rhythm and extended form than anything Davis had produced. (What Rollins did with tenor saxophone, bass, and drums has still to receive the critical recognition it deserves.) And compare Davis's much-lauded improvisation on "Sid's Ahead" from *Milestones* of 1958 with Louis Armstrong's "Wild Man Blues" of 1957: you will see a vast difference in subtlety, nuance, melodic order, and swing. As fine a player as he had become, Davis could not even approximate Armstrong's authority.

Still, of all the trumpet players who came to power during and after the first shock waves of Parker's innovations, Davis seemed the one who would eventually come the closest to Armstrong's emotional gravity. As he proved with his eerie, isolated, and mournful playing for the score of the murder thriller *Elevator to the Scaffold,* and in the better moments of his collaborations with the arranger Gil Evans (*Miles Ahead, Porgy and Bess, Sketches of Spain*), he had a talent for a transfixing musical logic and a scalding melancholy. It is true that those albums with Evans also reveal that Davis could be taken in by pastel versions of European colors (they are given what value they have in these sessions by the Afro-American dimensions that were never far from Davis's embouchure, breath, fingering); if Davis's trumpet voice is removed, in fact, a good number of Evans's arrangements sound like high-level television music. But these infirmities pale before the triumphant way that Davis summoned a range of idiomatic devices far richer in color and in conception than those of any of his fellow beboppers.

In the liner notes of *Porgy and Bess,* Davis noted a movement in jazz away from harmonic complexity toward simpler structures that emphasized melodic invention. In early 1959—the watershed year in which Ellington recorded *Jazz Party;* Coleman, *The Shape of Jazz to Come;* Coltrane, *Giant Steps;* Monk, *Orchestra at Town Hall;* and Mingus, *Blues and Roots* and *Ah Um*—Davis made *Kind of Blue.* Here the modal movement reached a pinnacle, precisely because Davis understood that blues should be the foundation of any important innovation in jazz. The record, which uses his sextet with Coltrane, Cannonball Adderley, and Bill Evans, has the feeling of a suite. It is dominated by the trumpeter's compositions. (On the one piece where straightout swing was called for, Davis used Wynton Kelly instead of Evans; but on the softer pieces the things that Evans had learned from Debussy, George Russell, and Mingus issued in voicings of simple materials with intricate details.) This set realized all of the possibilities of cool jazz without sinking into the vacuous, the effete, the pretentious.

By 1960 Coltrane and Adderley left to lead their own bands, and Davis began to cope with a jazz scene of expanding technical and emotional means. Davis's playing continued to grow in power and intensity, but for all his success he was no longer the center of the discussion. The centers, instead, were Coltrane and Ornette Coleman, who were inspiring charlatans as well as serious musicians. It looked possible that the crown would slip from Davis's head, that he might be relegated to the neglect experienced by many of the older masters. Former Davis sidemen were leading the most imposing small bands of the day—Coltrane, Silver, Blakey, Adderley, Rollins. Musicians he had been associated with, such as Monk and Mingus, were either refining, or adding to, the art, especially to its formal scope. In terms of pure bebop, Gillespie's quintet with James Moody was playing extraordinarily well, as was the Modern Jazz Quartet, with its lyrical use of percussion and harmony instruments. When his second great rhythm section of Wynton Kelly, Paul Chambers, and Jimmy Cobb left him in 1963, Davis had to rebuild for what became his last great period.

He soon found the musicians who provided the foundation for his final creative years. With *Seven Steps to Heaven,* Davis introduced George Coleman on tenor, another of the fine tenor players who had followed Coltrane into the band, and the rhythm section of Herbie Hancock, Ron Carter, and Tony Williams, the force that was to shape the orchestration and the propulsion of his next phase. The band with Coleman made its finest music in concert performances, released as *Four,* and *My Funny Valentine.* Wynton Marsalis has noted that on the many fast numbers of *Four,* Davis produced unorthodox phrases that are technically challenging and demand unique fingerings. *My Funny Valentine,* by contrast, and particularly the title tune, captured Davis in a moment of heroic intimacy that he rarely reached again.

When Wayne Shorter joined him in the fall of 1964, Davis had what has been considered his best group since the *Milestones* ensemble. In

January 1965 the band recorded *E.S.P.*, and the music still sounds fresh. The trumpeter was in superb form, able to execute quickstep swing at fleet tempi with volatile penetration, to put the weight of his sound on mood pieces, to rear his way up through the blues with a fusion of bittersweet joy and what Martin Williams terms "communal anguish." The rhythm section played with a looseness that pivots off of Williams's cymbal splashes and unclinched rhythms, Carter walking some of the most impressive bass lines of the day, and Hancock developing his own version of the impressionism that Evans was making popular.

Shortly afterward, Davis went into the hospital for surgery and didn't return to work until late in the year, when he recorded *Live at the Plugged Nickel* in Chicago. At the Plugged Nickel he and his musicians were staring right in the face of the avant-garde of the period, spontaneously changing tempi and meters, playing common or uncommon notes over the harmonies, pulling in harsh timbres, all the while in a repertoire that was roughly the same as the trumpeter had been using for a decade. Again, as with *My Funny Valentine,* the pieces were remade. Shorter was in such startling form that his improvisations remained influential through the 1980s. Davis himself seemed to be having trouble with his instrument; his authority on *E.S.P.* is rarely heard here. His "Stella by Starlight," however, with its masterful touches of brass color, is one of his supreme late efforts: it swells with intimacy, voices an elevated bitterness that seems to argue with the human condition, rises to a victorious swing.

The remainder of Davis's studio recordings with that band drew on the chromaticism of Warne Marsh and Lennie Tristano, who influenced Shorter and Hancock—and, to the surprise of almost all concerned, on popular dance music, on rhythm and blues and rock 'n' roll. Though the albums vary in quality, though they sometimes lack definitive swing or cohesive fire, even the weaker ones have at least a couple of first-rate performances. The range of ideas heard from the rhythm section put it in line with the best of the day, and Shorter wrote many fine compositions, especially on *Nefertiti*. But the clues to Davis's course were in his own pieces, in "Stuff" and in much of the work for *Filles de Kilimanjaro*. His extended "Country Son," which features perhaps Shorter's finest studio improvisation with Davis, revealed that he was capable of a flirtation with pop rhythms. He was headed, in fact, in the direction of Motown, the English bands, and the black rock of Sly Stone and Jimi Hendrix.

"Mademoiselle Mabry," on *Filles,* is a brilliant example of Davis's ability to elevate pop material. An innovation in jazz rhythm, it is an appropriation and an extension of Hendrix's "The Wind Cries Mary," and proof of what Davis might have done had he kept control of his popular sources, rather than succumb to them. The borrowing was in perfect keeping with the tradition begun by Armstrong's alchemical way with banal popular songs. In fact, what Davis does with popular influences throughout this recording shows off his sophistication and his ability to transform yet another universe of music in his own image.

That Davis was able to initiate what became known as fusion, or jazz rock, and with it to inspire musicians as different as Hancock, Rollins, Hubbard, and Coleman, shows what a powerful position he had in the minds of Afro-American jazzmen. Jimmy Heath described his position this way:

> Miles led the way for a lot of people because he was one of the few who got through. He had the fine clothes, the expensive cars, the big house, all the magazine articles and the pretty girls chasing him. He seemed he was on top of *everything.* Then you had all of this rock getting all of the press and it was like Elvis Presley all over again. Miles stepped out there and decided he was going to get himself some of that money and a lot of musicians followed his lead. It was like if Miles had led the pack for so long they didn't know how to stop following him, even if the music wasn't any good.

And then came the fall. *In a Silent Way,* in 1969, long, maudlin, boasting, Davis's sound mostly lost among electronic instruments, was no more than droning wallpaper music. A year later, with *Bitches Brew,* Davis was firmly on the path of the sellout. It sold more than any other Davis album, and fully launched jazz rock with its multiple keyboards, electronic guitars, static beats, and clutter. Davis's music became progressively trendy and dismal, as did his attire; at one point in the early 1970s, with his wraparound dark glasses and his puffed shoulders, the erstwhile master of cool looked like an extra from a science fiction B-movie. He was soon proclaiming that there were no Negroes other than Sonny Rollins who could play the saxophone, and that musicians like Ornette Coleman and Mingus needed to listen to Motown, which was "where it was at." Many hoped that this would be only a phase, but the phase has lasted 20 years. In his abject surrender to popular trends, Davis sank lowest in 1985 in *You're Under Arrest,* on which record one hears what is supposed to be the sound of cocaine snorting. His albums of recent years—*Tutu, Siesta, Amandla,* and the overblown fusion piece that fills two records on *Aura*—prove beyond any doubt that he has lost all interest in music of quality.

As usual, where Davis led, many followed. His pernicious effect on the music scene since he went rapaciously commercial reveals a great deal about the perdurability of Zip Coon and Jasper Jack in the worlds of jazz and rock, in the worlds of jazz and rock criticism, in Afro-American culture itself. The cult of ethnic authenticity often mistakes the lowest common denominator for an ideal. It begets a self-image that has succumbed to a nostalgia for the mud. What we get is the bugaboo blues of the noble savage, the surly and dangerous Negro who will have nothing to do with bourgeois conventions. (This kind of Negro has long supplied the ammunition for the war that many jazz and rock critics have waged against their own middle-class backgrounds.)

Davis's corruption occurred at about the time that the "oreo" innuendo became an instrument with which formerly rejected street Negroes and thugs began to intimidate, and often manipulate, middle-class Afro-Americans in search of their roots, and of a "real" black culture. In this climate, obnoxious, vulgar, and anti-social behavior has been confused with black authenticity. This has led to blaxploitation in politics, in higher education, and in art—to Eldridge Cleaver, Huey Newton, and the Black Panthers; to black students at San Francisco State demanding that pimps be recruited to teach psychology classes; to the least inventive and most offensive work of Richard Pryor and Eddie Murphy; to the angry cartoon coons of Spike Lee and the flat, misogynist, gutter verse of Ice-T and racist rap groups like Public Enemy.

Davis provides many unwitting insights into such phenomena in his autobiography, *Miles,* written with Quincy Troupe. His is, at least in part, the story of a jet black Little Lord Fauntleroy attracted to the glamour and the fast life of the jazz world during the period when heroin was as important to the identity of the bebop generation as LSD was to the youth culture of the late 1960s. The book draws a number of interesting portraits—of Dexter Gordon, of Sugar Ray Robinson, of Philly Joe Jones—but it is overwhelmingly an outburst of inarticulateness, of profanity, of error, of self-inflation, and of parasitic paraphrasing of material from Jack

Chambers's *Milestones*. Would Simon and Schuster publish such a book, without sending the manuscript to any number of experts for evaluations and corrections, if it were written by a white man? Perhaps the editors assumed that since Quincy Troupe is a Negro, he should know.

Davis's book is divided against itself. His sensitive and lyrical recollections of experience are constantly overwhelmed by his street corner poses. The trumpeter's desire to be perceived as the hippest of the hip has destroyed his powers of communication. This is particularly unfortunate, since his story falls far outside the clichés of jazz and racial lore. His father was a successful dentist and a gentleman farmer who reared his children to have a high sense of self-esteem. Davis recalls riding horses and living on a 300-acre estate; there was a cook and a maid. It was a world as full of sophistication as it was of superstition, as full of privilege as prejudice.

Davis tells of what he heard about the St. Louis Riot of 1917, of his father looking with a shotgun for the man who called his son a nigger, of a preference Negro bands had for light-skinned musicians that blocked a young friend of his from working with Jimmie Lunceford, of the way women started throwing themselves at him as he grew into his late teens. His involvement with music is well described, as are the personalities of many musicians he grew up with, some of whom fell by the wayside. There are powerful evocations of certain aspects of the times: of how drugs took over the lives of musicians, of the difficulties musicians had negotiating the territory between the cult world of bebop and the more general kind of success enjoyed by Ellington. And some of what is probably Troupe's best writing has nothing to do with music; the brief section on Sugar Ray Robinson sheds unexpected light on the influence of boxing on Davis's playing. If one listens to Davis's jabbing, suspenseful, aggressive improvisation on "Walkin'" from the 1961 Black Hawk recording, one hears not only Monk, but also, we can now say, Robinson:

> Sugar Ray Robinson would put an opponent in four or five traps during every round in the first two or three rounds, just to see how his opponent would react. Ray would be reaching, and he would stay just out of reach so he could measure you to knock you out, and you didn't even know what was happening until, BANG! you found yourself counting stars. Then, on somebody else, he might hit him hard in his side—BANG!—after he made him miss a couple of jabs. He might do that in the first round. Then he'd tee-off on the sucker upside his head after hitting him eight or nine more times hard in the side. Maybe he'd hit him four or five times hard in the ribs, then back to the head. So by the fourth or fifth round, the sucker don't know what Ray's going to do to him next.

Once our memoirist gets to New York, however, the book begins to lose itself in contradictions and obscenities. On one page Davis will say that Parker was "teaching me a lot about music—chords and shit—that I would go play on the piano" when he went to Juilliard, and then a few pages later that "Bird didn't teach me much as far as music goes." Davis claims that he became the musical director of Parker's group, but Max Roach, who was also in the band, vehemently disputes the claim. (It is proof, he says, that the trumpeter has "become senile.") Davis recalls being taken to Minton's in Harlem for the great jam sessions by Fats Navarro, whom many considered second only to Gillespie, but then says, "I would tell him shit—technical shit—about the trumpet." Jimmy Heath has a rather different memory of what Davis did or did not learn from Navarro: "Fats ate Miles up every night. Miles couldn't outswing him, he couldn't outpower him, he couldn't outsweet him, he couldn't do anything except take that whipping on *every* tune."

On things racial, it's impossible to figure out from this book what Davis really felt. "I could learn more in one session at Minton's than it would take me two years to learn at Juilliard. At Juilliard, after it was all over, all I was going to know was a bunch of white styles: nothing new." But only one page later he says:

I couldn't believe that all them guys like Bird, Prez, Bean, all them cats wouldn't go to museums or libraries and borrow those musical scores so they could check out what was happening. I would go to the library and borrow scores by all those great composers, like Stravinsky, Alban Berg, Prokofiev. I wanted to see what was going on in all of music. Knowledge is freedom and ignorance is slavery, and I just couldn't believe someone could be that close to freedom and not take advantage of all the shit that they can. I have never understood why black people didn't take advantage of all the shit that they can.

Of the interracial couples that he saw in the clubs on 52nd Street, Davis observes:

A lot of white people, though, didn't like what was going on on 52nd Street. . . . They thought that they were being invaded by niggers from Harlem, so there was a lot racial tension around bebop. Black men were going with fine, rich white bitches. They were all over those niggers out in public and the niggers were clean as a motherfucker and talking all kind of hip shit. So you know a lot of white people, especially white men, didn't like this new shit.

And then, explaining why he didn't want to do an interview for *Playboy,* he declares, "All they have are blond women with big tits and flat asses or no asses. So who the fuck wants to see that all the time? Black guys like big asses, you know, and we like to kiss on the mouth and white women don't have no mouths to kiss on."

Davis's treatment of women is disgusting. He details the way he destroyed the career of his first wife, Frances Taylor, who was a dancer, and later, claiming that black women are too bossy, he cites Taylor as an example of the way a good colored woman ought to be. He volunteers tales of slapping Cicely Tyson around, though she was probably responsible for his not dying from a binge of cocaine that spanned nearly six years.

The cavalier way that Davis imputes drug use to black musician after black musician is no less objectionable. (He claims repeatedly that the white jazz press didn't start paying attention to white guys being junkies until Stan Getz was arrested, but Leonard Feather has shown that in fact white musicians got the bulk of the attention for using drugs.) And the morality of the trumpeter's memory is oddly selective. About a woman who helped him during his time as a drug addict, Davis says, "I was seeing this same rich white girl who I'd met in St. Louis; she had come to New York to check me out. Let's call her 'Alice,' because she's still alive and I don't want to cause her trouble; plus she's married." And the customers of a white call girl were "very important men—white men mostly—whose names I won't mention." It seems that militant Inky respects the privacy of those mouthless, gluteus minimus white women and those white johns more than he does the dignity of his fellow musicians, some of whom were his very close friends.

One of the most disturbing things about *Miles* is its debt to Jack Chambers's *Milestones,* a critical biography written in two parts between 1983 and 1985 and now available in one volume from Quill. Pages 160–61 of *Miles,* for example, look alarmingly like pages 166–67 of *Milestones.* (There is even a cavalier reference to Chambers as "some writer.") Davis and Troupe:

> Bird had an exclusive contract with Mercury (I think he had left Verve by then), so he had to use a pseudonym on record. Bird had given up shoot-

ing heroin because since Red Rodney had been busted and sent back to prison at Lexington, Bird thought the police were watching him. In place of his normal big doses of heroin, now he was drinking an enormous amount of alcohol.

Chambers:

> . . . the man behind the pseudonym was Charlie Parker. Parker was under some pressure, not only because he had an exclusive contract with Mercury, but also because the trumpeter in his regular band, Red Rodney, had been arrested and committed to the federal prison in Lexington. Parker believed that he was being watched by narcotics agents, according to Ross Russell, and he had given up narcotics for the time being and was consuming large quantities of alcohol instead.

Much of the material used in *Milestones* and again in *Miles* comes from interviews done over the years. Troupe denies using any of it, then says that "the man can quote himself," then blames the publisher for "messing up" by omitting a discography and a bibliography, and by not checking facts.

But the important point, finally, is that *Miles* paints the picture of an often gloomy monster. It is full of stories that take the reader down into the sewers of Davis's musical, emotional, and chemical decline. Once the rage at his cruelty and his self-inflation has passed, we are left aghast at a man of monumental insecurity who, for all his protests about white power and prejudice, is often controlled by his fear of it, or of any other significant power. (One example of many: Davis asserts that he never listens to white music critics, and blames many of the woes of the music business on them, but then he admits that once they had him worried that he sounded inferior to Chet Baker, who was his imitator.) Obsessed with remaining young, and therefore willing to follow any trend in pop music, Davis is now a surly sellout who wants his success to seem like a heroic battle against the white world.

To that end, this former master of musical articulation often reduces himself to an inarticulate man. Davis has worn the mask of the street corner for too long; he thinks, like Pryor and Murphy and Lee, that his invective gives him authenticity. Gone is the elegant and exigent Afro-American authenticity of the likes of Ellington, at ease in the alley as well as in the palace, replaced by youth culture vulgarity that vandalizes the sweep and substance of Afro-American life. The fall of Davis reflects perhaps the essential failure of contemporary Negro culture: its mock-democratic idea that the elites, too, should lie down in the gutter. Aristocracies of culture, however, come not from the acceptance of limitations, but from the struggle with them, as a group or an individual, from within or without.

HOMAGE TO MILES DAVIS
AMIRI BARAKA

Amiri Baraka's homage to his "ultimate culture hero" appeared in the Sunday magazine section of *The New York Times* on June 16, 1985, five days before Davis's band opened the Kool Jazz Festival. Baraka's piece is an extended reflection on Miles Davis's significance to the author, the jazz world, and the African-American community. While conducting research for his appreciation, Baraka spent four hours in New York interviewing Davis in the bar of the United Nations Plaza Hotel. Some material from their conversation appears in the piece. Also included are comments about Davis's preeminence from Dizzy Gillespie, Max Roach, Reggie Workman, Steve McCall, Olu Dara, and Craig Harris. The "big-name jazz critic" that Baraka originally specified but the *Times* editorial staff deleted is Nat Hentoff. Hentoff's name is mentioned in the much longer version of this article that was published two years later in Baraka's book *The Music: Reflections on Jazz and Blues.*

For many years of my life, Miles Davis was my ultimate culture hero: artist, cool man, bad dude, hipster, clear as daylight and funky as revelation. His influence and effect on the music called jazz and its players is still somewhat astonishing. Davis, as composer and musician, has been at the center of one stream of African-American music and its variations and performers for 40 years—since he first arrived in New York City in 1944 from East St. Louis, Ill., to look for Charlie (Yardbird) Parker, the saxophone genius, and enroll at Juilliard.

But like the music itself, Davis's influence has not been limited to jazz musicians. Davis is almost as well known by contemporary European and Euro-American classical composers and followers; he was the recipient of Denmark's Sonning Prize for lifetime achievement, the first time a jazz musician has received the award. Blues people, rock folk, reggae runners, gospel chanters, neoclassical or neoromantic revelers and on out—all know his music. And the most sensitive have been directly changed by it.

Davis is perceived by a wide cross section of artists as a creative artist of the highest and most intense level. Few artists of my generation, whether writers, painters or dancers, do not know the trumpeter's work. Few, too, remain uninfluenced in some way by his work. Many, for instance, sculpted or painted while "Kind of Blue" intoned its modal hipness. Many used such pieces as "Sketches of Spain" or "Round About Midnight" to create their dances. Many stayed up all night whacking away at the typewriter while "Walkin'" or "Steamin'" made the darkness give up its lonely esthetic to art.

The prospect of finally doing a piece on the man, of having to interview him, meet him up close, was very important to me for these reasons and more. I remember one night in 1960 when I was a little boy of 25 trying to be a jazz critic. I had gone without benefit of a sponsor to the Village Vanguard where Davis was playing.

I don't remember the exact group he had with him then, but John Coltrane, the brilliant tenor saxophonist, was gone. Sax man Hank Mobley, one of my road buddies whom I'd met in Newark, was with Davis.

When I went into the back room, which still passes as a dressing room, the musicians were spread out, casually rapping, Davis all the way to the rear like a point. He waved off my timid request, mumbling something, I guess, about how he didn't want to be bothered.

With that youthful mixture of angry rejection and bold daring, I spat back, saying he would have talked had I been a big-name jazz critic.

The prospect of an interview raised the memory of that history and made me smile a little. Now, coming into the well-appointed, mirror-sparkling bar at the United Nations Plaza Hotel, I wondered would he remember.

My very first impression, watching this beautiful man moving gracefully yet walking with a cane and talking to waiters he knew, is that Miles Davis, who recently turned 59, looks like a real celebrity. His dress sets the rest of him off—as he means it to. His deep, black-brown skin is still a marvel of the African esthetic. At once, his old sobriquet—the Black Prince—comes back. He handles the gold-topped cane like a casual guidon of elegance. The cane becomes the focus, rather than the condition that once required it. Davis wears an unbelievably hip fisherman's cap made of what looks like black raffia, a black military-style jacket, ballooning, black pants and black clogs—along with some extremely expensive-looking sunglasses and the cane.

Old-time Miles Davis worshippers have always dug Davis's "vines" (clothing)—whether the cap pulled down around his ears on the hot 1950's "Dig" album, or the green button-down shirt, sleeves rolled up, and the impenetrable shades on "Milestones." He was always stylish. Although—and this is instructive as to our perception of the whole esthetic—as Davis got more into the music called "fusion" (the merging of cool jazz lines with rhythm-and-blues), he began to wear some wild, Sly and the Family Stone-styled threads we oldtime neo-Ivy intellectuals thought of as frankly out. ("Red brightens you up," Davis says at a later point. "Audiences love you even if you ain't doing nothing—even if you're terrible." Then he adds, "If I don't have on something I like, I can't play.")

What I got from Miles Davis in conversation and from his manner is a man always, as the writer Richard Wright said the intellectual and artist must be, "at the top of his time," aware of who he is and what they are and astride them both.

Dizzy Gillespie recently told me the night the Blue Note jazz club celebrated the famed trumpeter's birthday, as well as its own, that Davis "was like a man who had made a pact with himself . . . to never repeat himself." Davis himself has said it is like a "curse" to constantly change. But change is a manifestation of his deep sensitivity, forever impressed with the real, and the real is in constant motion.

The introductions are going round as Davis sits. We shake hands; he says, "The mystery man." Me!, a "mystery man"—you never know how people perceive each other across the clouds of time and distance, what they look like to each other, what they mean to each other.

A quiet, soft-spoken, even gentle man with a bright, quick sense of humor, Davis does not appear the overbearing ogre some have made him out to be. He banters with the waiters as he eats poached salmon and drinks Perrier.

I had said I only needed an hour. Most people dislike drawn-out interviews—I know I do. I also thought I knew so much about Miles Davis over the years. But being there with the man, the herd of questions his presence occasioned was actually embarrassing. I knew I couldn't ask most of them, coldly probe someone who had in one sense actually given me consciousness.

How did he get to here, to playing "The Man With the Horn" and "Star People," albums I do not care very much for? What brought him from the sublime heights of "Ornithology" and "Venus De Milo," or the myriad other anthems of the deep hip, to an overheavy back beat blocking the light, whirring, metal ideas?

It was not only in the asking and the telling that something changed for me. His latest albums, "You're Under Arrest" and "Decoy" (particularly the title tune), are a clear return to a much higher level of performance, more competent technically, more emotionally rewarding esthetically.

The reasons behind his development became clearer to me as we talked (and we would talk for four hours). I went back to his music to test and confirm the understanding his words compelled me toward.

"What can you say about Miles?" Gillespie says. "He's always changing— you never know what he's going to do next. Plus he's got . . . a kind of . . ."

Another younger musician breaks in, "an aura."

"Naw," says Gillespie, "I don't know about that. It sounds too much like some other word."

"Mystique," the younger man rejoinders.

"Yeh," he replies, "that's it. Miles got a mystique about him—plus he's at the top of his profession." Gillespie begins his hoarse laughter. "And he's got way, way, way, *way* more money."

He sums it up as only the Diz can: Davis constantly changes; he possesses a mystique that sometimes threatens to obscure his music yet is created in part by the deepness of that music as well as by his legendary personality. Davis, who earns between $30,000 and $50,000 per concert, may have even snatched a few coins in tribute to his "topness" and longevity.

For me, his music has always had that single vulnerable feeling, like a person, beautiful and solitary, moving gracefully, sometimes arrogantly, through the night. What does he think of his own music, from those first records and residence with Charlie Parker to his later changes?

"We were always playing way up there," says Davis, referring to the tempo. "It was all so fast, nobody knew what we were playing. *Blam.* It was over. I thought people needed a bottom, something to refer to."

He is recalling the 1945-to-1949 tenure with Parker around 52d Street—where the revolutionary music of be-bop and the hottest of the swing players merged downtown after the initial experimental developments uptown. Be-bop was the rebellion against the stiff swing arrangements of the 1940's. It re-emphasized small groups, improvisation, the restoration of African polyrhythms and the primacy of the blues. Such sound scientists as Parker, Gillespie, Thelonious Monk, Bud Powell and Kenny (Klook) Clarke led the charge.

Miles Davis was a young, middle-class intellectual seeking high art— a student of the hottest new musical innovations, yet a product of a conservative, professional, land-owning class. He could study at Juilliard by day and hang out with the artistically brilliant but socially incorrigible Parker the rest of the time. They lived on a weekly allowance sent by his father, an East St. Louis dentist. "I thought everybody in New York was hip," he says. "I came to New York City expecting everybody was sounding like Dizzy!"

When I ask Davis how he knew it was music he wanted and why the trumpet, his answer has that confirming yet mystifying near-rationalism. "Basically, it was how they looked when they were playing," he says. "I liked that. I wanted to look like that, too. I liked the way they held the horn, the way they stood. I wanted to do that." (It reminded me again of myself, a neophyte trumpet player imitating Davis in the ancient 1950's, a leather gig bag in my hand.)

"I have to hold my horn a certain way," explains Davis, who was performing with professional groups by the age of 16. "When I went to St. Louis with my boys, to check out how a band looked, I could tell by the way a musician holds his horn. If he don't hold his horn right, he can't play."

The photographs of Davis during the be-bop period show a young blood swimming in New York drape suits, his hair "gassed" (straightened), standing next to Bird—in the eye of the hurricane. His cracked notes and flubs from the period are legendary, alongside the awesomely articulate Parker, soaring past the stratosphere into the musical "way-gonesphere." Davis was a striking contrast—anxious, young, archly lyrical, his sprouting musical voice as much a question as a statement.

A few minutes later, Davis had hooked up with Gil Evans and Gerry Mulligan, and some of the young white players drawn by Evans's arranging for the Claude Thornhill Orchestra. Evans's cool, lush harmonies and even the innovative use of brass and Ellingtonian scoring (reeds) had a profound effect on Davis. A number of Davis's major successes commercially and artistically, including "Sketches of Spain" and "Porgy and Bess," make use of Evans's orchestral approach and arrangements.

Later, the 12 sides on "Birth of the Cool" became the first important result of the Davis-Evans collaboration, the symphonic quality transferred to a small group. For me, "Venus De Milo," "Move," "Godchild," "Budo" and "Darn That Dream" were the highest art I had ever contemplated, and they still are inestimable road signs of mastery.

I asked him how he got from the very hot of bop to "the cool," the prototype setting a whole musical, social and commercial movement in motion. Davis says Thornhill's music drew him because he wanted a music with more melodic access and a "cushion" (bottom) of harmonies that made his own simple voice an elegant, somewhat detached "personality" effortlessly perceiving and expressing.

What seems *subdued* in him, as his middle-register light-vibrato tone would seem to confirm, shows up elsewhere as tension, which is *dramatic* and rhythmically very funky, earthy. That undercurrent of tension comes with the smallest sound of his horn. He can wail with one or two notes placed, dropped, fired, drawled, sung, whispered, as light, reason, sweetness, regard, elation. His solos are extensions of the rhythm yet divide it, as time can be divided, even seemingly obliterated, but be as abstract and as unpredictable as our hearts.

After talking to Davis, I viewed his music video, "Decoy," and an interview filmed by Columbia Records, for whom Davis has recorded since the mid-1950's. Both gave aspects of Davis's abiding passions and his most recent pursuits. "I'm doing a video because I can," he said in the interview. "I'm gearing the video to all colors. Not just white. I won't be acting silly. I don't look silly and I don't act silly."

The video is Davis, playing, somewhat exaggerated in his gestures, his tongue pushing out. He seems whirled slowly in place, electronic graphics—much like his own spare drawings—bouncing from his horn.

In the interview, Davis, with his usual clarity and understated hilarity, talked about hiring white musicians, which he has increasingly done over the years and which once generated negative response from black musicians and fans. He explained that he wants to play "today music." Over the years, he has had to tell many musicians—black and white, "Don't play what you know but what you hear.

"White musicians usually are overtrained, and black musicians sometimes are undertrained," he said. "You have to mix the two. A black musician has his own sound, but if you want it played straight, mix in a white musician and the piece will still be straight, only you'll get feeling and texture—up, down, around, silly, wavy, slow, fast—you have more to work with. There's funky white musicians. But after classical training, you have to learn to play social music. You have to learn to underplay. I tell 'em, 'Don't practice all the time or you'll sound like that.'"

Davis described how he went "with his feelings" in playing, how much he loved music. "I always play the blues . . . my body's full of rhythm. I like broken rhythm—strong melodies, chords on the synthesizer. I use the DX 7. It's a whole other attitude. It's like sketching." The film showed Miles drawing and painting (an example of which appears on the inside jacket of "Decoy").

The coolness of the early 1950's gave way to a stomping sound; people marching, the assertion of gospel music and Africa expanded the music stylistically. These developments in the music coincided with a rising national consciousness among the African-American people characterized by the civil-rights movement.

Horace Silver, the pianist and composer, introduced contemporary gospel into postbop jazz. It was a quick, funky music, with a sharper eye on arrangement, in response to the cool. It had a free, screaming, rhythmic emphasis, even whispered. Miles Davis became its most sophisticated master. He developed a new black, postbop, postcool ensemble and solo style: He was laid back yet hot, melodic yet tense—searching. The next few years of his work were a measure of *all* the music of that period.

In 1955, Davis assembled a group that included the pianist Red Garland, the drummer Philly Joe Jones, the bassist Paul Chambers and, most important, the tenor saxophonist John Coltrane. The quintet—without peers during that period—combined the finger-popping urban funk blues of the hard-bop era with a harmonic cushion and Davis's gorgeous melodic invention. It caused a sensation among jazz people. Later, the alto saxophonist Julian (Cannonball) Adderley would join Davis.

"I used to tell them, 'The bass got the tonic. Don't play in the same register as the sax. Lay out. Don't play'"—the Milesian esthetic for his band. When he listens to his own music, Davis says: "I always listen to what I can leave out."

Davis's quintet and sextet, the most popular jazz groups of the times, carried the sound and image of the contemporary, urban American intellectual and artist. The albums "Milestones" and "Round About Midnight" were great social events as well as artistic triumphs. "Kind of Blue" led us into new formal and intellectual vistas. So powerful and broadly expressive was the classic group—with Adderley the formalist on one side and Coltrane the expressionist on the other—that it contained the elements for establishing or redefining two significant jazz styles that have dominated to one degree or another the music for the last 30 years. And though Adderley's later band and the music and the musicians he developed were prototypes for fusion, Miles Davis is the music's real originator.

Coltrane's direction and legacy were to redefine avantgarde—to transform the social upsurge to a musical revolution.

Davis talks about the two directions Coltrane and Adderley represented. "I showed Trane all that," he says, casually accepting credit for the chordal experimentation and chromatic lyricism that the saxophonist began to be identified with, and which in turn revolutionized the music. "Cannonball just played funk. But he could interpret any feeling."

Davis was not only the cool hipster of my be-bop youth, but also the embodiment of a black attitude that had grown steadily more ubiquitous in the 1950's—defiance. All the stories about Davis, who shook off a four-year heroin addiction during this time, told us he was "bad." He even had the unfortunate but spiritually-in-tune-with-the-times experience in 1959 of being beaten by racist policemen outside Birdland as he took a breather between sets. Black newspapers called it a "Georgia head whipping," comparing it directly with the beatings black activists got marching against "Jim Crow."

My road buddies and I knew he regularly went to the gym and boxed. We had even been close enough a couple of times when the quintet opened at the Bohemia in Greenwich Village to hear the fog-horn bass that was his voice. That was the way he was supposed to sound: hip and somewhat mysterious with a touch of street toughness.

"When I think of Davis's influence, I think he's had a positive influence on black people in general," says Steve McCall, drummer and an elder statesmen of the new music. "He transcended the slave mentality. I remember when he was setting all kinds of styles. The artist. He had class. Good taste. His music had a density."

By the time he recorded "Miles Ahead" in 1957, Davis understood enough about the entire American esthetic—its lushness and pretension—to make the cool statements on a level that was truly popular and which had the accents of African America included not as contrasting anxiety or tension but as an equal sensuousness.

"Sketches of Spain" and "Porgy and Bess" are high American musical statements, their tension being between a functional impressionism, serious in its emotional detail, and mood without significance. It is the bluesiness of the Miles Davis conception, even submerged in all the lushness, that gives these moods an intelligence and sensitivity. His horn probes like a dowser for beauty. The horn itself is so beautiful the listener feels that, maybe, all is a dream.

"Miles just shows several aspects of being creative," says Max Roach, the drummer and another of the genius teen-agers to hook up with Parker to create the explosion of be-bop. "If you're being creative, you can't be like you were yesterday. Miles exemplifies it. The record industry keeps reading us out . . . ," categorizing the music as an antiquated music form.

"But Miles will step out. Lester Young did that . . . always looking. It's the law of everything. Miles is that way . . . Ella"—Fitzgerald—"and Miles breathed new life into the record companies. I think what Miles is doing is in keeping with our creative people today."

The classic 1950's Davis group expressed both the soul and the rage. The 60's restatement with such future fusion stars as Herbie Hancock and Wayne Shorter does not carry the balance. Yet Davis says he told them the same thing, told them what "not to do too much of." Davis's group became the vehicle for the increasing use of the pop-commercial aspect of his mind.

By the end of the 1960's, his music had begun to take on a somber, somewhat formal tone. He was still trying to move, as always, trying to develop new forms, use different materials. The cushion and the use of electrified instruments—once thought to be the exclusive property of rhythm and blues—were also gradually rising.

Davis was moving to change his music and, one would suppose, himself once more. In my own mind, the album "In A Silent Way" in 1969 is the beginning of the elaboration of what came to be known as fusion. Davis had come up with a new direction. The music is contradictory, subdued yet bright. Now cushion and soloist—background and foreground seemingly exchanged places constantly.

"Bitches Brew" was made the same year and demonstrated not only that Davis's music had changed, but that he was ready to elaborate on the changes. The result—the incorporation of a definite back beat and electric instruments—was controversial.

The long passage of the 1960's had worked its magic on Davis. When he came out of his conservative, neo-Ivy threads in the 70's, it was not for loose, flowing African dress; it was for the fringed leather that the Black

Panther or the hippie might wear. Davis identified more completely with what finally is the more secular, more "integrated" and ultimately more popular and commercial consciousness of rhythm and blues or rock or fusion that led him to the music he is making today. The "new" infusion of such white musicians as Joe Zawinul and Keith Jarrett on a "permanent" basis in Davis's bands in the early 1970's was akin to the coalition politics of the Panthers. What is clear, though, is Davis carried them and many, many others in *his* direction.

But by 1975, Davis had dropped out of sight, neither recording nor touring. He had consistent health problems, one leading to the insertion of a prosthetic hip joint in 1983.

By the time of his "cooling out," lasting from 1975 until 1981, Davis had made still more personnel changes—adding a permanent electric bass and guitars: Mike Henderson, Pete Cosey, Reggie Lucas, Larry Coryell, and young players such as the drummer Al Foster or the percussionist Mtume. The albums recorded in this period were musically less than dynamic, but their song titles had a politically evocative mood—"Red China Blues," "Calypso Frelimo" and "Zimbabwe."

The new star trumpeter, Olu Dura, tries to assess Miles Davis's concept and contributions: "Miles bridged the gap to both Americas. He's hip to the whole culture here. He is playing it in his music. Miles was dealing with all that America had to say. He makes you a true American. He's off the Mississippi River," a reference to Miles's Midwest birthplace. "He's like the center of the pendulum. He goes where the history is—East, West, North, South. He's a consummate musical scientist."

Davis, both in print and in person, seems a man not only anxious to be appreciated and celebrated by blacks, but sensitive to the tragedy of race in this country, particularly as it relates to his musical and social life. His wife, the actress Cicely Tyson, appears to be like-minded. Davis has had run-ins with the critics, mostly white, particularly about their opinions over the years about his playing. *Down Beat*, the magazine viewed by many as the official jazz chronicle, published new favorable reviews of the Bird-Miles records (the original review was uniformly negative). In a *Down Beat* readers' poll, "Decoy" was voted the jazz album of 1984.

"I don't pay no attention to these white critics about my music," he says. "Be like somebody from Europe coming criticizing Chinese music. They don't know about that. I've lived what I played."

Of late, Davis has been trying to reconnect jazz with its most popular and commercial forms, r & b and blues. A great deal of outcry has come from people who revered classical Davis, charging that since "Bitches

Brew," he has sold out. Yet jazz is impossible without blues—it is the child of the blues, Langston Hughes told us. The business world, however, categorizes life for the marketplace, and an artificial separation has resulted.

Reggie Workman, the bassist, points out that Davis is doing the same thing, just using the electronics to reach people. "Miles's music is what he's always been playing," he says. "He's surrounded himself with electronics as a mediator between himself and today's market."

The results—"You're Under Arrest" and "Decoy"—clearly stand head and shoulders above his earlier "out of retirement" efforts. Most important, Davis is getting his "chops" back. One cannot lay off the trumpet, a notoriously taxing instrument, and pop up crackling. The latest recordings show Davis stronger, piercing through the electronic environment tellingly.

"Miles survived," explains Craig Harris, the trombonist. "He kept his mind open. He understands business, and he's doing what he wants to do. Miles don't care who agrees or disagrees with him. Miles says, 'This is what I'm gonna do.' And he sticks by his guns. And everybody follows Miles."

THE CONCEPTION OF THE COOL
RICHARD WILLIAMS

In 1948 Gil Evans lived on West 55th Street in midtown
Manhattan, three blocks from the vortex of 52nd Street. His
apartment was nestled behind a Chinese laundry, and many musicians, such as Miles Davis, George Russell, John Lewis, and Gerry
Mulligan, congregated there at all hours. One outgrowth of these
nondescript socials was Miles Davis's first band as a leader, a
nonet that featured arrangements by Evans and others from the
Evans salon.

A total of twelve arrangements (only two by Evans) were
recorded under Davis's leadership for Capitol during the period
1949–1950. Unfortunately, these recordings have been overgener-
alized as emotionally restrained by recent commentators—a kind
of critical payback for propagating a markedly less-intense style of
jazz on the West Coast. While it's true that some of the writing for
the Davis nonet is airy and does not convey the crackling intensity
of bebop, John Lewis's arrangements of Denzil Best's "Move" and
Bud Powell's "Budo" are undeniable uptempo flag-wavers, relent-
lessly pushed ahead by drummer Max Roach and bassist Al
McKibbon. Even some of the medium-tempo tunes swing rather
hard despite softened timbres and a texture thickened by deep
brass instruments.

The change of scenery, of course, is what interested Davis in
the first place, and these arrangements showcase his dry, plaintive

sound, which floats above and snakes through the charts. The significance of this first Evans and Davis project, that several years later was collectively dubbed the "Birth of the Cool," is explained in the following Richard Williams piece, excerpted from his 1993 book, *Miles Davis: The Man in the Green Shirt*.

The apartment was on West 55th Street, behind a Chinese laundry. Dark and airless, it belonged to Gil Evans, a thin, fair-haired, Canadian-born arranger who had made a small reputation arranging songs like "Polka Dots and Moonbeams" for the struggling big band of pianist Claude Thornhill. To that unprepossessing pad in the summer of 1948 came a procession of restlessly brilliant young men whose efforts would change the sound of popular music.

Just three blocks uptown from the heaving bars and nightclubs of 52nd Street, the thoroughfare known as "Swing Street," they met and conspired. There was John Lewis, 27, a thoughtful pianist-composer who had worked with Charlie Parker and Dizzy Gillespie, and would go on to form the Modern Jazz Quartet. There was Gerry Mulligan, the crew-cut baritone saxophonist who had written "Disc Jockey Jump" for the popular swing band of Gene Krupa and was to lead one of the most influential jazz combos of the early Fifties. There was George Russell, 24, a music professor's son who, during a lengthy period in hospital with tuberculosis, had formulated a new system of harmonic principles that he would later publish as the *Lydian Chromatic Concept of Tonal Organisation*. And, most significantly, there was a 21-year-old trumpeter called Miles Davis.

A dentist's son from East St Louis, a scion of the black middle class, Davis had arrived in New York four years earlier—ostensibly to study classical composition at the Juilliard Conservatory, in fact to find Parker, Gillespie and the fount of modern jazz. He succeeded so well that he gave up his studies almost immediately, spending three years with Parker's band, until he could no longer stomach the great saxophonist's perennial unreliability and slipperiness over money. By the time Miles Davis met Gil Evans, he was ready to make his own move.

At 35, Evans was the senior of the group that convened in the apartment on West 55th Street—although his diffident charm made him seem beyond questions of age. (In his seventies, he would be found in London, collaborating with Sting and David Bowie.) The big bands of the swing era were music factories, machines that demanded regular maintenance and strict supervision—qualities entirely inimical to Evans's bohemian temperament. But he had found in Claude Thornhill an unusually constructive employer, who—even at the cost of his own commercial success—

firmly encouraged his arranger's attempts to lead the ensemble away from the clichés of swing and into its own artistic territory.

Both Thornhill and Evans were inspired by unusual textures (Evans admired Ravel and Fauré as much as he loved Armstrong and Ellington), so the band was expanded to include a pair of French horns and a tuba, while the saxophone section made use of a wide variety of auxiliary wood-wind instruments, from piccolo to bass clarinet. Thornhill and Evans also shared a distaste for music that moved too fast: like other big bands, they played for dancers, but it must have been hard to do anything other than smooch to Thornhill's largely slow-motion repertoire, with its rich inner voicings and exotic detailing. Inevitably, such a band could not outlast the boom years of swing: when Thornhill came out of the US Navy in 1946 he reassembled many of his old sidemen, but when even Benny Goodman and Count Basie were feeling the economic pain, there wasn't much hope for an overmanned and idiosyncratic outfit such as his. Among musicians, though, his prestige was unusually high; normally contemptuous of commercial big-band leaders, they recognised a rare measure of altruism struggling against the odds in an environment which encouraged conformity.

It was certainly symptomatic of Thornhill's disastrous commercial judgment that in 1947, not long before the band met its end as a permanent unit, he allowed Evans to add arrangements of three Charlie Parker tunes—"Yardbird Suite," "Donna Lee" and "Anthropology"—to the repertoire. Bebop was music for listening, not dancing, which was why it became the first form of jazz to avoid broad popularity. If dancers had trouble with the dark ballads normally favoured by the Thornhill band, they must have been tied in knots by Evans's attempts to retain the fleetness and angularity of tunes originally played by a skeletal bebop quintet, even though the tones and textures were fleshed out with the broader instrumental palette at his disposal. The single unresolved tuba notes ending two of the pieces were a clear indication of Evans's understanding of the elliptical weirdness of bebop, but were hardly the calibre of ammunition with which Thornhill could mow down the likes of Les Brown or Tommy Dorsey in the fight for public favour.

Davis had co-written "Donna Lee," and it was when Evans came looking for the sheet music that the two met. Somehow, the aggressive young trumpeter and the serene older arranger recognised each other as a kindred spirit, and a crucial 40-year relationship began.

They were looking for something new. Jazz, since its early days on the streets of New Orleans, had been a music with a strong component of competitive machismo: the trumpeter Buddy Bolden could be heard, according to legend, 30 miles away on a clear night, while in Kansas City in the Thirties, the ethos of the "cutting contest" had turned jam sessions into musical wrestling matches. Indeed, *faster, higher, stronger* could have been a motto for virtually all trumpeters before Miles Davis, all arrangers before Gil Evans. But these two were hearing something different: a music with deeper currents and softer, subtler colours, the product of a sensibility formed by factors other than strength and endurance. Davis, too, was a competitive man, but his superiority was not the kind established by toe-to-toe slugging. It could be expressed only in something far less mundane: the development of a style so cool as to render its owner beyond competition—untouchable, unknowable, invulnerable.

The place to start was with the sound and speed of the music, and it was here that Gil Evans made his contribution. He could structure music that was delicate without being effete, that could sing of the blues without needing to drench itself in sweat. Against that background, Davis could begin the true evolution of a voice that had found little room to grow within the brisk technical rigour and repetitive formal routines of bebop.

Evans had always liked the idea of writing for individual soloists: a *concerto grosso* approach evolved from Ellington's practice of forming a piece with specific sidemen in mind. His ambition to work with Louis Armstrong foundered on the indifference of the trumpeter's manager, while an approach to Parker fell victim to the saxophonist's unwillingness to concentrate. In Davis, though, he found the perfect voice—and an utterly sympathetic sensibility.

Their plan called for a scaled-down version of the Thornhill band, retaining as far as possible its wide range of pitch and timbre. In Davis's mind, the structure would mimic the divisions of a vocal quartet: bass, baritone, alto and soprano. A rhythm section of piano, bass and drums would support six horns: tuba at the bottom, then baritone saxophone, trombone and French horn in the middle, trumpet and alto saxophone at the top. Each horn had its own voice, separated by air and space but deployed with a flexibility that permitted many different combinations and contrasts.

The rhythm section—Lewis on piano, the bassist Al McKibbon, and the drummer Max Roach—came from bebop, bringing with them that idiom's rhythmic intensity. Joining Davis and Mulligan in the horn chairs were a young trombonist, Mike Zwerin; a French horn specialist, Junior Collins; and two graduates from the Thornhill academy, tuba-player Bill Barber and alto saxophonist Lee Konitz. Davis, in fact, had wanted Sonny Stitt, a gifted Parker disciple; for once, he had his mind changed—by

Mulligan, who saw that Konitz's pale, translucent tone and oblique phrasing would provided a different sort of inner voice.

Since Evans was a notoriously slow worker, and each piece had to be tailor-made to fit the unorthodox instrumentation, it took them some time to assemble even a minimally adequate repertoire. Mulligan and Lewis pitched in with arrangements, while Davis took upon himself the tiresome burden of calling the musicians, organising rehearsals and hustling for gigs. In his first real shot at leadership, he was clearly making an effort to turn this unconventional outfit into a credible working proposition. Monte Kay, an agent who worked with many jazz musicians, eventually booked the nine-piece ensemble into the Royal Roost, a popular bop joint on Broadway, where it opened in August 1948, second on the bill to the Count Basie Orchestra, under a sign reading *Miles Davis's Nonet: Arrangements by Gerry Mulligan, Gil Evans and John Lewis*—an unusual form of billing which clearly reflected the band's unique selling point.

That first fortnight attracted the attention of some of the more inquiring minds among their fellow musicians. Basie himself listened hard, and is reported to have told Davis that the band's music was "slow and strange, but real good". Surviving transcriptions of radio broadcasts from the Royal Roost show a spirited and confident ensemble. The critics were less certain, although there was constructive interest from Pete Rugolo, the musical director of Capitol Records. A skilled arranger himself, having helped establish Stan Kenton's controversial "progressive jazz" approach in the mid-Forties, Rugolo could not rush the band into the studio, since the American Federation of Musicians had instigated a recording ban which lasted through 1948. Since there was no other interest from booking agents, the project was put on hold and the musicians went off to earn a living by various other means—Davis turning down an offer to join Duke Ellington's trumpet section in order to freelance around the New York club scene. But in January 1949, the record ban over, Rugolo reconvened the nonet in a Manhattan studio for the first of three sessions that would change the sound of jazz for a decade and more.

The sessions were spread over a period of 15 months and, given the unpredictability of jazz musicians' lives, featured several musicians who had not taken part in the debut at the Royal Roost. Others who passed through included the drummer Kenny Clarke, the pianist Al Haig, the trombonist J J Johnson. Four titles were recorded at each of the three-hour sessions, and six of the total of 12 pieces were released on 10-inch 78rpm discs: Lewis's arrangements of two bop classics, Denzil Best's "Move" and Bud Powell's "Budo"; Mulligan's swinging treatment of George

Wallington's "Godchild" and his own "Jeru"; plus "Boplicity" and Johnny Carisi's "Israel." Initially, public reaction was lukewarm; only Rugolo's enthusiasm kept the sessions coming. Gradually, though, musicians across America began to pay attention to the smooth, serene sound of this strange little band. After the power of the big bands, the raw freneticism of jump music and the high intensity of bebop, this new sound, with its porcelain surface, proposed an entirely different direction: disdaining obvious exertion and explicit emotional involvement.

Not everybody liked it. Dizzy Gillespie, for one, was ambivalent about the way it had discarded the emotional heat of his kind of jazz. "It was a natural progression," he admitted, "because Miles had definitely come out of us, and he was the leader of this new movement. So it was the same music, only cooler. They expressed less fire than we did, played less notes, less quickly, and used more space, and they emphasised tonal quality. This music, jazz, is guts. You're supposed to sweat in your balls in this music. They sorta softened it up a bit."

But for Davis, the music of Gillespie and Parker had been too complex for a mainstream audience. "If you weren't a fast listener," he said, "you couldn't catch the humour or feeling of their music. Their musical sound wasn't sweet, and it didn't have harmonic lines that you could easily hum out on the street with your girlfriend trying to get over with a kiss."

You could hear what he meant most clearly in Evans's work on a song called "Moondreams," a commercial ballad which began in a gentle reverie but gradually accumulated an intense luminosity until, in the final measures, the rhythm section disappeared along with the tempo, the alto saxophone held a series of unearthly whistling high notes, the trumpet and tuba wandered beneath it, the trombone stuttered and each voice appeared to be acting in autonomy until the piece tapered away in a sort of constructive anti-climax. No rhetoric, no obvious virtuosity, not even any improvisation (although Evans's genius made the whole thing sound improvised). There had been nothing like it.

It took years for the nonet's effect to work its way through the system of American music. But a new generation was listening. In California, especially, young arrangers like Shorty Rogers and Marty Paich found the airy sound of the nonet to be in tune with the post-war mood of optimism, expansionism, modernism. When the results of all three sessions were compiled into an album, they called it *Birth of the Cool*. The cool world was here.

MILES: NOT IN A SILENT WAY
NAT HENTOFF

In 1955 Davis's five-year struggle with heroin addiction and his conspicuous absence from the jazz scene finally came to an end. His July performance with Thelonious Monk at the Newport Jazz Festival was universally acclaimed as "triumphant." By autumn he had assembled a new touring band that included Sonny Rollins, Red Garland, Paul Chambers, and Philly Joe Jones. And by virtue of the overwhelmingly positive reviews of the Newport concert, he was leaving Prestige, a small, independent label with limited distribution, for Columbia Records, a major company with unlimited resources.

In an effort to mark his return as a bandleader and reclaim his audience, Davis consented to be interviewed by Nat Hentoff for the November 2, 1955 issue of *Down Beat*. Davis doesn't look back at his troubled past or speak about his life in transition. Instead he comments on the jazz scene that he had in a sense rejoined. Big band and small group writing, West Coast jazz, and some of Davis's favorite music of that time, including John Lewis's "Django," Charles Mingus's "Mingus Fingers," and Alex North's music for *A Streetcar Named Desire,* is discussed. Davis also comments on the work of Dave Brubeck, Lennie Tristano and Lee Konitz, Charlie Parker, Max Roach and Clifford Brown, Stan Kenton, Carl Perkins, Frank Sinatra, and J. J. Johnson.

In his introductory remarks Hentoff mentions Davis's desire to collaborate again with Gil Evans, as he did in 1949 and 1950 for Capitol Records. Fortunately, Davis's wish would be realized several years later with the important Davis-Gil Evans projects *Miles Ahead* and *Porgy and Bess,* among others.

After a time of confusion and what appeared to be a whirlpool of troubles, Miles Davis is moving rapidly again toward the forefront of the modern jazz scene. He has just signed a contract guaranteeing him 20 weeks a year in Birdland (the first three dates—two weeks each—Oct. 13, Nov. 24, and Jan. 19). He has been added to the three-and-a-half-week all-star Birdland tour that begins Feb. 5, and there are reports—at present unconfirmed and denied by Prestige—that Miles may leave Prestige for one of the major record companies.

Miles already had shown clearly this year how important a jazz voice he still is by his July performance at the Newport festival, a performance that caused Jack Tracy to write: "Miles played thrillingly and indicated that his comeback is in full stride." A few weeks later, Miles surprised the international jazz audience by tying Dizzy for first place in the *Down Beat* Critics' poll.

But those listeners who had heard several of his Prestige records over the past year (particularly the *Walkin'—Blue 'n' Boogie* date with Lucky Thompson, J.J. Johnson, Kenny Clarke, Horace Silver, and Percy Heath) decided on second thought that there really should have been no cause for them to have been surprised.

So Miles is now in the most advantageous position of his career thus far. He has the bookings, the record outlet, and he has the group that he's been eager to assemble for some months. As of this writing, on drums there's Philly Joe Jones, described by Miles as "the best drummer around today." On bass is the young Detroit musician, Paul Chambers, who's recently been working with George Wallington at the Bohemia and of whose ability Miles says only "Whew! He really drives a band. He never stops." On piano is Red Garland from Philadelphia. The tenor is Sonny Rollins, for whom Miles has deep respect. Miles has been trying to convince Sonny to leave Chicago and go on the road with him and finally, to Miles' great delight, he has succeeded.

"I want this group," says Miles, "to sound the way Sonny plays, the way all of the men in it play individually—different from anyone else in jazz today. We've got that quality individually; now we have to work on getting the group to sound that way collectively. As we get to work regularly, something will form up and we'll get a style."

As for records, Miles is dissatisfied with most of his recent output, since his standards call for constant growth and change, and his criteria for judging his own works are harsh. "The only date of mine I liked in the last couple of years was the *Walkin'* session (Prestige LP 182). And the one with Sonny Rollins (Prestige 187). The rest sounded too much alike."

Of the records he made in the years before, Miles looks back with most satisfaction to the set with J.J. Johnson that included *Kelo* and *Tempus Fugit* (Blue Note LP 5022), the earlier albums with Rollins (Prestige LP 124, 140) and the 1949–'50 Capitol sides with Gerry Mulligan, Lee Konitz, Al Haig, Max Roach, J.J. Johnson, John Lewis, and Kenny Clarke (Capitol LP H 459). He remembers, however, how tense those Capitol sessions were, and wishes he had a chance to do a similar date, only with a full brass section and with writing that would be comfortable for all.

Miles, as his sharply perceptive *Blindfold Test* (*Down Beat,* Sept. 21) indicated, is an unusually knowledgeable observer of the jazz scene. In a recent, characteristically frank conversation, he presented his views about several key figures and trends in contemporary jazz. This is a record of his conversation:

The West Coast: "They do have some nice arrangements. Jimmy Giuffre plays real good and Shelly is good, but I don't care too much for the other soloists. Carl Perkins, though, is an exception—he plays very good piano, but he doesn't record enough. I wish I could get him to work with me. You know, that man can play bass notes with his elbows!

"My general feeling about what's happening on the coast is like what Max Roach was saying the other night. He said he'd rather hear a guy miss a couple of notes than hear the same old cliches all the time. Often when a man misses, it at least shows he's trying to think of something new to play. But the music on the coast gets pretty monotonous even if it's skill-fully done. The musicians out there don't give me a thrill the way Sonny Rollins, Dizzy, and Philly Joe Jones do. I like musicians like Dizzy because I can always learn something from him; he's always playing new progressions, etc. Kenny Clarke, too, is always experimenting."

Brubeck: "Well, Dave made one record I liked—*Don't Worry About Me.* Do I think he swings? He doesn't know how. Desmond doesn't swing, either, though I think he'd play different with another rhythm section. Frankly, I'd rather hear Lennie. Or for that matter, I'd rather hear Dizzy play the piano than Brubeck, because Dizzy knows how to touch the piano and he doesn't play too much. A lot of guys are so conscious of the fact that the piano has 88 keys they try to do too much. Tatum is the only man who plays with a whole lot of technique *and* the feeling too. Along with Bud Powell, he's my favorite pianist.

"Getting back to Brubeck, I'd say first he ought to change his drums. Another thing is that if Brubeck could play the piano like that pianist in Sweden—Bengt Halberg—in combination with the way he himself already thinks, he would please a lot of musicians. Brubeck has wonderful harmonic ideas, but I sure don't like the way he touches, the way he plays the piano."

Tristano and Konitz: "Lennie has a different problem. He's wonderful by himself. He invents all the time, and as a result, when he works with a group, the bass player generally doesn't know what Lennie's going to do. I don't think, therefore that Lennie can be tied down to writing one bass line. He should write three or four bass lines, so that the bassist can choose.

"As for Lee Konitz, I like the way he plays. With a different rhythm section, he swings—in his way. Sure, there are different ways of swinging. You can break phrases and you can play 7 or 11-note phrases like Lee does, and they swing, but you can't do it all the time."

Bird: "Bird used to play 40 different styles. He was never content to remain the same. I remember how at times he used to turn the rhythm section around when he and I, Max, and Duke Jordan were playing together. Like we'd be playing the blues, and Bird would start on the 11th bar, and as the rhythm sections stayed where they were and Bird played where he was, it sounded as if the rhythm section was on one and three instead of two and four. Everytime that would happen. Max used to scream at Duke not to follow Bird but to stay where he was. Then eventually, it came around as Bird had planned and we were together again. Bird used to make me play, try to play. He used to lead me on the bandstand. I used to quit every night. The tempo was so up, the challenge was so great.

"Of the new altoists, Cannonball plays real good. He swings and has real drive, but he doesn't know the chord progressions Bird knew. Bird used to play things like Tatum. But if Cannonball gets with the right musicians—men like Sonny Rollins—he'll learn."

MJQ: "I was talking about small groups before. I can't omit the Modern Jazz Quartet—that's the best group out. That piece, *Django,* is one of the greatest things written in a long time. You know, John Lewis teaches everyone all the music in that group."

Max Roach–Clifford Brown: "I don't like their current group too much because there's too much going on. I mean, for example, that Richie Powell plays too much comp. Max needs a piano player that doesn't play much in the background. Actually, Brownie and Max are the whole group. You don't need anybody but those two. They can go out onstage by themselves. What happens is that the band gets in Brownie's way the way it is now."

Writing: "With regard to big bands, I liked some of the arrangements this last Stan Kenton band had at Birdland, and, of course, Count Basie sounds good, but that's just swinging. I also admire the big band writing Billy Strayhorn does. Do you know the best thing I've heard in a long time? Alex North's music for *Streetcar Named Desire* (Capitol LP P-387). That's a wild record—especially the part Benny Carter plays. If anybody is going to be able to write for strings in the jazz idiom or something near to it, it'll be North. I'd recommend everyone hearing that music.

"Now as for Kenton, I can't think of anything he did original. Everything he did, everybody else did before. Kenton is nowhere in the class with somebody like Duke. Duke has done more for jazz than anyone I could name. He takes in almost everything when he writes, he and Billy.

"You can really tell how a man writes when he writes for a large band. But funny things happen, too. Like if it weren't for Neal Hefti, the Basie band wouldn't sound as good as it does. But Neal's band can't play those same arrangements nearly as well. Ernie Wilkins, on the other hand, writes good, but the Basie band plays Neal's arrangements better.

"About the kind of things Charlie Mingus and Teo Macero are writing for small groups, well, some of them are like tired modern pictures. Some of them are depressing. And Mingus can write better than that. *The Mingus Fingers* he did for Lionel Hampton is one of the best big band records I ever heard, but he won't write like he did on that number any more. For one thing, in his present writing, he's using the wrong instrumentation to get it over. If he had a section of low horns, for example, that would cut down on some of the dissonance, he could get it over better. I heard one of Teo's works at Newport, but I don't remember it. And if I didn't remember it, I didn't like it.

"My favorite writer has been Gil Evans. He's doing commercial things now, but if you remember, he did the ensemble on *Boplicity* and several other fine things around that time. In answer to that critic who recently asked why a song like *Boplicity* isn't played by modern groups, it isn't played because the top line isn't interesting. The harmonization is, but not the tune itself.

"Other writers I like are Gigi Gryce—there were several nice things in the last date he did with Art Farmer—and Gerry Mulligan is a great writer, one of my favorites. Bill Russo is interesting, too—like the way he closes the harmony up. He sure loves trombones. He uses the brass section well.

"A lot of musicians and writers don't get the full value out of a tune. Tatum does and Frank Sinatra always does. Listen to the way Nelson Riddle writes for Sinatra, the way he gives him enough room, and doesn't clutter it up. Can you imagine how it would sound if Mingus were writing for Sinatra? But I think Mingus will settle down; he can write good music. But about Riddle, his backgrounds are so right that sometimes you can't tell if they're conducted. Billy Eckstine needs somebody like Sinatra, by the way, to tell him what kind of tunes to sing and what kind of background to use."

Instrumentalists: "There are other musicians I like. Stan Getz is a wonderful musician, and Bobby Brookmeyer is real good. The man I like very much is J.J. Johnson, because he doesn't play the same way all the time. And he's a fine writer. If J.J. would only write for a big band, then you'd hear something. The best small band arrangements I've heard in a long time are the ones J.J. writes for the Jay and Kai group, and that's only two horns. I liked, too, what he wrote for me on the Blue Note session. J.J. doesn't clutter it up. He tries to set the mood. He has the quality Gil Evans has, the quality I hope Gerry Mulligan doesn't lose.

"As for trumpets, Brownie plays real good. Yes, he plays fast, but when you're playing with Max, you play real fast almost all the time, like the time I was with Bird. Art Farmer is real good, but he has to get his tone together. Thad Jones, if he ever gets out of the Basie band, then you'll really hear him. Playing in a big band makes you stiff. It doesn't do a horn man good to stay in a band too long. Conte Candoli, for example, told me he hasn't been the same since Kenton. He can't keep a flowing line going. His lips tighten up and he has to play something high even though he doesn't like to play like that. I told him to lay off three weeks and start over again. Dizzy had to do the same thing after he had the big band. Part of that stiffness comes from playing the same arrangement again and again. The only horn players a big band didn't tie down were Bird and Lester.

"Now about drummers, my five favorites are Max, Kenny Clarke, Philly Joe Jones, Art Blakey, and Roy Haynes. Roy though has almost destroyed himself working with Sarah so long. He's lost some of his touch, but he could pick up again if he had a chance to play more freely. Elvin Jones, the brother of Thad and Hank, is another drummer who plays real good. Elvin comes from the Detroit area which is producing some very good musicians."

Tradition and Swinging: "Bird and Hawkins made horn players realize they could play fuller progressions, play more of the chord, and still swing. I saw Stan Getz making fun of Hawkins one night and I said to Getz, 'If it weren't for Hawkins, you probably wouldn't be playing as you are!' Coleman plays just as well as anybody you can name. Why, I learned how to play ballads by listening to Coleman. I don't go for putting down a man just because he's older. Like some guys were once looking at a modern car, and they said, 'A young guy must have designed that car!' Why does he have to have been a young guy?

"On clarinet, I only like Benny Goodman very much. I don't like Buddy DeFranco at all, because he plays a lot of clichés and is very cold. Tony Scott plays good, but not like Benny, because Benny used to swing so much. No matter what form jazz takes—Lennie or Stan or Bird or Duke—jazz has to swing.

"What's swinging in words? If a guy makes you pat your foot and if you feel it down your back, you don't have to ask anybody if that's good music or not. You can always feel it."

MILES'S JAZZ LIFE
NAT HENTOFF

Other than Ralph J. Gleason, Nat Hentoff was the only well-known American jazz journalist that Miles Davis trusted. In the following profile Hentoff conveys a sense of that intimacy by offering rare glimpses of the Miles Davis behind the public mask. Here the author presents the full breadth of Davis's personality—his moods, his habits, his coping styles and opinions, and his humanity—at a time of enormous financial success and worldwide popularity. The author has also woven additional commentary about Davis's music by Art Farmer, Gil Evans, Cecil Taylor, and Herbie Mann to broaden his portrait.

Hentoff's piece, published in his 1961 book, *The Jazz Life,* is wrenched from the chapter "Three Ways of Making It: John Lewis, Miles Davis, Thelonious Monk," hence the slightly stilted beginning and the reference to Monk's family. Several pages have been deleted, with the author's permission, to better mesh with other pieces in this collection.

Francis Newton in the *New Statesman* terms Davis "a wraith-like artist . . . a player of surprisingly narrow technical and emotional range." He admits Davis communicates an absolutely unmistakable sound and mood. ". . . The mood, as one might expect, is one of total introversion and ranges from a reflective melancholy to naked desolation; but these sound as though felt by someone who, though not quite suffering from nightmares, is never quite awake. It is a sleepwalker's art, a lonely sound which plays before, after and besides, but rarely *with* other players." Newton, from hearing only the music, reacts to Davis as "this strange personality whose power lies in Davis' uncompromising hostility to the outer world." He concedes that Davis has "the rare ability to suggest vistas beyond the sound of his horn, stretching into some sad sort of infinity. I do not think that he is a great artist, because as yet he lacks both the tragic and the comic dimension. But there are few more genuine poets in jazz. . . . The present vogue for him is justified; but I should feel happier if the young men and women for whom jazz is the only adequate expression of their view of life, chose for their symbol a player whose art was less close to self-pity and the denial of life."

It's understandable that the brooding intensity of Davis' music should have led Newton to so misunderstand the man. Far from denying life, Davis enjoys existence more than most of his contemporaries, in or out of jazz. He is subject to moods of depression and extreme irritability, but more often in recent years has "made it" in most areas of his life.

Davis is more solvent than most jazzmen. He invests successfully in the stock market and in real estate. Characteristically, Davis makes his own decisions on what stocks to buy, often based on his own empirical testing of a company's product or his observance of current supply-and-demand balances in the various areas through which he travels. Davis owns a brownstone in New York's West Seventies, is buying additional real estate, and does not worry about when his career will end and what will happen to him then. As a property owner he gets grim satisfaction when, as recently, an electrician rang the bell, took Davis for the janitor, and asked to see the owner.

"You're looking at him," says Davis.

Concerning his music, Davis has said in *Playboy,* "I'm too vain to play anything really bad musically that I can help not doing. If ever I feel I *am* getting to the point where I'm playing it safe, I'll stop. That's all I can tell you about how I plan for the future. I'll keep on working until nobody likes me. If I was Secretary of Defense, I'd give the future a lot of thought, but now I don't. When I am without an audience, I'll know it before anyone else, and I'll stop. That's all there is to life. You work at what you do best, and if the time comes when people don't like it, you do something else. As for me, if I have to stop playing, I'll just drive my Ferrari, go to the gym, and look at Frances."

Frances is Mrs. Davis, a lissome dancer who is devoted to her husband. He also has two boys and a girl by a previous marriage. He enjoys playing with them and teaching the boys boxing. His children's reactions to him are not usually those set off by a man who denies life. His teen-age daughter said to him shortly after his marriage to Frances, "I know some girls have an infatuation for their father, but I tell you that if Frances hadn't married you, I would have."

Miles is similar to Thelonious Monk in the closeness he feels to his family and the extent to which he can be absorbed in his music. He is seldom satisfied with anything he has done musically, but his impatience with himself leads not to frustration but to the constantly renewed excitement of finding and coping with the next challenge. Like creators in many fields, Davis is more involved in the continuing process of discovery than in what *is* discovered at each stage.

Davis' disinclination to coast on clichés is similar to the credo of Duke Ellington—a musician Davis admires more than anyone else in jazz—as expressed in a conversation I had with Ellington some years ago. As a composer, Ellington was saying that "the fun, the challenge is writing for musicians who have weaknesses. The fun of writing and participating in music is the motivating force that keeps me going on and on. . . . I enjoy solving problems. Take *Boy Meets Horn*. There's one note with a cocked valve on the trumpet that has that sound I wanted—E natural. The big problem was to employ that note logically and musically within the overall structure of a composition. It was something to have fun with. It has nothing to do with conquering the world. You write it tonight and play it tomorrow, and that's it."

Ellington added his regret, in a sense, that the young jazzman can now "play anything you set down. I remember when cats with trombones used to say, 'Man, this thing ain't got no keys on it, you know.' Now they don't say it; they just play it. The problems of writing for individual musicians with their particular advantages and their particular weaknesses are reduced. So, you try to make new problems for yourself another way. You try to think in terms of combinations. . . . It's gotten so adult and civilized and that sort of thing. The other way, the old way, was like a kid playing with blocks. The first time he sees a Q, he says, 'Now what'll we do with this?' He hasn't perhaps gotten beyond A, B, and C in his alphabet up to that point."

As a player, Davis is fortunate from Ellington's point of view in that he does not have the seemingly effortless facility in all registers that many other modern jazz trumpet players do. Conversely, not having technical bravura to rely on when ideas falter, Davis never gives the impression of vacuous glibness. As trumpeter Art Farmer has said of Davis: "When you're not technically a virtuoso, you *have* to be saying something. You've got no place to hide."

Davis has made maximum use of his assets. He plays with a burnished tone that can be more expressive in the lower register than that of any of the modernists; and his general musical conception and temperament are annealed to a spare style that fits well with the fact that his technique is somewhat limited.

Davis' capacity for the tragic dimension, Newton notwithstanding, is startlingly evident in his Columbia *Sketches of Spain* album in which, with Gil Evans' arrangements, he has blended flamenco patterns and jazz with surprising success, particularly in his personalization of the flamenco *cante hondo* ("deep song"). Davis' playing in the set is remarkable in its authenticity of phrasing and timbre. It is as if he had been born of Andalusian gypsies but had also grown up with American blues. I doubt if any other American jazz musician could have so thoroughly absorbed the emotional nuances of an alien music and still retained his own personal jazz inflections.

Davis and arranger Gil Evans, who has provided him with uniquely sympathetic orchestral textures in several albums, had, as is their custom, planned the Spanish sketches for months. They also took as much time as they felt they needed to edit the tapes. In contrast to his earlier attitude toward recordings, Davis is extremely careful now as to what performances he allows to be issued.

Newton is as wrong in ascribing self-pity to Davis' playing in the past several years as he is in finding life-denial in his work. Davis' personality is complicated, but he consistently strikes out for what he wants. His direct aggressiveness is not characteristic of those who soothe themselves with pity. A small man with deceptively fragile-looking features, Davis at times resembles a choirboy who has been playing chess with the Devil and winning. Not quite in keeping with his freshness of mien is a voice that was left much hoarser than Louis Armstrong's after an operation a few years ago to remove nodes from his vocal chords. When Miles decides to speak in what is now his characteristic rough whisper, usually punctuated by a coughed chuckle, the choirboy turns into a mocking deflator of pomposity who will usually become serious only about music.

"Miles is a leader in jazz," says his long-time friend, arranger Gil Evans, "because he has definite confidence in what he likes and he is not *afraid* of what he likes. A lot of other musicians are constantly looking around to hear what the next person is doing and worry about whether they themselves are in style. Miles has confidence in his own taste, and he goes his own way."

Davis has become in the past few years the most influential modern jazz trumpet player since Dizzy Gillespie. The bristling introspectiveness of Davis' playing and his questioning, intensely personal tone have led to a frequent misconception that his music is delicately cool with only glints of the fire that marks more explosive hornmen such as Dizzy Gillespie and Roy Eldridge. In fact, the most quoted and least accurate description of Davis' playing compares him to a man walking on eggshells. If Davis walked on an eggshell, he'd grind it into the ground.

The essence of Miles Davis can be determined by listening to the men he has surrounded himself with on his regular jobs. There is his favorite drummer, for example, Philly Joe Jones (not to be confused with Basie alumnus Jo Jones). Philly Joe is a fearsomely aggressive, polyrhythmically swinging athlete who often uses his sticks as if he had been trained in Sherwood Forest. Philly Joe's excitability propels him at times to play louder than would be necessary for a military band, but Miles was undismayed when Philly was with his combo, because the excitement Joe generates is more important to Miles than any volume problems.

"Look," Davis said before Philly Joe left the band, "I wouldn't care if he came up on the bandstand in his B.V.D.'s and with one arm, just so long as he was there. He's got the fire I want. There's nothing more terrible than playing with a dull rhythm section. Jazz has got to have *that thing*. You have to be born with it. You can't even buy it. If you could buy it, they'd have it at the next Newport festival."

"You must realize," says Gil Evans, "that underneath his lyricism, Miles *swings*. He'll take care of the lyricism, but the rest of the band must complement him with an intense drive. And it's not that they supply a drive he himself lacks. Actually they have to come up to him. There's nothing flabby or matter-of-fact about his rhythm conception. As subtle as he is in his time and his phrasing and his courage to wait, to use space, he's very forceful. There is a feeling of unhurriedness in his work and yet there's intensity underneath and through it all."

"Miles Davis' conception of time," adds pianist Cecil Taylor, "has led to greater rhythmic freedom for other players. His feeling, for another thing, is so intense that he catapults the drummer, bassist and pianist together, forcing them to play at the top of their technical ability and forcing them with his own emotional strength to be as emotional as possible."

When he's not playing, Davis also will not be hurried. Unlike most jazzmen with a reputation as established as his, Davis will not take all the dates he can get, however well they pay. "I never work steady. I work enough to do what I want to do. I play music more for pleasure than for work." And he seldom yields to any of the intersecting, extra-musical pressures in the business. When a powerful entrepreneur once asked him to let a protégé sit in with his combo while Davis was working at his club, Miles refused. The potentate, paternalistically amiable only so long as his demands are being met, threatened Davis: "You want to work here?"

Miles said with obscene gusto that he didn't care and told the man he was going home. The club owner tried to smooth over the hassle, and asked Miles to return to the stand. Later in the night, however, the protégé was sent up to the band. Miles and his men simply walked off.

Miles claims it was one of his frequent arguments with this particular club owner that prevented his throat from healing properly after his operation. "I wasn't supposed to talk for ten days. The second day I was out of the hospital, I ran into him and he tried to convince me to go into a deal that I didn't want." In the course of the debate, to make himself clear, Miles yelled himself into what may be permanent hoarseness.

Miles Davis' albums sell in sizable figures for jazz sets. Most former skeptics concerning his talent—like John S. Wilson of *The New York Times*—are being converted. For years Wilson had found Davis' playing to have been characterized by "limp whimpering and fumbling uncertainty," but now he feels Miles' recordings of the past few years are examples of "hitherto diffused talent" suddenly taking a turn "that brings it sharply into focus."

Miles is unimpressed by what little he reads about himself, favorable or not, having small respect for any American critics except Ralph J. Gleason of the San Francisco *Chronicle*. Miles does allow that his playing has come somewhat closer to his own exacting criteria in the past few years.

"Do you find," a record company official, George Avakian, once asked Miles, "there are many things you do now that a few years ago you wouldn't have dared to do?"

Miles laughed. "A few years ago I used to do them anyway. Now maybe I use better taste than then."

Some observers feel that Miles' "comeback," after several years during which his career seemed to be on a slowing treadmill, dates from his appearance at the 1955 Newport Festival where all the reviews underlined the ardor and freshness of his brief contribution. Miles, like many jazzmen angered at the way the Newport supermarket is stocked and serviced, does not agree: "What are they talking about? I just played the way I always play."

Actually, the renaissance of interest in Miles coincided with the fact that by 1955 he had matured emotionally to the point at which he could handle the multiple pressures of keeping a combo together. He has since led a unit which, despite its shifting personnel, is considered by musicians throughout the country to be one of the most stimulating forces in contemporary jazz. Miles' rejuvenation enabled him finally to establish a consistency in his playing and to develop from night to night in the company of musicians who challenged him and whom he in turn fused into a coherent unit.

Miles is now booked—at the highest prices of his career—in the major American jazz rooms, occasionally spends playing time in Europe, and has ad-libbed the score for a French film, *L'Ascenseur pour L'Echafaud*. Among younger American jazzmen, his intransigent musical integrity and strongly personal "conception" (as a man's style is described in the jazz idiom) make him part of the consistory of modern jazz along with Dizzy Gillespie, Thelonious Monk, the pervasive memory of Charlie Parker and a few others, including a protégé of Miles, tenor saxophonist Sonny Rollins.

Miles' playing is still unpredictable and it may be necessary to sit through two or more sets of an engagement before he indicates fully what all the hosannas have been about. "All of us," says one of his sidemen, "are affected in our playing at night by what's happened to us during the day, but of all those in the band, Miles is the most easily influenced by outside events. He reflects everything he feels in his playing immediately."

"Miles," notes a French musician, "doesn't take you by storm like Dizzy. He's more insidious, more like somebody calling you from the other shore." Herbie Mann, a flute player, has explained that Miles, rather than any other flutist, was his primary inspiration when he started trying to make the flute a jazz instrument. "The attraction of Miles to me as a flutist was that he could be masculine, could communicate strong feeling with his horn and still be subtle and rarely sound beyond the volume level of the flute. He proved you don't have to yell and scream on your instrument to project feeling."

According to Gil Evans, "A big part of Miles' creative gift is in the creation of sound. He arrived at a time when, because of the innovations of modern jazz, all new players had to find their own sound in relation to the new modes of expression. Miles, for example, couldn't play like Louis Armstrong because that sound would interfere with his thoughts. Miles had to start with almost no sound and then develop one as he went along, a sound suitable for the ideas he wanted to express. Finally, he had his own basic sound which any player must develop. But many players then keep this sound more or less constant. Any variation in their work comes in the actual selection of notes, their harmonic patterns and their rhythmic usages. Miles, however, is aware of his complete surroundings and takes advantage of the wide range of sound possibilities that exist even in one's basic sound. He can, in other words, create a particular sound for the existing context. The quality of a certain chord, its tension or lack of tension, can cause him to create a sound appropriate to it. He can put his own substance, his own flesh on a note and then put that note exactly where it belongs."

It was with Evans as the dominating influence and young writer-players Gerry Mulligan, John Lewis and others assisting that Miles assembled an influential nine-piece unit for a series of Capitol recordings in 1949–1950 (now available in *Birth of the Cool,* Capitol T 762). These recordings, more than any other single event, shaped the growing active movement in modern jazz toward carefully integrated "chamber" groups. The Davis Capitol sessions helped establish in the consciousness of many modern jazzmen, here and abroad, an unprecedentedly challenging realization of the subtle possibilities of group dynamics and group expression as a whole in which the solos are a flowing part of the entire texture and structure of the work. The records illustrated further how much more colorful the background textures for jazz improvising could become.

Davis has continued to suggest other directions in modern jazz. He has also prospered, but unlike many jazzmen who begin to achieve relatively wide success, he refuses to adhere to the usual rules for celebrities in any field. With very few exceptions, he will not do radio interviews and will not make guest appearances on local television programs for scale to help advertise the club in which he's appearing. First of all, he feels that he's paid for playing and is entitled to spend the rest of his time his own way. Also, he believes that "people either like what you're doing or they don't. If they don't, I'll know it, and no amount of publicity is going to help."

Although often surfacely churlish, Davis often helps younger players with advice and sometimes gets them jobs. As a leader, he is not a strict disciplinarian, taking care to hire only musicians whom he likes personally. He does let a sideman know if he disapproves of a particular way of playing; but in terms of such infractions as being late on the job, Davis is a permissive employer. He rarely rehearses his band, depending on the constant contact between his sidemen and himself on a job to develop the cohesiveness that any jazz unit must have to sustain attention.

Davis has a rare capacity to fuse a unit into an organically integrated whole. Because the performances of his groups often consist of long solos by the sidemen with only rhythm backing and because Davis himself often strolls offstand during a number, some listeners form an impression of a disorganized band. Davis' combos, for all the freedom he gives his sidemen, unmistakably reflect his musical ideas and personality. There is a noticeable difference between a Davis combo with the leader present and the same men if Davis has gone home before the last set.

Davis is less annoyed than many other jazzmen by noisy night club audiences. "I figure if they're missing what Philly Joe Jones is doing, it's their tough luck. I wouldn't like to sit up there and play without anybody liking it, but I just mainly enjoy playing with my own rhythm section and listening to them. The night clubs are all the same to me. All you do is go in and play and go home. I never do know what people mean when they talk about acoustics. All I try to do is get my sound—full and round. It's a challenge to play in different clubs, to learn how to regulate your blowing to the club."

"Miles has changed much in the past few years," says an old European friend. "He has become more master of himself. He knows what he wants to express, and he expresses it well, with control."

"I'll tell you," says Miles with a grin, "if I can play good for eight bars, it's enough for me. It's satisfaction. The only thing is," he puts his finger on his nose, "I don't tell anybody which eight bars are the good ones. That's my secret."

Nat Hentoff, Martin Williams, and Hsio Wen Shih's short-lived monthly, *The Jazz Review*, often gave musicians an opportunity to critique the latest recordings, to respond to issues swirling about, or to make their views known. For the magazine's November 1958 inaugural issue, valve trombonist and arranger Bob Brookmeyer was invited to review two LPs: *The John Lewis Piano* and Miles Davis and Gil Evans's collaboration *Miles Ahead*. In his short and witty critique of the Davis-Evans project, Brookmeyer offers some perceptive observations of Evans's work that reveal the author's vast experience as a musician and listener. Brookmeyer's humble, engaging style, written solely from his own point of view, is a refreshing change from the more typical, haughty approach to jazz criticism in which reviewers, serving as mouthpieces for the masses, use terms such as "we" and "our" to make sweeping, magisterial pronouncements on behalf of their assumed brethren.

For this, as for the John Lewis Piano album, I say (and will continue to do so in future reviews) that it is a superior and important album and for my money that's all you need to know. However, when a record says something new to you, there is naturally a need to translate this impact into words. After all, not everyone speaks good music but all of you can read and that's how *The Jazz Review* came up the river.

For a starter I shall state that Mr. Evans is the most influential, revolutionary writer (that is, one who used the dance band for a medium of expression—the only one open to composers until the advent of super-sonic sound) since Duke Ellington and his lovely orchestra broke fallow ground in the thirties. His work for the lamented Thornhill band was purely a delight to play and it is a pity that so much worthwhile music has to lie about rotting in a trunk in someone's cellar. However, to be succinct, he has succceeded in translating the Berg/Schoenberg/Webern idiom into practical, personal expression as successfully as did Ralph Burns and Neal Hefti for Woody Herman's 1946 Stravinsky-influenced group. His exotic textures, use of internal doubling to create sheen and his humanist sophis-tication all remind me strongly of the expressionist composers and their allied companions—i.e., it may be a doomed and dying world but it sho' is purty with the right brand of opium. Ah well, onward.

Maids of Cadiz begins with a faintly sinister, "haunted house" passage until a more All-American influence takes hold and continues to alternate throughout the piece. Miles plays flugelhorn exclusively in the album and its diffused quality perfectly complements both the arrangements and his own, unique brand of wistful yearning for the better life upstairs. They have a self-acknowledged mutual admiration society and no wonder! Immediately one becomes aware of waves and waves of gorgeous sound, an almost Oriental sensuality with a basic logic that is the essence of musi-cal expression.

All of the pieces are connected in some manner, either gradually merged or abruptly mated and I found the result quite pleasing. *The Duke, Springsville, My Ship* (with some accurate mid-Atlantic sounds) and *Miles Ahead* (what if they had christened him Irving?) round out the first side.

At the beginning of *Blues for Pablo* I was overcome by a sense of wide, desolate, endless plains; hollow and lonely with a very Spanish flavor, not the *Latin From Manhattan* variety, currently used as a crutch by some fellows. I must, in all honesty, say that by this time the highly stylized writ-ing became evident to me but that is in no sense derogatory, lest I be mis-understood. *New Rhumba*, composed by Ahmad Jamal (a Chicago pianist who has had, I understand, considerable influence upon Miles) is best characterized by the term "exquisite simplicity" and pits the solo horn against the varying combinations of instruments for a prolonged question-and-answer period. Mr. Davis plays extremely well which, for him, is very well indeed.

A quote from the 2nd movement of Berg's *Violin Concerto* segues into *The Meaning of The Blues*—along about this time I glanced at the liner notes and was struck by the word "seductive"—I concur and would add "shimmering, limpid and nocturnal"—Gil's use of inner dissonance to create that moonlit effect is awful nice indeed. A sterling performance of J. J.'s *Lament* moves surprisingly into a humorous, almost giggling *I Don't Wanna Be Kissed,* a relief from romance for a while. The bizarre, rich orchestration was beginning to wear a little thin on me by then but I could easily attribute it to many things other than the music, though there is some validity in the "too much cherry pie" reaction. The record ends with Berg upside down, resolving to a more consonant chord and there you have it.

MILESTONES
BENNY GOLSON

Benny Golson's review of the Miles Davis LP *Milestones* appeared in the January 1959 issue of *The Jazz Review*. At that time the author was tenor saxophonist and music arranger for Art Blakey's Jazz Messengers. Much earlier in his career, of course, Golson was an up-and-coming saxophonist in his hometown of Philadelphia. The dynamic North Philadelphia jazz scene of Golson's youth was rich with promising young musicians—some of the very best of his generation. Jimmy and Percy Heath, Clifford Brown, John Coltrane, and Red Garland were just some of musicians learning their craft in the clubs around Broad and Columbia Avenue. (Philly Joe Jones also was a product of the Philadelphia scene, but left for New York after his stint in the Army rather than return home.) Golson's insightful remarks about Coltrane, who in less than a decade would be regarded as one of greatest soloists and bandleaders in jazz history, seem remarkably prescient now, some forty years after their publication.

Side 1: Dr. Jekyl, while not especially melodic, gives the group an excellent opportunity to "stretch out." The eights and fours between Miles and Philly Joe Jones are fiery and invigorating. Paul Chambers, in spite of the fast tempo, takes a soulful solo. The exchange of choruses between Coltrane and Cannonball is the high point of the track, and the rhythm section is very stable throughout.

Sid's Ahead is, in reality, the old, and now classic, *Walkin'*. During his solo, Coltrane is very clever and creative in his handling of the substitute chords. Miles strolls (without piano) beautifully. He is a true musical conversationalist. Cannonball is quite "funky" at times, and Chambers exemplifies his ability to create solo lines in the manner of a trumpeter or saxophonist.

The third track, *Two Bass Hit,* opens with everyone on fire—particularly Philly, whose punctuation and attack are as sharp as a knife. Coltrane enters into his solo moaning, screaming, squeezing, and seemingly projecting his very soul through the bell of his horn. I feel that this man is definitely blazing a new musical trail. Philly and Red Garland back the soloists like a brass section, an effect which always creates excitement.

Side 2: The theme of *Milestones* is unusual, but surprisingly pleasant—particularly the bridge where Miles answers the other horns, achieving an echo effect. Philly's use of sticks on the fourth beat of every bar is quite tasteful. Cannonball cleverly interweaves melodies around the changes. Miles is as graceful as a swan, and Coltrane is, as usual, full of surprises.

Red Garland, who is undoubtedly one of today's great pianists, is spotlighted in *Billy Boy* with Philly and Paul. The arrangement is tightly knit and well played. Red employs his block chord technique on this track and plays a beautiful single line, as well. Philly and Paul do a wonderful job, both soloing and in the section.

Straight No Chaser is a revival of a Thelonious Monk composition of a few years ago—the spasmatic harmony makes it quite interesting. Cannonball is excellent on this track. I may be wrong, but he seems to have been influenced somewhat by Coltrane. Miles paints a beautiful picture, as surely as with an artist's brush. He has a sound psychological approach in that he never plays too much. He leaves me, always, wanting to hear more.

I have heard no one, lately, who creates like Coltrane. On this track, he is almost savage in his apparent desire to play his horn thoroughly.

Red plays a single line solo with his left hand accompanying off the beat. He closes the solo with a beautiful harmonization of Miles' original solo on *Now's The Time.* Here, Philly goes into a subtle 1-2-3-4 beat on the snare drum behind Red's solo, setting it off perfectly. This is the best track of the album.

In closing, I'd like to say—keep one eye on the world and the other on John Coltrane.

MILES IN ENGLAND
BENNY GREEN

In September 1960, Miles Davis began his first tour of England. With Sonny Stitt replacing the recently departed John Coltrane, Davis's quintet opened in London at the Gaumont Cinema, where it played two shows for 7,500 people aroused by a torrent of pre-concert publicity. An excited British jazz press was in attendance too, of course, including Benny Green, whose review of the proceedings is below.

Green's piece, which was republished in his 1973 book *Drums in My Ear,* recounts some of the more striking aspects of the band's performance. His review also argues for Davis's exalted place in jazz history. For the author, Davis was a revolutionary because his uniquely melancholic trumpet sound, judicious economy of notes, and "concern with the release of tension" established introspection as an entirely new aesthetic.

Davis's British tour coincided with the release of *Kind of Blue,* cited by jazz fans and historians as one of the most important recordings in the jazz canon. Interestingly, the first issue of *Kind of Blue* available in England was produced by the Fontana label and featured liner notes by Benny Green, not the well-known commentary by pianist Bill Evans that has graced the Columbia jacket for more than thirty years.

The myth that jazz is essentially a good-time music was finally laid to rest last week when the American trumpeter Miles Davis opened his long-awaited British tour. At the Gaumont, Hammersmith, Davis somehow managed to re-create, and even intensify, the hypnotic effect of recordings which have obliged us all to stop in our tracks and ask once again, 'What is jazz anyway?'

The power of Davis's originality is most effectively proved by the astonishing way in which his playing places that of the rest of his quintet on a subordinate plane. His saxophonist, Sonny Stitt, prolific and irresistible, is an instrumentalist of immense culture and personality. It is hard to imagine even a partial eclipse of so dynamic an artist. But Davis, with a few notes selected with diabolonian cunning, forces us to examine the classical methods of players like Stitt from a new perspective.

The one very real dilemma of jazz music is the problem of the limitations of improvising on chord sequences. Within the framework of a harmonic progression the musician is free to trace whatever melodic patterns he can. But one senses, in the work of the most gifted soloists and in the fidgeting of younger rebels, a certain resigned acceptance of the theory that the utmost limits have almost been reached.

The attempt by Davis to solve this problem was admirably posed at Hammersmith by the sharp contrast between the material Davis first introduced on his albums, and the more orthodox themes which form perhaps half of the quintet's repertoire. Significantly, Miles opened and closed his first British concert with two themes from his 'Kind of Blue' recording, one which questioned the tenets of jazz-making more searchingly than anything since Charlie Parker. With those two themes, 'Freddie Freeloader' and 'All Blues,' Davis cast a spell already familiar to those who know the recordings.

What is it about this spell which makes it so very different from any other jazz? To put it briefly, Davis has succeeded in introducing into the jazz context a new aesthetic. Every note he plays is tinged with the disturbing melancholia of a highly sophisticated and super-sensitive artist. Nowhere is there any trace of the unselfconscious joy at being alive of Louis Armstrong, or the irrepressible good spirits of Davis's great contemporary, Dizzy Gillespie. Suddenly, through the prism of Davis's conception, all other jazz appears a Panglossian affair concerned with the release of tension rather than the exploration of it. With Miles Davis, introspection enters the jazz world, and just as Lester Young, when he introduced the qualities of wit into the idiom, used new weapons, so Davis has been obliged gradually to evolve an approach of his own.

Tonally he has dramatically distilled the sound of the trumpet, so that it now possesses a deathly purity evoking all kinds of poetic images.

Vibrato has almost disappeared completely, and forgotten is the old avowed intention of the instrumentalist to suggest the overtones of the human voice, still very apparent in contemporaries like Ellington's Clark Terry. When Miles, using a mute, improvises on 'Green Dolphin Street' and 'Round Midnight,' he achieves a spectral evocation which makes even Lester Young's pre-war legerdemain sound like jolly extroversion. Were I limited to one adjective in reference to Miles Davis, I would probably settle for 'crepuscular.'

The 'Kind of Blue' material reflects Davis's attempt to escape from the cage of normal progression from discord to resolution without shattering the jazz form entirely. The themes are based less on chord progressions than on a series of modal scales, whose possibilities Davis probes with consummate delicacy, employing a more rigorous selection and economy of notes than anybody before him. To find any parallel at all with this introversion I can think only of the piano fragments of Bix Beiderbecke thirty years before, although these were necessarily quite different in harmonic conception.

Davis's originality is underlined by Stitt when the group plays a conventional blues theme like 'Walkin'.' Here Stitt is positively brilliant, playing with masterly execution and producing a cascade of ideas completely overwhelming to the listener bred on a diet of derivative homegrown jazz. The contrast between Stitt and his leader serves also to remind us that Davis is limited by the very nature of his development to a single mood, but that within its confines he is one of the great jazzmen.

The presentation of this new approach has given rise to some touching confusion on the part of the audiences. Davis says not a single word throughout most of his concerts. He makes no announcements and even leaves the stage when not actually playing. Some people have used this austerity as an excuse to talk of Miles Davis's 'failure to project' or even his bad professional manners. The truth is that Miles projects with his trumpet, and that his so-called snubbing of the audience is merely a flattering assumption that any audience which pays to see him knows enough about what is going on to be spared announcements of the 'For my next number' variety.

As for the benumbing jocosities of most jazz group leaders, Davis is quite justifiably contemptuous of such attempts to milk his followers. He is trying to invest a jazz performance with the same dignity and self-assurance which he himself possesses to such a remarkable degree. Those knockabout comics, the Modern Jazz Quartet, would do well to study him a little more closely. Rarely have I witnessed a more impressive concert of jazz.

The April 1961 Blackhawk performances were Davis's first live recording dates and Davis wanted everything the band played that weekend—including the "mistakes"—to be put on the records. For Davis a "mistake" was not merely a chord, phrase, or drum roll that could've been executed better and unfortunately had to be retained because it was recorded on tape. In Davis's mind a "mistake" was a positive thing; something a soloist or rhythm player did in the heat of performance that went awry when stretching for something original. To Davis, who strove for originality at every turn, mistakes were, paradoxically, symptomatic of music-making of the highest order.

As Ralph J. Gleason points out in his liner notes to the Blackhawk sessions, at this stage of his career Davis wasn't at all interested in tinkering with his recordings in the studio. But all would change in a few years. Increasingly, splicing and overdubbing would become the norm. Davis, with mad scientist Teo Macero (his producer), would become the Doctor Frankensteins of jazz. Together they would create in their laboratory entirely new recordings by disemboweling countless Davis tapes left for dead.

It has become as fashionable to write of Miles Davis as a social symbol and as one of the charismatic personalities in the religious symbolism of jazz as it is to write of him as a jazz musician. And these things are true, even if now commonplace. Miles does occupy a position in the jazz culture far beyond that of a jazz soloist (even though based on that). His mode of dress sets styles ("Pin-stripes are coming back," a hipster remarked when Miles appeared opening night at the Blackhawk in San Francisco in a pin-striped suit. "I got to get me one"), his language and his attitudes are aped by thousands for whom he has the status of a social leader. Long before Eva Marie Saint brought a four-letter expletive to the attention of the country in her impromptu remarks after a laudatory introduction at a motion picture industry dinner, Miles Davis had made acceptance of liberal use of that same word a prerequisite for conversation in most jazz circles, though with characteristic individuality he had transformed it from one syllable to two.

The debate over his onstage attitude has raged wherever he has appeared: Is it pretense? Is it real? His refusal to make announcements, his habit of leaving the stage when others are soloing, his occasional turning of his back to the audience, are either vigorously defended or attacked depending on one's point of view. Do we get announcements from the Budapest String Quartet? Or do jazz musicians owe their public more? But one thing Miles Davis is and that superbly: He is controversial. He is never dull. His basic attitude from which all the rest springs, is realism and antipretense. That he is aware of what is said and argued about him, he occasionally implies in one aside or another. "They're all worried about making records with me," he said at the Blackhawk on one of the nights this album was being made. He paused and looked up, deadpan, with his eyes gleaming. "An' I'm just standing here, minding my own business, being my own sweet self." Miles' own sweet way has been to do exactly as he pleased with his own music throughout his entire career. The fact that he is now, like Picasso and a very few other artists, a great commercial success in his own lifetime is a tribute to his courage and his sanity and his basic good sense. It is also, whether or not he wills it, a rare symbol to all artists everywhere of the complete triumph of uncompromising art. At the Blackhawk, for instance, he almost never played the last set at night and never played the Sunday afternoon session. "I shouldn't complain," Guido Cacienti, the owner, said, "as long as the people come." And, of course, what makes Miles right is that they *do* come.

Despite his legendary intransigence, he mingles with the audience at the Blackhawk, signs autographs and answers questions, idiotic as they may be, with surprising patience if not exactly a loquacious manner. He will leave the stand when the other men solo and walk back by the entrance and stand with the cashier, Elynore Cacienti, Guido's wife, the

At the Blackhawk
83

center of a small crowd of admirers too awed, usually, to speak to him. He is capable of devastating bluntness on occasion. Once he told me he had been past my house that afternoon en route to Dave Brubeck's. "Why didn't you stop in?" I asked in a stereotyped social response. "What for?" he answered with shattering frankness.

The nights this album was being made were tense ones, whether Miles wanted it that way or not. Everyone *was* worried about whether or not the idea would come off. Photographers, imported especially for the occasion, were ordered not to use flash and everyone walked on tiptoes for the first part of the evening. Miles, imperturbably smoking and sipping champagne, exchanged anecdotes with singer Bill Rennault, a fellow veteran of the Howard McGhee band, and with trumpeter Benny Harris, then working in town. At one point, almost as if seeking to get his mind off recording, he gave a vivid lecture, with illustrations, on the theory and practice of the art of picking pockets. A tape recording of this would have been useful to any sociologist examining the mores of "whiz mobs." Right in the middle, he turned to Wynton Kelly and asked him to go next door to the 211 Bar, where the recording equipment was set up, to check on the sound, and then continued his lecture to a fascinated group at the bar.

Miles likes to shock reporters with his statements. "I'm going to retire and go to Europe. I can't stand this, it's too much work," he's said every time he's played the Blackhawk for the past three years. And if it looks like you are taking him seriously, he will go into it at length. When a case-hardened cynical newspaper photographer asked him to pose for a picture at the club, Miles completely stopped him with the statement: "I wouldn't go in where you're working and take *your* picture." Neither Nikita Khrushchev nor any other visiting VIP had ever thwarted that particular photographer before.

But none of these things for one moment means that Miles isn't totally concerned with his music. Of course, this is obvious if you think about it. But many people refuse to go beneath the surface and think his attitude means he doesn't care. How could he play the way he does if he wasn't totally concerned? For all the improvisation that is inherent in jazz, I have a deep conviction that Miles does nothing in his playing that isn't deliberate. He may make surprising turns and twists, by accident or design, but it is all part of a deliberate plan of approach, a definite conception of music. And of course the history of his career proves this. What other artist in jazz, with the sole exception of Louis Armstrong, has been so consistently the leader of highly influential groups from which a whole host of players, themselves influences in turn, have come? Bunk Johnson once put it this way: "Playin' jazz is from the heart. You don't lie." That applies with equal force to Miles Davis and is, really, the best summation.

The recording of this album, the first recording of his group in performance in a club that Miles has ever made, was treated with exactly the same concentration and pains that mark everything he has ever done. "When they make records with all the mistakes in, as well as the rest," he said, "then they'll really make jazz records. If the mistakes aren't there, too, it ain't none of you." After the album was completed, I asked Miles if he had anything he wanted to say about it for the notes. "I've been trying to get Irving [Irving Townsend, the Columbia A&R man] for years to put out these albums with *no* notes," Miles said. "There's nothing to say about the music. Don't write about the music. The music speaks for itself." And so it does, and what it says—here and in everything else he has ever recorded, whether or not he now admires the records—is a celebration of the human truth of the creative artist telling his story of the world as he sees it.

AN AFTERNOON WITH MILES DAVIS
NAT HENTOFF

This piece was conceived by Nat Hentoff as a variation on the blindfold test that Leonard Feather conducted routinely for *Down Beat*. Hentoff asked Miles Davis to listen to and comment on several recordings, which, unlike Feather, he identified beforehand. The recordings Davis heard that afternoon were the 1937 Billie Holiday performance of "I Must Have That Man," the Oscar Peterson Trio's performance of "Joy Spring," an excerpt from *Kenny Clarke Plays André Hodeir* featuring pianist Martial Solal, Miles Davis's *Porgy and Bess,* "Now's the Time" as recorded by the Modern Jazz Quartet, Louis Armstrong's 1927 "Potato Head Blues," "But Not for Me" by Ahmad Jamal, "Ruby My Dear" as played by Coleman Hawkins and Thelonious Monk, and Bessie Smith's 1926 recording, "Young Woman Blues." Davis's candid reactions ranged from pure, unalloyed admiration to outright revulsion, quite a departure from the typically staid responses that Feather attributed to musicians in his column.

Hentoff's piece was first published in the December 1958 issue of *The Jazz Review* and later republished in Martin Williams's book *Jazz Panorama*. Although it was intended to be the first in a series of regularly published "observations" by Davis, it was the only one printed, probably due to the *Review*'s brief two-year run and consistently shaky financial status.

Miles lives in a relatively new building on Tenth Avenue near 57th Street. The largest area in his apartment is the living room. Like the other rooms, it is uncluttered. The furnishings have been carefully selected and are spare. Miles has a particular liking for "good wood" and explains thereby why his *Down Beat* plaques—and even his Four Roses Award from the Randall's Island "festival"—are all displayed. He has a good piano and an adequate non-stereo record player.

The idea of the afternoon—the first of a series of observations by Miles to be printed at regular intervals in this monthly—was to play a variety of recordings for him and transcribe his reactions. This was not a blindfold test, for while I find those adventures in skeet shooting entertaining, I doubt if they serve much purpose except transitory titillation.

First was Billie Holiday's 1937 *I Must Have That Man* with Wilson, Clayton, Goodman, Young, Green, Page and Jo Jones. "I love the way Billie sings," Miles began. "She sings like Lester Young and Louis Armstrong play, but I don't like all that's going on behind her. All she needed was Lester and the rhythm. The piano was ad libbing while she was singing, which leads to conflict, and the guitar was too loud and had too much accent on every beat."

Miles was asked whether he agreed with most of the writers on jazz that the Billie of 20 years ago was the "best" Billie and that she is now in decline. "I'd rather hear her now. She's become much more mature. Sometimes you can sing words every night for five years, and all of a sudden it dawns on you what the song means. I played *My Funny Valentine* for a long time—and didn't like it—and all of a sudden it meant something. So with Billie, you know she's not thinking now what she was in 1937, and she's probably learned more about different things. And she still has control, probably more control now than then. No, I don't think she's in a decline.

"What I like about Billie is that she sings it just the way she hears it and that's usually the way best suited for her. She has more feeling than Ella and more experience in living a certain way than Ella. Billie's pretty wild, you know.

"She sings way behind the beat and then she brings it up—hitting right on the beat. You can play behind the beat, but every once in a while you have to cut into the rhythm section on the beat and that keeps everybody together. Sinatra does it by accenting a word. A lot of singers try to sing like Billie, but just the act of playing behind the beat doesn't make it sound soulful.

"I don't think that guys like Buck Clayton are the best possible accompanists for her. I'd rather hear her with Bobby Tucker, the pianist she used to have. She doesn't need any horns. She sounds like one anyway."

Miles' reaction to Clifford Brown's *Joy Spring* as played by the Oscar Peterson Trio on *The Modern Jazz Quartet and The Oscar Peterson Trio at the Opera House* (Verve MG-V 8269) was intensely negative. "Oscar makes me sick because he copies everybody. He even had to *learn* how to play the blues. Everybody knows that if you flat a third, you're going to get a blues sound. He learned that and runs it into the ground worse than Billy Taylor. You don't have to do that.

"Now take the way he plays the song. That's not what Clifford meant. He passes right over what can be done with the chords," and here Miles demonstrated on the piano, as he did frequently during the afternoon. "It's much prettier if you get into it and hear the chord weaving in and out like Bill Evans and Red Garland could do—instead of being so heavy. Oscar is jazzy; he jazzes up the tune. And he sure has devices, like certain scale patterns, that he plays all the time.

"Does he swing hard like some people say? I don't know what they mean when they say 'swing hard' anyway. Nearly everything he plays, he plays with the same degree of force. He leaves no holes for the rhythm section. The only thing I ever heard him play that I liked was his first record of *Tenderly*.

"I love Ray Brown. As for Herb Ellis, I don't like that kind of thing with guitar on every beat—unless you play it like Freddie Green does now. You listen and you'll hear how much Green has lightened his sound through the years. If you want to see how it feels with a heavy guitar, get up to play sometimes with one of them behind you. He'll drive you nuts.

"Back to Oscar. He plays pretty good when he plays in an Art Tatum form of ballad approach. And I heard him play some blues once at a medium tempo that sounded pretty good. But for playing like that with a guitar, I prefer Nat Cole. I feel though that it's a waste to use a guitar this way. If you take the guitar and have him play lines—lines like George Russell, Gil Evans or John Lewis could make—then a trio can sound wonderful."

The next record was a track from *Kenny Clarke Plays André Hodeir* (Epic LN3376). It was Miles' own *Swing Spring* and these are Hodeir's notes on the arrangement: "*Swing Spring* is also treated as a canon, after an introduction featuring an elaboration of the main element of the theme, the scale. Martial Solal's brilliant solo is followed by a paraphrase with integrated drum improvisations. Both Armand Migiani (baritone sax) and Roger Guerin (trumpet) take a short solo."

Miles hadn't looked carefully at the liner notes and was puzzled for the first few bars. "That's my tune, isn't it? I forgot all about that tune. God damn! Kenny Clarke can swing, can't he? That boy Solal can play, but the pianist I like in Europe is Bengt Hallberg. Damn! You know, I forgot I wrote that. That's the wrong middle—in the piano solo—why does he do that? Because it's easier, I suppose. The arrangement is terrible. It was never meant to be like that. It sounds like a tired modern painting—with skeletons in it. He writes pretty good in spots, but he overcrowds it. Kenny and Solal save it. I think I'll make another record of this tune. It was meant to be just like an exercise almost." Miles went to the piano and played the theme softly. "It was based on that scale there and when you blow, you play in that scale and you get an altogether different sound. I got that from Bud Powell; he used to play it all the time."

Miles started to talk about his strong preference for writing that isn't overcrowded, especially overcrowded with chords. He found some acetates of his forthcoming Columbia *Porgy and Bess* LP which Gil Evans had arranged but for the scoring of which Miles had made a number of suggestions. He put *I Loves You Porgy* on the machine.

"Hear that passage. We only used two chords for all of that. And in *Summertime,* there is a long space where we don't change the chord at all. It just doesn't have to be cluttered up."

From the same Verve Opera House LP, I played the Modern Jazz Quartet's version of *Now's The Time*. "If I were John," Miles began, "I'd let Milt play more—things he'd like to get loose on—and then play these things. It would be all the more effective by contrast. You can do a lot by setting up for contrast. Sometimes I'll start a set with a ballad. You'll be surprised at what an effect that is."

The conversation turned on pianists. "Boy, I've sure learned a lot from Bill Evans. He plays the piano the way it should be played. He plays all kinds of scales; can play in 5/4; and all kinds of fantastic things. There's such a difference between him and Red Garland whom I also like a lot. Red carries the rhythm, but Bill underplays, and I like that better."

Miles was at the piano again, indulging one of his primary pleasures— hearing what can be done with voicings, by changing a note, spreading out the chord, reshaping it. "You know, you can play chords on every note in the scale. Some people don't seem to realize that. People like Bill, Gil Evans and George Russell know what can be done, what the possibilities are."

Miles returned to the MJQ recording. "John taught all of them, Milt couldn't read at all, and Percy hardly. All John has to do is let Milt play with just a sketch of an arrangement. That's what we do all the time. I never have anybody write up anything too difficult for us, because then musicians tighten up.

"I love the way John plays. I've got to get that record where he plays by himself. I usually don't buy jazz records. They make me tired and depressed. I'll buy Ahmad Jamal, John Lewis, Sonny Rollins. Coltrane I hear every night. And I like to hear the things that Max Roach writes himself. A drummer makes a very good writer. He has a sense of space and knows what it feels like to be playing around an arrangement. Philly Joe plays tenor and piano, and he's starting to write."

The talk came to Coltrane. "He's been working on those arpeggios and playing chords that lead into chords, playing them fifty different ways and playing them all at once. He's beginning to leave more space except when he gets nervous. There's one frantic tenor in Philadelphia, by the way, Jimmy Oliver."

Then came Louis Armstrong's *Potato Head Blues* of 1927 with Lil Armstrong, Kid Ory, Johnny Dodds, Johnny St. Cyr, Baby Dodds, and Pete Briggs on tuba. "Louis has been through all kinds of styles," Miles began. "That's good tuba, by the way . . . You know you can't play anything on a horn that Louis hasn't played—I mean even modern. I love his approach to the trumpet; he never sounds bad. He plays on the beat and you can't miss when you play on the beat—with feeling. That's another phrase for swing. I also love the way he sings. He and Billie never made a record, did they?" Miles was informed they had, but the material was poor (c.f. Billie's *The Blues Are Brewin'*, Decca DL 8707).

"There's form there, and you take some of those early forms, play it today, and they'd sound good. I also like all those little stops in his solo. We stop, but we often let the drums lay out altogether. If I had this record, I'd play it."

Before four bars of Ahmad Jamal's *But Not for Me* on Argo LP 628, Miles said happily, "That's the way to play the piano. If I could play like Ahmad and Bill Evans combined with one hand, they could take the other off. Jamal once told me he's been playing in night clubs since he was eleven. Listen to how he slips into the other key. You can hardly tell it's happening. He doesn't throw his technique around like Oscar Peterson. Things flow into and out of each other. Another reason I like Red Garland and Bill Evans is that when they play a chord, they play a *sound* more than a chord.

"Listen to the way Jamal uses space. He lets it go so that you can feel the rhythm section and the rhythm section can feel you. It's not crowded. Paul Chambers, incidentally, has started to play a new way whereby he can solo and accompany himself at the same time—by using space well.

"Ahmad is one of my favorites. I live until he makes another record. I gave Gil Evans a couple of his albums, and he didn't give them back. Red Garland knew I liked Ahmad and at times I used to ask him to play like that. Red was at his best when he did. Bill plays a little like that but he sounds wild when he does—all those little scales."

Miles by now was back at the piano, talking with gathering intensity about the need for more space and less chord-cluttering in jazz. "When Gil wrote the arrangement of *I Loves You, Porgy,* he only wrote a scale for me to play. No chords. And that other passage with just two chords gives you a lot more freedom and space to hear things. I've been listening to Khachaturian carefully for six months now and the thing that intrigues me are all those different scales he uses. Bill Evans knows too what can be done with scales. All chords, after all, are relative to scales and certain chords make certain scales. I wrote a tune recently that's more a scale than a line. And I was going to write a ballad for Coltrane with just two chords.

"When you go this way, you can go on forever. You don't have to worry about changes and you can do more with the line. It becomes a challenge to see how melodically inventive you are. When you're based on chords, you know at the end of 32 bars that the chords have run out and there's nothing to do but repeat what you've just done—with variations.

"I think a movement in jazz is beginning away from the conventional string of chords, and a return to emphasis on melodic rather than harmonic variation. There will be fewer chords but infinite possibilities as to what to do with them. Classical composers—some of them—have been writing this way for years, but jazz musicians seldom have.

"When I want J. J. Johnson to hear something or he wants me to, we phone each other and just play the music on the phone. I did that the other day with some of the Khachaturian scales; they're different from the usual Western scales. Then we got to talking about letting the melodies and scales carry the tune. J. J. told me, 'I'm not going to write any more chords.' And look at George Russell, his writing is mostly scales. After all, you can feel the changes.

"The music has gotten thick. Guys give me tunes and they're full of chords. I can't play them. You know, we play *My Funny Valentine* like with a scale all the way through."

The next record was *Ruby, My Dear* with Thelonious Monk, Coleman Hawkins, Wilbur Ware and Art Blakey (from *Monk's Music,* Riverside RLP 12-242).

"I learned how to play ballads from Coleman Hawkins. He plays all the chords and you can still hear the ballad. Who's playing bass? He doesn't know that tune. As for the performance as a whole, the tune wasn't meant to be played that way. I guess Hawkins figured that with young cats, he should play 'young.' It's a very pretty ballad and should be played just even. This way you can't hear it the way it is; I'd play it more flowing. Monk writes such pretty melodies and then screws them up.

"You have to go down to hear him to really appreciate what he's doing. I'd like to make an album of his tunes if I can ever get him up here.

"Monk has really helped me. When I came to New York, he taught me chords and his tunes. A main influence he has been through the years has to do with giving musicians more freedom. They feel that if Monk can do what he does, they can. Monk has been using space for a long time.

"The thing that Monk must realize is that he can't get everybody to play his songs right. Coltrane, Milt Jackson and maybe Lucky Thompson are the only ones I know that can get that feeling out of his songs that he can. And he needs drummers like Denzil Best, Blakey, Shadow, Roy Haynes, and Philly.

"I love the way Monk plays and writes, but I can't stand him behind me. He doesn't give you any support."

The final record was Bessie Smith's *Young Woman's Blues,* 1926, with Fletcher Henderson, Joe Smith and Buster Bailey.

"Listen to Joe Smith's tone. He's got some feeling to it." Miles laughed while listening to the lyrics. "They're pretty hip. This is the first time I've heard this record. I haven't heard much of Bessie, but I like her everytime I hear her. She affects me like Leadbelly did, the way some of Paul Laurence Dunbar's poetry did. I read him once and almost cried. The Negro southern speech.

"As for those lyrics, I know what she means about not being a high yellow and being a 3/4 brown or something like that. In those days high yellow was as close to white as you could get. It's getting more and more mixed though and pretty soon when you call somebody an m.f., you won't know what kind to call them. You might have to call them a green m.f.

"I'd love to have a little boy some day with red hair, green eyes and a black face—who plays piano like Ahmad Jamal."

MILES—A PORTRAIT
MAX GORDON

Max Gordon was the owner of the Village Vanguard, arguably the world's most famous jazz club, for 54 years until his death in 1989. As a businessman and talent scout who presented Davis in the 1950s and '60s, Gordon's relationship with Davis was markedly different from that which Davis had with musicians or writers. In Gordon's brief profile of Davis that is taken from the author's 1980 autobiography, the age-old dance of employer and employee is the dominant theme: Gordon and Davis joust over salary, Davis walks off the job or threatens not to return, Gordon complains about Davis's disregard for his customers, Davis is unhappy with the workplace, and Davis refuses to change his job description. According to Gordon, Davis was the hardest act he had to handle. But it was worth enduring, Gordon wrote, because Davis was "money in the bank."

What do you do on a Saturday night when the place is jammed and the star of your show walks off the bandstand in the middle of a set because his girlfriend is drunk in some uptown joint and phoning him to come and get her? Of all the jazz men who have worked at the Vanguard, Miles Davis was the toughest to handle.

Miles always liked to get one thousand dollars front money before he'd open. If I didn't have it, he might open, but after the first set on opening night, he'd come up to me and, scanning the crowd, whisper, "Don't forget the grand if you want me to come in tomorrow night." Miles's voice

93

is like no other voice I've ever heard. A loud whisper through fog and haze you can barely hear. You can hear it once you get used to it. And I was used to it.

"And move that fuckin' spot out of my eyes. Or turn the goddamn thing off altogether. I'll work in the dark, if that's the way you wanna run your place."

But whatthehell, he was money in the bank.

Miles belongs to the cool school of jazz. He invented it. You go up and you play what you're gonna play. If the audience likes it, OK; if they don't like it, OK. Sure, you expect people to be quiet and listen, but if they don't, they don't. You play the same, quiet or no quiet.

Miles never asks an audience to be quiet, as I've heard some jazz musicians do. In fact he never talks to the audience, never says a word to them. I asked him once, "Why not announce a number? Why not take a bow at the end of a number? Why not announce the names of the men in your band, let people know that you're Miles Davis? They don't know you, never saw you before, some of them."

He looked at me with a puzzled, suspicious look, as if I were crazy. "I'm a musician, I ain't no comedian. I don't go shooting my mouth off like Rahsaan Roland Kirk. Don't get me wrong, I like Rahsaan. If you want a big mouth in your place, don't hire me. I don't smile, I don't bow. I turn my back. Why do you listen to people? The white man always wants you to smile, always wants the black man to bow. I don't smile, and I don't bow. OK? I'm here to play music. I'm a musician."

I knew enough after a speech like that to leave Miles alone, and I did, except once when I asked him to play for a girl singer who used to hang out at the Vanguard Sunday matinees. It was in the late fifties.

"She's great," I told him. "I heard her at a benefit."

"I don't play behind no girl singer. Ask Herbie (Herbie Hancock, the piano player in Miles's sextet); if he wants to play for her, it's OK with me."

When Miles heard the three numbers she did—and the applause, he said, "What's her name? Bring her in, if you want to, but hire a trio to play for her. I won't play behind no broad."

The girl singer was Barbra Streisand. I put her into The Blue Angel later.

The Vanguard doesn't run Sunday jazz matinees any longer. Miles didn't mind playing them, but some musicians hated it. They felt that playing six nights straight in one week was enough. Thelonious Monk put it to me this way: "Man, I ain't gonna work no seven nights a week—not me."

When people ask me why the Vanguard doesn't run Sunday matinees anymore, I tell them, ask Thelonious Monk.

Sunday jazz matinees were great while they lasted. Most important, they brought in the kids in the afternoon, who grew up later to become full-fledged Vanguard customers at night.

When Gary Giddins, the jazz critic, was fifteen, he used to spend the two-dollar allowance his father gave him to go to the Vanguard to hear Miles Davis on Sunday afternoon. He'd come early, get a front seat. Miles was one of his jazz heroes. One Sunday, Miles, walking off the bandstand at the end of the first set, stopped to rub out his cigarette in the ashtray on Gary's table. "Here, save it," he said to Gary. "Some day it's gonna be worth some money."

Miles didn't coddle his audiences, or his boss either. "You talk, 'Man, this, man that!'" he once growled at me. "Don't talk to me like a black man. You're a white man and don't forget it."

I was in his house on West Seventy-seventh Street. Miles, neat, immaculate, in a tailored suit, dark glasses, asked me, "Did you go up to see my tailor like I told you?"

"Who can afford three hundred for a suit?"

"You're too goddamn cheap."

"If I was making the kind of money I'm paying you, I'd get myself one." I was paying him thirty-five hundred a week.

Miles used to like to putter around in his all-electric open-faced kitchen after playing all night. That's when he was hungriest—at five in the morning. Once he pan-fried a three-inch filet mignon, put a second one on for me without even asking me did I want it, could I eat it. We were in his living room and I was watching him wash it down with a bottle of beer, when a blonde girl I'd seen him with at the Vanguard the night before came ambling sleepily down the stairs from the bedrooms, awakened by the kitchen noises he was making. She sat herself on a chair, yawning, saying nothing.

Miles barely recognized her presence.

"Do you like her?" he whispered to me. "Go upstairs with her if you're not gonna eat."

"Miles, you're a bastard."

"What, you don't like her?"

He invited me to see the changes and improvements made in his house since the last time I was there. He led me into the bathroom to demonstrate the outsized, square-shaped, whirlpool bath.

"Try it," he said. "Have yourself a bath in a real bathtub."

"When are you opening at the Vanguard?" I asked Miles once when he hadn't worked there for a year. "I got a week open in May."

"Tomorrow night," he said. Miles believed in straight, fast answers.

"How much?" I asked.

"Six thousand," he said.

"You know the Vanguard can't pay that kind of money," I replied.

"Get yourself a bigger place. I don't like nightclubs anyway. I don't want to work a nightclub anymore."

(That's Miles's way of turning down a gig—asking for an impossible amount of money.)

"What's the matter with nightclubs? You've worked in 'em all your life."

"They stink! I make more in one night on a college date than you pay me in a week. And I don't have to take all that shit!"

"What're you talking about?" I knew what he was talking about: the unemployed musicians and ex-musicians; the pundits; the reviewers, columnists, and salesmen promoting fly-by-night jazz mags; the writers of liner notes on album covers; the record collectors; the heavyweights from Harlem; college kids bearing cassette recorders; the gossips, punks, and freeloaders who hang out in rooms where jazz is played.

"You know what I mean, Maaax."

Miles draws out my name like that when he wants to make a point.

"I can't stand the whole fuckin' scene. The cats comin' around, the bullshit, the intermissions. I hate intermissions. And you looking sore because I ain't up on the bandstand. And the people! "Play 'Bye, Bye Blackbird!' Shit! I don't drink now. I work out in Stillman's Gym four hours a day. I used to have to come down every night. Down to your plantation. Now I come when I want to come. On a college concert I do two short sets and I'm through. I don't have to hang around, listen to a lot of bullshit!

"I was playing Birdland one week. We're out front during intermission, standing around minding our own business. Broadway was crowded. A convention or something. A cop comes over. 'Move over,' he says.

"Sure. It's me. I'm the one blocking the goddamn sidewalk. I don't move. 'Move!' the cop shouts. I don't move. He gets his club out. I don't move. Lets me have it on the head. I wipe the blood off my head, but I don't move. I don't move for no goddamn cop. I don't move for nobody.

"It's like I say, I've had it with nightclubs. At the intermission during a college concert the kids come up asking for autographs. That's about as tough as it gets. I can take it. No sweat."

"How're you getting along with Jack these days?" I asked Miles. Jack Whittemore had been his agent for ten years.

"I'm getting rid of him!" he said.

"What happened? After all these years?"

"I was in Paris last year," he began. "I needed a few albums, a cut of my latest record. Friends, critics, broads wanted one. So I called up Jack in New York. 'Call CBS,' I told him, 'and tell 'em to call Paris and have their wholesaler here deliver a dozen albums to me in my hotel.' So what d'you think Jack said to me? 'Who do you think you are, Frank Sinatra?'"

"I'm getting rid of the bastard. What's Sinatra got I haven't got?"

Jack Whittemore called me the next day.

"Miles called, said he saw you yesterday. By the way, how's Miles feeling these days? I haven't seen him in a month. He said something about a week in May, that you got a week in May open. Right?"

"Right."

"He sounded interested. Maybe I can get him to take it."

"How much money?" I asked.

"Forty-five hundred."

"I paid him thirty-five hundred the last time."

"Miles said forty-five."

"Thirty-five," I screamed.

"Make it forty and I'll talk to him."

"Talk to him. Talk to the bastard. And wrap it up, Jack."

"You got him for forty—OK?" was the first message on my answering box when I walked in the next day.

Nights when Miles wasn't playing at the Vanguard he'd bring his current girl to The Blue Angel and order Piper Heidseick champagne. One night I told the waiter to hand him the check. He tore it in two and sent the waiter back with this message: "Tell your boss I'll never pay a check here. Tell him he's been underpaying me at the Vanguard for years. I gotta get even somehow."

MILES IN THE SKY
STANLEY CROUCH

Miles Davis's 45 years of music was a constantly evolving organism, always pushed ahead by Davis's restless mind. As Stanley Crouch points out in his assessment of Davis's 1961–1965 period, from at least 1955 right through the mid-1960s, Davis's highly original music was advancing steadily, albeit under the overarching influence of pianist Ahmad Jamal. For one thing, the Ahmad Jamal Trio's group concept, which "blurred any significant distinction between foreground and background," led Davis to a more egalitarian, interactive style of quintet and sextet writing not heard in his earlier work for Prestige.

The Jamal approach, as described by Crouch in the August 1986 *Village Voice* jazz supplement "Miles Davis at 60," suited Davis for roughly ten years. Nevertheless, by the early '60s Davis was groping for something new. According to Crouch, Davis's desire to move his music forward can be heard in the four live albums—*Miles Davis in Person, My Funny Valentine, Four and More,* and *Live at the Plugged Nickel*—that Davis recorded from 1961–1965. In these performances standard Davis tunes were being abstracted, sometimes almost beyond recognition, and new compositions contributed by Davis band members, particularly Wayne Shorter, were edging the repertoire in entirely new directions.

For Davis, change during the first half of the '60s was steady and incremental, just as it was during his entire career. The dramatic shift, the new thing Davis was after, would come, much to the author's dismay, at the end of the decade with Davis's adoption of electric instruments, dreamy Stockhausen soundscapes, and rock rhythms. Yet a look at the Davis discography reveals that this too was phased in over time.

A signal period in Miles Davis's development took place between 1961 and 1965. Four Columbia albums recorded in performance—*Miles Davis in Person, My Funny Valentine, Four and More,* and *Live at the Plugged Nickel*—tell an illuminating tale of self-imposed evolution. What we hear is how Davis largely finished off his involvement with jazz standards and popular songs, preparing the way for his last great period, which ended with *Filles de Kilimanjaro.* Davis was between schools then and was looking for something that would rejuvenate his style. He was coming to the end of a phase that had been mightily influenced by the work of Ahmad Jamal and was about to focus on a repertoire in which the bulk of material was the original music of Wayne Shorter.

Because Davis desired a musical role more substantial than that of an improvising paymaster with a "back-up" group, it was no surprise that Jamal's influence permeated Davis's work. Like a composer/arranger, Jamal was concerned with more detail than the improvised line "played over" the rhythm section. His imagination was essentially orchestral and, as his trios developed, they blurred any significant distinction between foreground and background. Through use of rests and shifts of rhythm and tempo, Jamal's groups invented a sound that had all the surprise and dynamic variation of an imaginatively ordered big band. The pianist's right and left hand, and the use to which he put his bassists and guitarists, often took on roles that paralleled those of brass and reeds, harmony and rhythm. Jamal's sense of drama put to remarkable use all he had learned from the big bands and perhaps from the ensemble shifts of New Orleans masters like Morton, or even the startling arrangements of the George Kirby Sextet. Miles Davis heard it all perfectly and made superb use of his understanding.

In June of 1955, when Davis recorded with Red Garland, Oscar Pettiford, and Philly Joe Jones, the Jamal influence was overt. In "Will You Still Be Mine?" Davis's phrasing shows the impact of the pianist—the pungent phrases that appear in the middle of fleet bursts, the determination to make each idea different from the last, the understanding of how overall shapes are achieved through the understanding of the song's basic structure, allowing for reiteration of central elements, whether melodic or harmonic, rhythmic or textural. As Philly Joe Jones once told me, "Miles used to *study* Jamal. I'll show you how brilliant he was. Once when we were in Chicago listening to Jamal when he didn't use a drummer, we kept hearing an accent on the fourth beat, but there wasn't no gaddam drums up there *anywhere*. Miles kept looking and noticed that Ray Crawford was hitting the guitar with his thumb on the last beat, swinging the hell out of the band. Miles said to me, 'Joe, if you took your drumstick and hit the rim of the snare on four, it would swing the band to death.'"

Later in 1955, Davis hired John Coltrane and Paul Chambers, kept Garland and Jones, and thus formed his first quintet. Over the next six years, Davis adapted many things from Jamal. Different rhythms were used to support featured instrumentalists, there were interludes, and the piano had a position as dramatic as it was musical, functioning as a harmonic and rhythmic force that could change the texture of the ensemble through register, voicing, attack, and silence. The bassist's role included vamps and riffs, and the drums were as important for color as they were for meter and rhythm. Garland, Chambers, and Jones had such resilient authority at any tempo that their combined musicality made them into the most accurately praised rhythm section of the mid-'50s, from musicians to lay listeners.

By 1961, with groups that included Coltrane, Cannonball Adderley, Bill Evans, and Philly Joe Jones behind him, Davis had made some classic small band recordings and had experimented with his sound in a variety of orchestral situations arranged by Gil Evans. On *In Person,* Davis's working group includes tenor saxophonist Hank Mobley, pianist Wynton Kelly, bassist Paul Chambers, and drummer Jimmy Cobb. Though he plays well at almost every opportunity, Mobley, in Coltrane's shoes, fails to provide the bewildering excitement of his predecessor—who wouldn't? Davis plays many extended improvisations, almost as though he intends to make up for the lessening of ensemble power in the wake of Coltrane. By that point, Jamal's sensibility and his skill at dynamic variety and textural shock had provided Davis with a perfect angle from which to apply what he had learned from Armstrong, Young, Holiday, Parker, and Monk. The trumpeter's counterbalancing of pianissimo phrases against shouts, his use of rests for suspense or pathos, the puckish bounce of his time, and the range of his inflections fused into a style where mood, tempo, and volume were extensions of syncopation, were soothing surprises or startling excitements. And, as "Neo" shows, his experiments with pitch were successful and offer a brass adventurousness superior in technique to "avant-garde" trumpeters even 25 years later.

Other than Davis, the dominant force on the recording is Wynton

Kelly. Perhaps the most swinging jazz pianist to emerge in the last 30 years, Kelly had a sound of pure, idiomatic nobility, a sense of space and drama, a gift for sustained melodic development, a sense of humor much like Davis's, and a special swiftness of conception and execution. Like Ellington, Monk, Silver, and John Lewis, Kelly also enjoyed improvising arrangements, structures with rising and falling sections, staccato punctuations, and clear extensions of thematic material. Consequently, he often moves beyond comping chords to cunning backgrounds and lightening dialogues with Davis that result in contrapuntal variations.

By February of 1964, when *My Funny Valentine* and *Four and More* were recorded at a single concert, Davis was moving further and further away from bebop, even his version of it. He was at the mountain top of his trumpet technique and with a band that included tenor saxophonist George Coleman, pianist Herbie Hancock, bassist Ron Carter, and drummer Tony Williams, the leader was adventurously pushing his material into fresh areas. On the first album, Davis's interpretation of the title track is as bold as Parker's "Embraceable You" or Monk's "I Should Care." The melody is abstracted to the point of near-disappearance and Davis's mastery of timbral variety, phrasing, dramatic silence, and tension and release allows for an astonishing statement. The same is true of "Stella by Starlight," where Davis sounds like Gabriel remade as he ends his first improvisation with *nine* high E naturals! No album better displays his greatness. On the second record, we hear the overtly powerful side of Davis's playing in contrast to the reflective grandeur of *My Funny Valentine*. Most of the material is fast and Davis doesn't back off from any challenges. Not everything he tries for is within his reach, but there are so many passages hot with audacity—unusual note selections, tricky rhythms, and sweeps across the range of the horn—that the thrill of performance adventure nearly overwhelms the listener. Though Hancock didn't have the soul or the swing of Kelly, there are moments when it is obvious that Davis had a much looser rhythm section, and one prepared to follow him into his next evolution.

In December of 1965, Davis and his men (now including Wayne Shorter) were looking the avant-garde right in the eye. Where previous changes of color and tempo in the Davis bands had been prearranged, metric and tempo modulations became spontaneous, as they had been for years in the music of Charles Mingus. Forms weren't discarded but they were more elastic, extending the single composition into the feeling of a suite, or a work with movements. The rhythm section was ever ready to challenge the horns. Tony Williams would sometimes, as on "Agitation" and "So What," push the rhythms into a jumble that eschewed meter in favor of a convoluted pulse. Hancock and Carter stretched and bent the harmonies, avoiding clichés as often as possible. Davis played devil-may-care with his tone, with the time, and even toys with some Don Cherry licks on "All Blues." His most successful playing is on "Green Dolphin Street" and "Stella by Starlight," where he invents another classic statement. Wayne Shorter, however, is fascinating in every feature. His synthesis of Coltrane, Rollins, and Warne Marsh has a spontaneous authority that makes for some of the most inventive tenor work of the '60s. Like Rollins and Coltrane, Shorter plays his horn better than any of the "official" avant-garde tenor saxophonists, then or now. His exceptional fluidity, intonation, and harmonic depth give compositional sophistication to his features, especially "Green Dolphin Street," "Stella," "'Round Midnight." But there are quite a few younger musicians who consider his playing on the "Rhythm" changes that follow "Yesterdays" a handbook of contemporary harmony.

In retrospect it is easy to see why Davis went into directions other than those that quickly became cliché among "avant-garde" jazzmen. Doubtless, Davis and his men could play like that, but the great Columbia recordings that were to come from that wonderful quintet were more musically demanding and more enduring. In those final years of seriousness, Davis was continuing to test his talent and his idiom, finishing up with *Filles de Kilimanjaro*. Since then, his relationship to jazz has largely rotted away. And though Miles Davis is now no more than a winged death's head floating on the hot air of insipid writers and gullible listeners, the invincibly splendid artistic victories of his past will never cease to intrigue.

"I DON'T HAVE TO HOLD THE AUDIENCE'S HAND"
ARTHUR TAYLOR

As a well-respected jazz drummer and a colleague of musicians here and abroad since the late-1940s, Arthur Taylor has had access to musicians far and wide. Starting in 1968 Taylor began taping "musician-to-musician" interviews, 27 of which were collected in his book *Notes and Tones*. First self-published in Liège, Belgium, in 1977, Taylor's influential anthology included conversations with Max Roach, Sonny Rollins, Elvin Jones, Dizzy Gillespie, Art Blakey, Ornette Coleman, and Miles Davis, among others. Taylor's interview methodology was straightforward. He would engage artists in candid talk about themselves and the jazz scene, and always ask about Charlie Parker and Bud Powell with the hope of amassing "accurate" information about them. In the Miles Davis interview that Taylor conducted in New York on January 22, 1968, Davis openly discusses boxing and other hobbies, his influence on Philly Joe Jones and Tony Williams, the absence of realistic roles for black actors in Hollywood films, and his strained relationship with promoter George Wein.

Hopefully the author's estate will publish a second collection of interviews that Taylor first promised in 1984, when he was the host of a live radio interview program for WKCR in New York.

Do you have a list of things you want to ask me?

No, I would like to ad-lib.

Hello, hello, hello, hello my ding. Look out, look out, my duke. What do you want to talk about, Arthur?

Why do you go to the gymnasium so often, Miles?

I go to the gym to keep my body in shape, so I can hold notes longer, so my stomach will be flat and so I'll look handsome.

How long have you been doing this?

Let's see . . . ever since I can remember. The reason I started doing it was to make my legs stronger.

Do you think boxing is comparable to music?

I think it is. You have to have rhythm and good time to do both. Timing has to be good on both of them. Doing exercise makes you think clear and your blood circulate. It makes you think stronger, feel stronger, and you can play whatever instrument you play with greater strength, whether it's wrong or right.

What about drums? Do you remember we were talking about drums the other day?

Drums? Drums? Oh, yeah! I think all musicians should have some kind of knowledge of drums and piano; not necessarily the bass, but at least piano and drums. Because drummers scare a lot of musicians. Like Tony [Williams]—a lot of musicians can't play with him because they're used to playing on the first beat and he accents on the second and third beats if you're in 4/4 time. Sometimes he might accent on any beat. And he might play 5/4 time for a while, and you've got to have that. You've got to know about rhythms and the feel of different rhythms in order to play with him, because he might haul off and do anything rhythmically. If you don't have any knowledge of time and different time changes, he'll lose you. You have to have it when you first start out, so it'll be back in your head, so it'll be natural.

How do you go about picking a drummer for your band?

First I look at my ding! When I look at a drummer, it's just like when I look at a fighter. I watch his reactions to different things, his quickness, whether he's on time and whether he can clean up, you know what I mean?

Would you be more explicit about that?

Say a guy makes a phrase and the phrase isn't exactly what he wants it to be; well, the drummer is supposed to be hip enough to sorta add to the finished phrase. If you know your drummer is capable of doing that, then you won't feel funny if you miss a certain phrase you're thinking of. It might be one of those off-beat phrases, or out of time.

The first thing I listen for in a drummer is if he can roll. You know, a lot of drummers can't roll. When you end a song, a roll is the most natural way for it to die off, and you can cut off. I also watch to see how fast his hands move. I look at a drummer's hands to make sure that he does not play with his arms but with his wrists and to see how his wrists are. If they are nice and fast, then he can be cultivated and you just let him go. I listen to check if he has good time and he doesn't play the bass drum too loud. The bass drum has to be played even. And I listen to the top cymbal to hear whether he plays it even or not. He may not play it like I want him to play it, but he can be taught how to play it if he plays even. I changed Joe's [Philly Joe Jones] top cymbal beat. He was kind of reluctant at first, but I changed it so it could sound more ad-lib than just straight dang-di-di-dang-di-di-dang: I changed it to dang-di-di-dang-di-di-di-di-dang, and you can play off that with your snare drum.

But you sometimes get a drummer who plays with his arms or else his foot is too heavy . . . it may be heavier than the group he's playing with or lighter than the group . . . well, it's best to be lighter, because you can always come up. Right? I made Tony play his bass drum, because he didn't play it at all. And he didn't play his sock cymbals, so I started him on the sock cymbals. I made him play the bass drum even, and all the rest he had. I suggested he cut all his phrases off on the fourth beat, so it wouldn't sound like you're starting in a chorus every time. Like 1-2-3-4, you say 1-2-3 . . . 1, accent on the fourth beat. Erroll Garner accents on the fourth beat. A lot of people don't know that. And let's see who else? Baby Laurence. It's like a pickup. Or else you can leave it. It's hipper to leave it. I also told Tony not to stop his roll but just to let it die out and keep the tempo.

Where did you get the idea of using a guitar for the record *Miles in the Sky?*

I got it from my head. I wanted to hear a bass line a little stronger. If you can hear a bass line, then any note in a sound that you play can be heard, because you have the bottom. We change the bass line quite a bit on all the songs we play. It varies. So I figured if I wrote a bass line, we could vary it so that it would have a sound a little larger than a five-piece group. By using the electric piano and having Herbie [Hancock] play the bass line and the chords with the guitar and Ron [Carter] also playing with him in the same register, I thought that it would sound good. It came out all right. It was a nice sound.

Did you compose all the music?

Well, Herbie, Wayne [Shorter] or Tony will write something, then I'll take it and spread it out or space it, or add some more chords, or change a couple of phrases, or write a bass line to it, or change the tempo of it, and that's the way we record. If it's in 4/4 time, I might change it to 3/4, 6/8 or 5/4.

Is there anything you want to add?

How about my ding? I want to add my ding.

I know you wanted to get that in. What interests you besides music and boxing?

Nothing other than music and girls. Let's see, what else? Drummers, bass players, money, slaves, white folks.

Do you have any particular hobbies?

Making fun of white folks on television. That's my main hobby. That's about it. Driving my Ferrari. I like driving a Ferrari. I don't like to drive anything else. That's a good, fast car.

You can't drive a car like that too fast in the city.

I drive that fast in this block. Whenever you can, you do it. You try not to hurt anybody. Those are about my only hobbies.

Do you go to sporting events often?

I only go to the fights. I like to see nice slick fighters, or else good enter-
tainers like Sammy Davis, Jr., but the rest of that shit ain't nothing.

Has New York changed much since the early days when you were on
Fifty-second Street?

They don't have anyplace to experiment for young guys who start play-
ing and who play their own stuff. It's because of all those records they
make nowadays . . . you know, the guys copy off the records, so they
don't have anything original. You can't find a musician who plays any-
thing different. They all copy off each other. If I were starting out again,
I wouldn't listen to records. I very seldom listen to jazz records, because
they all do the same thing. I only listen to guys that are original, like
Ahmad Jamal and Duke Ellington, guys like Dizzy Gillespie, Sonny
Rollins and Coltrane.

Can we start again, Miles?

What? Sock it to me! Come on out with it!

What kind of music interests you besides jazz?

Yesterday I listened to an album of music from Poland: Penderecki's
Threnody for the Victims of Hiroshima. *I have* Dr. Doolittle *here, which*
Columbia sent me, and Camelot.

Of all the music that's been sent to you through the years, how much
have you used?

It's all stacked up there. Most of the songs are so weak that you have to
rebuild them, so it's like composing yourself.

Is it better for you to compose your own music?

It's better because you can put what you want in it. Gil [Evans] and I
looked over most of this music, and it's kind of weak.

Have you and Gil recorded anything that hasn't been released?

We've been working on something for about three years. I don't know how it's going to turn out, though.

Do you think it will culminate soon?

It has to, because we've been working on it for so long.

When you say "working on it," what exactly do you mean?

You see these little sketches here at the piano? [He plays] Little things like this . . . trial and error. We write, and then we take out everything we don't like, and what's left is what we record. We try different combinations of instruments, different voices.

Three years seems like quite a long time to be working on one piece of music.

We do it off and on. Gil has to work, and he doesn't work that much. He has to do albums to get money to live on. So we just work on the side.

What about this piece of music on the piano?

Dr. Doolittle has about three songs in it that are worth something, but the rest have to be rebuilt.

Is *Dr. Doolittle* playing on Broadway?

No, they made a movie out of it.

Do you go to the movies often?

I haven't seen any I liked. Let's see, I saw The Graduate. *That was pretty good. But I can't stand those white movies about white problems. I'd like to see a movie dealing with Negroes as human beings with emotions, not just a black maid or a doctor. I'd like to see one in everyday life . . . like an executive, or the head of a company. One who falls in love and out of love; one who drives a sports car; and one who acts like me or like you; who has girls, white girls, colored girls, Chinese and*

Hawaiian and German and French, you know? They don't have that in the movies, so I don't go. Every time I go I feel like I'm giving my money away. Some money! I'd rather shoot tigers or something. I have a funny feeling all day after I've seen a movie with the same white problems. You know, full of girls with long hair and where everybody's having a lot of fun, and we don't have any fun. You don't see any Negroes. It makes me feel funny. It makes me feel like I just gave my money away. If I'm going to give my money away I can give it to something. It's a form of Jim Crow when you have white people dancing and having a good time, and they don't show any Negroes or what Negro feelings are, or any Chinese people, just white girls dancing, with their hair going and going. It's tiresome to me. I want to see somebody acting and living like I do or like you do. Not just white. I saw a movie last night on television. It was just all white all the way through. I figure if the white people keep on showing us their problems on television like they're doing, then we will be able to tell their problems by their facial expressions pretty soon, 'cause they're running out. I was telling Herbie the other day: "We're not going to play the blues anymore. Let the white folks have the blues. They got 'em, so they can keep 'em. Play something else."

Do you like traveling for your work?

It doesn't bother me as long as the band sounds good.

Do you get enjoyment from touring the world with your band?

No, because I'm bringing the pleasure, and whenever I go someplace, I'm going there to please somebody else. So I don't get any kick out of a foreign country unless I go there not to play but on a vacation.

Do you find traveling a strain?

It doesn't bother me, because I don't drink. I stopped drinking.

Do you feel better?

I feel better; a lot better. I don't tire myself out so quickly. When you do one-nighters, like we did in Europe, and you drink every time you eat, you wind up feeling real tired before a concert. You get up early in the morning . . . you might have a hangover and it carries on, and you won't be able to think right. I don't mind traveling, but it just bothers me when guys like George Wein did what he did in Spain and blamed it on me.

What was that?

He tried to slip two extra concerts in and told me he'd pay my room rent, which made me mad, so I left. At the plane I told him I wasn't going to make it. It's all right. He pays enough money and everything, but if he's going to put another concert in and have television, and get paid for it . . . I went along with it, but when it gets so you feel like you're being taken advantage of, it's best to leave, because he's not treating you like a man. I don't think the fact he married a colored girl changes anything. It doesn't matter to me who he married. He married her, not me. I take him for the way he treats me. But he gets real common after a while. He's all right except when he tries to get like one of the boys; then he gets sickening, because nobody's interested in that. All I want to do is play the concert and get the money. He said I stranded my band. They had already been paid, they had their transportation, you know, the tickets.

He wanted everybody to think he was my manager in Europe. I didn't say anything, but that's kind of disrespectful to a musician. And then he would ask me about how I live. It's none of his business. I told him so. I said: "George, you can't live like me because you don't make that much money." He asked me once, "What do you do with your money?" I told him to shut up and don't say nothing 'cause I'd break his neck. If I play a concert, Arthur, I like to play the concert and leave. You don't have to be nice to me or nothing. Let me play the concert and leave me alone. I'll play the music. Pay me off, and that's it. But don't come around to me trying to be a nice guy or a big shot, with some bitches or something, because it doesn't have any effect on me.

The only thing I asked George was, "Wherever we go, try to find a gymnasium in the town so I'll have something to do." He didn't do it. I figured he'd take care of it himself, but he had those in-between guys, the middlemen, who didn't think it was important. But to me it was important. I guess they thought it was a joke. I had a nice time in Europe, because the band played good. That was the only reason. The band plays pretty good sometimes. Oh yeah, George stopped a check because I didn't play in Spain. I was there for two days. So now I'm suing him for what he said. For always dropping all the weight on me. Well, promoters always do this, anyway.

Do you see any solution to problems like that?

Yeah, get your money first. That's what I do. I mean it was all right . . . I called him and said: "George, if we're doing an extra concert, give me some more money." And guess what he said: "Man, like I don't have no bread." So how you going to talk business like that? He tries to use slang and be hip, and: "I don't have no bread, man." I said: "If you don't have no bread, get somebody else, 'cause I'm leaving." So I left.

Do you think it's easier for someone like myself to interview you?

I think it's much easier, if you have something that you want to ask me about music. Because you think the same way, on the same line I think on. Most guys want to know about . . . well, they say I'm rude, and that I turn my back on the audience, and that I don't like white people. And that I don't like the audience. But the thing is, I never think about an audience. I just think about the band. And if the band is all right, I know the audience is pleased. I don't have to hold the audience's hand. I think audiences are hipper than musicians think they are. They wouldn't be there if they didn't want to hear some music, so you don't have to con them into believing that this music is great. I figure they can judge for themselves, and those who don't like it don't have to like it, and those who like it will have a nice time listening. If I go to a concert, I take it like that.

This piece, originally published in the September 3, 1970, issue of *Down Beat,* recounts two muggy summer afternoons the author spent with Miles Davis. On the first day an anxious Morgenstern arrives at Davis's New York City townhouse, where Davis plays excerpts from his upcoming recording, *Live at the Fillmore East.* Davis also demonstrates for his awed guest an amplified trumpet with a patched in wah-wah foot pedal. Davis was on the verge of totally transforming his sound with the wah-wah, which he would utilize for the next few years as guitarist Jimi Hendrix had done before him.

Their second day together gave Morgenstern a chance to see Davis in his typical routine. Together they zip around New York in the trumpeter's new Lamborghini, first picking up Davis's boxing trainer (probably Bobby McQuillen) in Harlem, then traveling north to Gleason's Gym in the Bronx where Morgenstern watches Davis work out. On the drive back to Manhattan, Morgenstern and Davis talk about Davis's current band, which included Chick Corea, Keith Jarrett, Jack DeJohnette, and Airto Moreira.

I approach the prospect of interviewing Miles Davis with some trepidation. We've had a nodding acquaintance for years—since the time, way back in '48, when a little trumpet player named Nat Lorber (they call him "Face") introduced us on Broadway. I remember that Miles was wearing a beautiful dark blue double-breasted pinstripe suit. (He's always been sharp.)

Since then, many brief encounters, in clubs, backstage at concerts, etc., Miles sometimes friendly, sometimes not. And nine years ago, an evening at his house, with a whole bunch of writers and players in a "confrontation," as they call it now, between critics and musicians arranged by a press agent. Miles was a beautiful host. So why am I up tight?

I remember the house, in the west 70s, but as the cab pulls up and I spot Miles lounging near the entrance, it looks different. Above the front door, there is now a moorish turret. Miles greets me, and we enter. There are men at work inside. The place is being completely redecorated. An Egyptian mural graces the patio walls. A tempting honeydew melon rests on the kitchen table.

"Want a piece?" Miles asks. It's a hot day. He cuts two slices expertly. The melon is delicious, tasting just right at room temperature. "It's best when it's not too cold," Miles comments. "Come in here—I want to show you something," he adds, moving toward the front room.

There stands a new Innovex unit. "They sent me this," says Miles, turning on the power and picking up his trumpet. "Dig this."

A foot pedal has been connected to the unit, and Miles works it while he blows. The sound is not unlike that achieved by moving the hand in front of the bell, in this case Harmon-muted. Miles obviously likes the sound; he's never played wa-wa style, and this way, he can also bend the notes subtly. He turns up the volume to show the power of the speaker system. Then he puts the horn away.

Glancing at the multiple controls atop the unit, I ask if he uses any of the other devices. "Naaah," he shrugs disdainfully. Like any musician with his own good and distinctive sound, he has no desire to distort it. He likes the pedal effects and the amplification, but that's all.

"Let's go upstairs," he says. It's a duplex apartment, and the redecorating upstairs is finished. The living room is like a cool oasis. Everything is built in—aside from a low, round table, there is no standing furniture. (A recent article about the house in the *New York Times* quotes Miles to the effect that he doesn't like corners. Everything is rounded off.) The soft, blue carpeting looks inviting, and when Miles answers the phone, he reclines on the floor. You can move freely in this place. The bedroom is so groovy that if it were mine, I might never leave it.

"You want to hear something?" Miles asks, approaching the wall that holds his music system—tape decks, amplifiers, turntable, some records, lots of tapes. He finds the reel he wants, unravels it, and puts it on. The speakers, invisible, built into the ceiling somewhere, are a gas, and so is the music, by Miles' new band, obviously recorded live. It's quite a change from *Bitches Brew*—this man doesn't stay in one place too long. I listen, and let the music carry me away.

What I've heard, I learn, is from a forthcoming Columbia album, recorded live on three consecutive nights at the Fillmore East. It will be released in September, and is the first live Miles LP in many years. Keith Jarrett is on the band (as well as Chick Corea—Chick on electric piano, Keith on Fender-Rhodes combo organ), and he is a significant addition. Miles is obviously pleased with him.

"Did you hear what Keith was playing behind me there?" he asks, rolling back the tape. "He's a bitch. Chick, too." After the passage has been replayed, he demonstrates at the piano, built into one side of the seating unit, and within easy reach from the hi-fi system.

"With a C going on in the bass, you can play anything against it," he explains. I ask if he does most of the writing for the group now, since Wayne Shorter's departure, and he says yes.

When he has to write something for a record date, he adds later, he usually does it at the last moment, so it will be completely fresh.

"You write to establish the mood," he points out. "That's all you need. Then we can go on for hours. If you complete something, you play it, and it's finished. Once you resolve it, there's nothing more to do. But when it's open, you can suspend it. . . ."

Suspension is a word Miles uses frequently when talking about his music. It is a music very much of today, in sound and feeling. Once again, Miles is setting the pace, as he has been doing at frequent intervals since 1948 and the Capitol Nonet. There was the pioneering quintet with Coltrane, Red Garland, Paul Chambers, and Philly Joe Jones; *Miles Ahead* and the other memorable collaborations with Gil Evans; the great sextet with Trane, Cannonball Adderley, and Bill Evans, which in *Kind of Blue* established a whole new syntax for jazz improvisation, and then the series of surprises beginning with *E.S.P.* and running on through *Bitches Brew*.

When the Fillmore album comes out, there'll be new surprises. In a sense, Miles is a perfectionist, but not the polishing kind. Once he has perfected a thing, he needs to move on to something new. His music today is in constant motion, ideas bouncing off each other, interacting; many things going on at once; cyclical, unresolved, suspended and full of suspense, electrified and electrifying.

Miles has some private business to attend to. He invites me to come back the following afternoon. "We'll go up to the gym. You can watch me work out. . . ."

Another sultry New York day. Inside, it's cool and dark. We join our host in a cup of refreshing mint tea, then take a stroll to a nearby garage.

Again a surprise—no more red Ferrari, but a new battleship grey Lamborghini; a magnificent machine, low and trim, built like a racer. We shoot out onto the West Side Highway, heading north.

Miles drives with the superlative reflexes of a pro, fast but not taking any dumb chances; not showing off, always in complete control. We learn that the Ferrari was "full of bullet holes," unwanted souvenirs of the stupid attempt on Miles' life by obviously amateur gangsters earlier this year.

What happened to them? "They're all dead," Miles answers matter-of-factly, not gloating. "I don't know how or where, but that's what I heard."

On our way to pick up Miles' trainer, we stop for a red light in Harlem. A young black man on a monumental yellow Honda pulls up next to us, eyeing the car with open admiration. "What kind is that?" he asks. "Tell him a Lamborghini," Miles instructs. The motorcyclist is on my side of the car, and Miles can't shout. I convey the information, repeating the unfamiliar name, and adding that it's an Italian make.

"Ask him how much is that Honda," Miles requests. "It's $1600," the cyclist responds proudly, obviously pleased at the question. The car is more than ten times the price of the Honda, but in asking, Miles has equalized them—two men admiring each other's strong machines.

At Bobby Gleason's Gym in the Bronx, a comfortable, old fashioned place where some of the city's best fighters work out, Miles, in bright blue trunks, is shadow boxing under the watchful eye of his trainer, a slim, trim, soft-spoken man who looks and acts not at all like the stereotype of the ex-boxer. He's been with Miles for years.

Afterwards, while Miles does exercises in a corner, the trainer tells me: "He's really coming along. His reflexes are getting better all the time. And he's in top shape."

As I have noticed. Not an ounce of excess fat. All solid muscle, but not of the bulging kind displayed by some of the men in the gym. Sleek and compact like a panther. It's obvious that everyone around the gym and on the street outside knows and likes Miles Davis.

"Boxing is like music," Miles says later, as we drive downtown. "You keep adding to it." He works out four times a week, he says, and does 40 pushups and 40 situps each day.

He talks some more about music. "We're not a rock band. Some people get that idea because we're amplified, but with amplification, we can be heard, and we can hear each other. This is a new day, and we can do what we want. With a good system, you can play soft or loud, and people can hear."

"For years," he goes on, "I've been going to clubs to listen to something—like Ahmad Jamal playing piano—and once I'm there, I can't hear anything." And there are other things he dislikes about most clubs: "You have to give people something, not just take from them."

But he doesn't mind playing clubs, he says, provided things are right and the music can be heard. "For a while, I thought we had something good at the Village Gate (where, earlier this year, Miles had worked out an arrangement with owner Art D'Lugoff enabling him to book acts of his own choice to work opposite his band, getting the admission gate while the club took in the proceeds from drink and food sales), but Art didn't seem to want to keep it going."

We're nearing our destination, and Miles gives me fair warning to hold on before he negotiates a hairpin turn that takes us off the East River Drive.

"Our music changes every month," he says. "We extend each other's ideas. I may start a phrase and not complete it because I hear something else behind me that takes me to a different place. It keeps going further. Our Latin drummer (Airto Moreira) gives us something else to play off. Most of the guys in the band can play other instruments, and that expands their conception. Jack (DeJohnette) can really play the piano, and Chick plays the shit out of the drums. Keith plays clarinet. So when they ad lib, you know it's going to be something you like to hear."

* * *

In jazz today, there are many seekers of new ways. Often, the searching seems forced, and the results not natural. Miles Davis, however, has that rare gift of being able to give birth and life to new things which, no matter how startling, always seem natural and logical, and open up new roads for others to travel after he has moved on.

The sole photograph in Miles' living room, unobtrusively displayed, is a color shot of a pensive John Coltrane, dating from his days with the trumpeter. It's pure speculation, of course, but if he were still among us, I have a feeling that Coltrane, that restless seeker, might well once again feel very much at home with Miles.

Leonard Feather's profile of Miles Davis was first published in his 1972 book *From Satchmo to Miles,* though serialized in *Penthouse* a few months prior to publication. Looking back at Davis's accomplishments, Feather writes, "For a quarter of a century [Davis] has to some extent controlled the direction of jazz . . . manifestly chang[ing] the entire course of an art form three or four times in 25 years—an accomplishment that no other jazz musician can claim." Feather states that Davis also "pioneered in the concept of segueing from one theme and mood to another, so that an entire set at a club would be a continuum." (Davis biographer Jack Chambers has pointed out that Davis began this approach around 1967.)

Interspersed among Feather's interview with Davis is additional interview material from Clark Terry, Dizzy Gillespie, Quincy Jones, and Herbie Hancock. Hancock states that Davis in 1972 was "setting up a criterion of excellence in the direction of rock that nobody else has achieved." Gillespie, for his part, reminded Feather that Davis "was the first one that came along in our business and figured he didn't have to smile at everyone, didn't have to tell no jokes or make no announcements, didn't have to say thank you or even bow. He figured he could just let the music speak for him, and itself. He succeeded in doing this. . . . I say more power to him."

The unnamed *Ebony* reporter that Feather cites is Marc Crawford. Interestingly, Davis tells Feather at one point that tenor saxophonist Joe Henderson had played in his group. According to Chambers, Henderson joined Davis's band in January 1967, augmenting the unit (already with Wayne Shorter) to a sextet. Henderson played gigs with the group at the Village Vanguard and then did a fifteen-city tour through March. Hopefully, recorded material of this band will surface.

Miles Dewey Davis III has learned as well as any musician alive how to make music, women, money, and headlines, not necessarily in that order of importance but probably in that chronological sequence.

The various sobriquets he has acquired along the way—Prince of Darkness, Public Enigma No. 1—attest to his ability to build around himself an aura of cultism and mysticism.

He inspires young musicians who are awed by his presence, instills fear in the hearts of young secretaries at Columbia Records whom he has called white bitches, leaves reporters ignored or confused, talks in absolutes and with seemingly total conviction. His words are at variance with his actions, particularly in the area of race, and some of his statements are total contradictions of others.

He has been called bitter, hostile, bigoted, capricious, undependable, often by some of the same observers who at other times have found him shy, warm, generous, sensitive, and witty. After denouncing white American society, he has emulated its most materialistic values by acquiring all the appurtenances and luxuries his millions could bring him over the years: the $15,000 Ferrari; the $100,000 town house on West Seventy-Seventh Street; the vast Italian-style wardrobe, including compensatory high-heeled shoes.

Much has been made of his background: unlike most black and many white musicians, he was born into a middle-class family with bourgeois values, and was urged by his mother to take up some genteel instrument such as the violin. That these advantages have not protected him from racism or other forms of dehumanization Davis considers irrelevant. "You don't know how to play better just because you've suffered," he says. "The blues don't come from picking cotton."

He is a maverick in much more than his social origins. It has been axiomatic through the history of jazz that once established, the great individual styles, whether conceived by Armstrong, Eldridge, Hawkins,

Hodges, Young, Gillespie, or Peterson, have remained basically unchanged through the years, evolving only within the original framework. Gillespie solos recorded in 1945 and 1971 are clearly recognizable as the work of the same artist. Davis, on the other hand, has changed so radically that most listeners not familiar with all his work would refuse to believe that a recent solo, on one of his rock-dominated records, was played by the same trumpeter heard on, say, "Out of the Blue" in 1951.

Davis, for all his changes of direction, is today more than ever a player of unquestionable originality and has an almost hypnotic influence on his contemporaries, as Gillespie had in the 1940s. Miles was the first to make a definitive switch from trumpet to flügelhorn, an instrument that has since become a double for hundreds of trumpeters. He was the first to make use of modal themes, a development later associated more closely with John Coltrane, but actually dating back to the late 1950s when Coltrane was a sideman in Davis' group. Davis' early career found him as a bebopper who had listened closely to Clark Terry and Gillespie; in a second phase, as a central figure in the breakaway from bop to cooler and more orchestrated conceptions through his collaboration with Gil Evans, John Lewis, Gerry Mulligan, and others on the *Birth of the Cool* recordings (1949–50); in a third stage, as leader of various small bands, quintets and sextets, and overlapping the latter, as partner with Evans in a series of large-scale orchestral albums that are assured a permanent place in musical history. Still later came the first intimations of "space music," and not long afterward the flirtation with rock.

With each of these directional shifts in the group style came substantial changes in Davis' entire approach to the horn. According to him each new move has represented a step ahead, a development evolving directly out of the previous period. Other musicians are sharply divided concerning the accuracy of this self-analysis.

Davis revels in the present and eagerly courts the future; in effect, although at times he may deny it, he rejects his past.

LF: When you hear the old records you made with Gil Evans, or the combo albums when Herbie Hancock and Wayne Shorter were with you, how do they sound to you today?

MD: *I don't listen to them.*

LF: Is that because you no longer find anything interesting in them?

MD: *The records sound funny to me.*

LF: Wouldn't you advise young musicians to go through those stages first before getting to what you're into now? These guys that you have now, didn't they at one time play songs with definite beginnings and endings?

MD: *Yeah, you have to come up through those ranks. They can always do that; but you don't hear anybody doing that old shit with me. You know, some guys are still playing all that shit we did years ago, things I did with Bird and stuff; they're still using those clichés and calling it jazz. Black guys as well as white guys. I hear it over and over again— shit that I've even forgotten.*

LF: Well, that's natural, Miles, as long as they get into something eventually.

MD: *No, it's not natural.*

LF: You could just as well say that Dizzy is still playing the blues and "Night in Tunisia" and all those things. Does that make him inferior?

MD: *How is he going to be inferior? How is he ever going to be inferior?*

LF: That's what I mean. So why shouldn't he continue to go on like that as long as it's valid?

MD: *He can do anything he wants to.*

LF: Do you believe the era of the 12-bar blues and the 32-bar song is dead?

MD: *No, you can add something to it. But when I write something, I don't think of anything I've ever heard. I don't try to be different; it's just that I figure, when whatever I wanted to write is finished, I stop. I don't count the bars. What's complete to me might not be complete to your ear; 'cause I never resolve anything that way. I hate to. But I'm not rejecting anything. You're not losing anything with what we're doing now; you're gaining everything you lost, because you heard all that other shit over and over again.*

LF: A lot of young people haven't heard it. The kids that heard you at the Fillmore or Shelly's Manne Hole may not even know about the Gil Evans albums, let alone the Capitol albums. I think it's wrong that they should be unfamiliar with the important innovations of the past.

MD: *There's so much more to music than just that. Like what I'm doing now, you know?*

LF: I'm saying that they should also recognize what you did then, because you accomplished something that was important to you and to jazz at that time.

MD: *I don't know whether they recognize it or not. Anyway everything that I do is recognized until somebody else does it.*

This last observation is irrefutable. Whether or not today's rock fans are conscious of it, some part of each Davis contribution has eventually filtered through into the mainstream of jazz. This means that he has manifestly changed the entire course of an art form three or four times in twenty-five years—an accomplishment that no other jazz musician can claim.

The Davis family has to its credit at least three generations of impressive achievements. Miles Dewey Davis the First was a well-to-do black man who at one time owned 1,000 acres of land in Arkansas. Miles II became a substantial landowner himself in addition to pursuing a lucrative career as a dentist and dental surgeon. Miles Dewey Davis III was born May 26, 1926, in Alton, Illinois. Soon afterward the family moved to East St. Louis, where Miles II increased his wealth still further by breeding hogs.

Pride of family was a conspicuous trait in the Davis household. Doc Davis once said: "The Davises historically have always been musicians. I would have been one myself, but my father forbade me to play, because Negroes at that time could only play in barrelhouses. By genetics and breeding, Miles III is always going to be ahead of his time."

LF: How many were there in the family?

MD: *I have an older sister, Dorothy; she's married. My brother, Vernon, was born in 1929.*

LF: How old are your own children now?

MD: *Cheryl is the oldest, then there's Gregory, and Miles. They're all in their twenties. I was married when I was sixteen. I have a grandson— he's five; he and Cheryl live in St. Louis.*

LF: You were pretty close to your mother, weren't you?

MD: *No, I've never been close to none of my family. Me and my mother fell out when I was thirteen. We were close at one time; we could talk to each other, but you know, I wasn't going to take none of that shit from her just because she was my mother.*

LF: What kind of shit?

MD: *Just real bullshit. It was a matter of either talk straight to me or not at all. When she did, we became real tight.*

LF: How was your relationship with your father?

MD: *Not bad. He just told my mother to leave me alone. He bought me a trumpet for my thirteenth birthday, and I'd only been playing two or three years when I had a chance to leave school and go on the road with Tiny Bradshaw's band. I went home and asked my mother . . . she said no, I had to finish my last year of high school. I didn't talk to her for two weeks.*

LF: What advantages did growing up black and middle class give you over growing up black and poor?

MD: *You're gonna run into that Jim Crow thing regardless of how wealthy you are. I can't buy no freedom. Having money has helped me once in a while, but I'm not looking for help. I'm even the one that's the helper, helping people by playing my music. There's no excuse for being*

poor anyway. You see, you're not supposed to wait on anybody to give
you nothing. My father taught me that.

LF: How old were you when your parents separated?

MD: *I don't remember, but I remember I sent my sister to school, to*
Fisk, when I was about sixteen—I was making $85 a week with Eddie
Randall's band. That was just before I went to New York.

LF: How did you get along that far musically in just a couple of years?

MD: *I just got onto the trumpet and studied and played. It would have*
been that or something else; a lot of black people think that to keep
from being Jim Crowed and shit like that you have to be a professional
man and know a little bit of something. But then if you want an engi-
neer or an architect or something, who do you get? You don't go to a
black man.

LF: Were there a lot of kids in school with you who became professionals?

MD: *Yeah. One of them is going to run for Mayor of Compton, Cal.*
East St. Louis was so bad that it just made you get out and do some-
thing. . . . See, I believe if you don't go to school you can still educate
yourself. I don't think you need formal schooling to get an education.
There's always a library. You know, I can't believe the library they got
in New York.

LF: Were you a good student?

MD: *Well, I taught my sister mathematics. See, if I had a book, I could*
look at it and remember the whole page. It came to me like that. I can
remember anything—telephone numbers, addresses. Even today I can
just glance at them and remember. That's the reason I used to take care
of band payrolls; I could remember all the tabs and shit.
    Music was easy. When I was a kid, I was fascinated by the musi-
cians, particularly guys who used to come up from New Orleans and
jam all night. I'd sit there and look at them, watch the way they walked
and talked, how they fixed their hair, how they'd drink, and of course
how they played.

Then of course I played in the school band. Around that time I met
Clark Terry. He was playing like Buck Clayton in those days, only
faster. I started to play like him. I idolized him.

Clark Terry, five years Miles's senior, grew up across the river in St. Louis.
"The first time I ever set eyes on Miles," says Terry, "was in Carbondale,
Illinois. His music teacher, who was a drinking buddy of mine, had told
me about him. 'I've got a little cat over there in East St. Louis who's a
bitch,' he said. 'You really got to hear him.' I said OK, OK, I'd hear him
sometime.

"Not long afterward I was working in a May Day affair when all the
schools would compete against one another in athletics. He was in this
school band, and he came up to me and very meekly said, 'Pardon me, Mr.
Terry, but would you tell me something about the horn? I'd like to know
how you do certain things.' And I was so preoccupied with all the beautiful schoolgirls around that I said, 'Why don't you get lost—stop bugging
me,' which is something I never normally do. Miles was maybe fifteen
then.

"A few months later, in St. Louis, I was on my way to an after-hours
jam session at the Elks, a place with a long staircase. On the way up this
long flight of stairs I heard this new sound, new trumpet. I thought I could
recognize everybody's style, but this stumped me. So I walked up to the
bandstand and there was this little fellow. I said, 'Hey, aren't you the cat
I ran into at Carbondale?' And he said, 'Yeah, man, I'm the cat you fluffed
off that night!' I was in the profession a long time before he was, and I
guess he used to come across the bridge many times to listen to bands I
was in. I know he credits me as his first influence and I'm flattered,
because he's not a cat that passes out compliments too easily.

"He was a nice, quiet little kid then, and I think the changes in him are
a cover-up. Deep down, basically, he's a beautiful cat. Many people have
misunderstood him and don't know the true Miles.

"If he seems to go to great lengths to conceal it, he's probably been
given a bad time by people who've mistreated him and he feels he doesn't
have to accept these things anymore. I can understand this, because there
were times in my own childhood when I was abused by Caucasians, so I
could have all the reason in the world to be anti-Caucasian and make a
career out of paying people back for things they've done to me. I've been
attempted-to-be-lynched twice, and spat on, and had my clothes ripped off

and been beaten, but I just refuse to lower myself to that level. Maybe many more things happened to Miles than to me, and some of them he just can't forget."

If Miles does not talk about childhood traumas, it is certainly not because they never existed. "One of the first things I can remember," he says, "was when I was a little boy and a white man was running down the street after me hollering, 'Nigger, nigger!'"

He is said to have been deeply hurt again when, living in a white neighborhood with his black middle-class parents, he was stopped by a white bigot who told him, "What you doin' here? This ain't no nigger street." Miles's father once told friends that his son would have won the first prize in the high school music competition, but traditionally whites had a hold on that honor.

Before leaving high school Miles had one brief fling in the big time, playing for two weeks as substitute for one of the regular trumpeters in the Billy Eckstine orchestra. This placed him in the exalted company of Dizzy Gillespie and Charlie Parker. (Eckstine recalls it differently: "When I first heard Miles, I let him sit in so as not to hurt his feelings, but he sounded terrible; he couldn't play at all.")

Mrs. Davis wanted her son to go to Fisk University, a predominantly black institution in Nashville, well known for its music department and renowned for having produced the Fisk Jubilee Singers. But Miles knew that this would be pointing him in the wrong direction for jazz. He opted for Juilliard and, with his father's blessing, headed for New York.

"I spent my first two weeks looking for Charlie Parker," he recalls. "That's who I wanted to learn from. I knew all that Juilliard shit already—I'd studied it all myself.

"Originally I went there to see what was happening but when I found out nothing was happening, I told my father to save his money. I stayed about a semester and a half. Shit, I did all the homework for summer school in one day."

"Isn't that," I suggested, "because you just naturally had a bright mind and a good feeling for it?"

"I had nothing on my mind *but* study. I wasn't even fuckin', man, you know?"

"I thought you said you were married when you came to New York."

"Yeah, but at that time she was pregnant."

Whatever the state of his education Davis soon drifted into the bustling Fifty-second Street scene of the mid-1940s and found a friend and sponsor in Charlie Parker. For a while they roomed together and Miles followed Bird around on gigs. "I'd make notes of the chords and stuff I was hearing, write 'em down on matchbooks, then next day at Juilliard, instead of going to class, I'd spend all my time trying out those chords."

Before long Davis was out of Juilliard for good and a regular member of Parker's quintet. As the early recordings show, his technique still had a long way to go; he had little control in the upper register and often fluffed in the middle. Over the years an elliptical sense of self-editing developed that enabled him to play less yet say more.

As a close associate of Parker he was inevitably brought into contact with the drug scene, yet to most observers around Fifty-second Street he was the abstemious, mild-mannered youth who neither smoked nor drank. A year or two elapsed before he became a part of the narcotics world. Heroin was then rampant among the young beboppers, but Miles, to all outward appearances, remained cool, taking care of business on the Bird job and subsequently with Coleman Hawkins's small band, on the road with Benny Carter's orchestra and with Billy Eckstine. By this time he was so improved, Eckstine says, that he was able to take over the parts previously played by Gillespie. He stayed with Eckstine until the band broke up in 1947, later working in the singer's small combo. It was during this period that he made headlines with his first arrest for possession.

"As strong as that man may seem to be outwardly," says Harry "Sweets" Edison, "his inward character may be a little weak just one time, and that's all it takes."

Although his private life was to remain chaotic for several years, Miles continued to progress as he became part of a workshop band, one that involved the use of two instruments never before heard in the new jazz, French horn and tuba.

"Gil Evans and I spent the better part of one winter hashing out the instrumentation for that nine-piece band," Gerry Mulligan once recalled. "But Miles dominated the band completely; the whole nature of the interpretation was his."

Miles's version of the band's evolution was predicated on his desire to play with "a light sound . . . because I could think better when I played that way. Gerry said to get Lee Konitz on alto because he had that light sound too. That whole thing started out as just an experiment; then Monte Kay booked us into the Royal Roost on Broadway for two weeks.

"As for that *Birth of the Cool* shit, I don't understand how they came to call it that. Someone just dropped that label on me. I think what they really mean is a soft sound—not penetrating too much. To play soft you have to relax . . . you don't delay the beat, but you might play a quarter triplet against four beats, and that *sounds* delayed. If you do it right, it won't bother the rhythm section."

The nine-piece band was short-lived, lasting for two public appearances and three recording dates, but it marked the beginning of the close, enduring friendship and association between Miles and Gil Evans. It was to bring out in Davis a lyricism, a soaring and ecstatic sound for which Evans provided the perfect setting.

"Gil has a way of voicing chords and using notes like nobody else," said Miles. "We work together great because he writes the way I'd like to write. In fact, years ago I used to do arrangements and give them to him to look over. He'd tell me my charts were too cluttered up, that I could get the same effect using fewer notes.

"Finally I decided the best thing to do was let Gil do the writing. I'd just get together with him—sometimes not even in person, just on the phone—and outline what I wanted. And he always has such a complete feeling for what I mean that it comes out sounding exactly like what I had in mind."

For younger jazz fans who know Davis only from his recent work, an entire new-old horizon may be opened up by the endless mixture of orchestral sounds, and the stark, mournful spareness of Davis' horn, in such masterpieces as *Miles Ahead, Porgy and Bess,* and *Sketches of Spain.* Davis and Evans were reunited in parts of the *Miles at Carnegie Hall* album and on a later LP called *Quiet Nights,* but the first three are the definitive works. (All five are still available on Columbia.)

Miles's career might have gained immediate momentum after the *succès d'estime* of the first (Capitol) collaboration with Evans, but the narcotics habit proved a formidable roadblock, wrecking his home life, limiting his musical development, and reducing him at times to a near-derelict.

"I remember one day on Broadway," says Clark Terry, "I found him sitting in front of one of those ham-and-eggs places. He was just wasted, actually sitting by the gutter. I asked him what was wrong and he said, 'I don't feel well.' After buying him some ham and eggs I took him around to my hotel, the America on West Forty-seventh Street. I was getting ready to leave on the bus with Basie's band, and I told him, 'You just stay here, get some rest, and when you leave just close the door.'

"The bus waited longer than I'd expected, so I went back to the room. Miles had disappeared, the door was open, and all my things were missing.

"I called home, St. Louis, and told my wife to call Doc Davis to see if he could get Miles, because he was obviously in bad shape and had become the victim of those cats who were twisting him the wrong way. And you know what? Doc Davis was very indignant. He told her, 'The only thing that's wrong with Miles now is because of those damn musicians like your husband that he's hanging around with.' He was the type of guy who believed his son could do no wrong. So he didn't come to get him."

As Miles found himself facing a bleak future, it became a case of physician's son, heal thyself. "It took me four years to break the habit," he told an *Ebony* reporter. "I just made up my mind I was getting off dope. I was sick and tired of it. You can even get tired of being scared. I laid down and stared at the ceiling for twelve days and cursed everybody I didn't like . . . I lay in a cold sweat . . . I threw up everything I tried to eat . . . then it was over." He had kicked the hard way—cold turkey.

Nonetheless illness continued to plague him. He had an operation for nodes on the throat. Warned by a doctor not to use his voice for a while, he began speaking too soon; as a result he was reduced to the famous whisper that has become chronic, a source of psychological and physical discomfort, and a subject he prefers to avoid.

The post-heroin years marked the start of an invigorated, productive phase. In addition to the large orchestral ventures with Evans, he headed a series of combos, each of which had its own catalytic effect on jazz.

In 1955, at the Newport Jazz Festival, he earned a rousing reception, scoring most strongly with a down-home swinging blues called "Walkin'." The recorded version of this number, on Prestige, became a classic. In the view of many critics it set the pace for a trend away from the cool phase, which Davis himself had done so much to initiate, into a period of funkier and more aggressive music. Even more influential was his *Kind of Blue* album, recorded after his switch to Columbia Records. Three members of the sextet heard on that LP were to develop as individual forces on disparate levels of jazz creativity: John Coltrane, who took Miles's modal pioneering many steps further and blended it with other idioms; Cannonball Adderley, and Bill Evans. (The other definitive unit flourished in the mid-1960s with Wayne Shorter, Herbie Hancock, and Tony Williams, all of whom also subsequently became leaders.)

"While I was in the band," Coltrane said, "I found Miles in the midst of a new stage of musical development. It seemed that he was moving to the use of fewer and fewer chord changes in songs. He used tunes with free-flowing lines and chordal direction. I found it easy to apply my own harmonic ideas . . . I could play three chords at once; but if I wanted to, I could play melodically. Miles's music gave me plenty of freedom."

Davis' method of assembling cohesive groups of major artists, usually finding them at the most crucial points in their evolution, is deceptively casual. Herbie Hancock, whose case is typical, recalls their first meeting, when Donald Byrd took him to the Davis house.

"I was introduced to Miles as Donald's new piano player. Donald said, 'Herbie, why don't you play something?' So I sat down and played a ballad. Miles said, 'He's got a nice touch.' And that was that until the following year, when he called me up and asked me to come over to his house.

"Tony Williams was there, and Ron Carter and George Coleman. I knew he was looking for a new group, so I figured this was an audition. We concentrated on one tune, 'Seven Steps to Heaven.' The next day we rehearsed some of Miles's older things but concentrated on a second tune. Miles didn't even play. He just came downstairs with me, said something to George, and then went back upstairs. I guess maybe he turned on the intercom and was listening to us.

"The next day, as I heard later, Miles called up Gil Evans and Philly Joe Jones and said, 'Hey, come over and listen to my new band.' On the third day Miles came downstairs and played a couple of notes, but he soon went back up. After we finished running things down, I'm still thinking that I'm auditioning, so Miles comes downstairs and says, 'You have to be at Columbia studios tomorrow afternoon at two.'

"It took me completely by surprise. I said 'Wait a minute—what? I thought you were auditioning. Are we recording tomorrow?' He said, 'Yeah.' I said, 'Does that mean that I'm in the group, or what?' He said, 'You're making the record, ain't you?'

"I left his house floating on a cloud. Just through that offhand conversation, I had a job that turned out to last five years and then enabled me to go out on my own."

During the incumbency of Hancock, Wayne Shorter (who replaced George Coleman), Williams, and Carter, Miles veered further and further away from his 1950s concept of playing structured popular songs and jazz standards. Although he continued for some time to hold on to "'Round Midnight" and a couple of others, most of the themes now were freer and more adventurous works written by members of the group. They became points of departure for displays of intracommunication that were tantamount to ESP—which logically became the title number of a 1965 album. Performances became longer as Davis pioneered in the concept of segueing from one theme and mood to another, so that an entire set at a club or concert would be a continuum.

Working at an ever-higher level of abstraction the quintet became more completely an expression of the leader's dominant personality as key sidemen left. The use of electric keyboards and bass, and of two or three percussion instruments, expanded the compass of the music still further. The switch from a floating, free rhythm to the incorporation of rock became a controversial element but one Davis sincerely believed in.

Herbie Hancock points out: "Miles has been going in his present direction ever since the time when I jumped on the electric piano. Back in 1968 the album *Miles in the Sky* had a hint of rock. The next year *In a Silent Way* showed the shape of things to come with its two or three electric keyboards. The essential difference was in the rhythmic complexity. *Bitches' Brew,* which shook everyone up in 1970, was totally different from *In a Silent Way,* yet you can hear the parallel; it blended all the complexities of the new modern jazz with an underlying rock beat.

"The next album, *Miles at the Fillmore,* showed how much he can be fed musically not only by his musicians but by the whole environment, the vibes of the people. This is something I totally respect. . . . But of course it didn't sound like John Mayall at the Fillmore or anyone else at the Fillmore. Miles was still playing Miles.

"The value of what Miles is doing now is that he is, in effect, setting up a criterion of excellence in the direction of rock that nobody else has achieved, in terms of instrumental efficiency, interaction, and all of those things that just hadn't happened too much in rock before.

"I realize that a lot of people were turned off by the strong rock element, especially in the sound track of the film he did, *Jack Johnson,* which was pretty much straight rock with Miles thrown on top. Obviously this has to be controversial to many of the people that were into his music during his traditional jazz days, but then periods shouldn't be compared. I don't think people should expect him to go back and play 'Stella by Starlight' again because it would only inhibit the direction he's going in.

"Sure, the best of music is timeless. But to the artist who is performing it the music has to be a reflection of where he is at any given moment, and where he is depends on the individual. Say, in the case of Oscar Peterson, there is a certain predictability about his playing, but his growth seems to be internal, whereas Miles's is external. There's room for both attitudes."

Hancock's view of Davis is of course an inside glimpse, offered by a musician who for years was an integral part of his music. Those on the outside have mixed reactions, especially musicians who were once regarded as Miles's main influences.

"I have listened to those recent albums time after time," says Dizzy Gillespie, "until I started getting cohesions. The guy is such a fantastic musician that I know he has something in mind, whatever it is. I know he knows what he's doing, so he must be doing something that I can't get to yet.

"He played some of it for me, and he said, 'How do you like that shit?' I said, 'What is it?' and he said, 'You know what it is; same shit you've been playing all the time,' and I said, 'Have I?' I said, 'Look, I'm going to come by your house and spend several hours and you're going to explain to me what that is.' But we never did get together. I'm sure he could explain it to me musically, though of course you can't explain anything emotionally.

"Miles should be commended for going off in a completely new direction, he's just as brave as shit. That's what it is, stark stone bravery, to have something that his fans all over the world liked so much, and then turn around and go on an altogether different course. Shit, I don't think I got that much guts. Sometimes I find myself playing those same old licks I used to play, till I get stale as a motherfuck. When I play something exactly the same way I did it some other time, I figure, 'Oh shit, you're getting lazy.' But I can no more change my spots. . . . Miles can, though.

"He has a knack of grabbing one of those notes in the chord, like, suppose you have a B flat minor sixth chord with a C in the bass, Miles would stop on an A flat or something like that—and hold it! He picks the dynamic notes to lay back on. He had the same thing going on in *Bitches' Brew*; he had a blues thing going, and he grabbed one of those notes, and when the chord changed he grabbed one of those other strange ones and held it.

"Whether it'll last, what he's doing now, that's not up to me to judge. You can't judge your contemporaries; you can only say what strikes you at the moment, but you can't assess the validity of the message. Time alone judges that, so I just sit here and wait until . . . well, if he's hooked that far in front, wait for time to catch up with it. Because I had the same experience with Ornette Coleman until somebody gave me an album one day and I sat down and really listened. I used to make jokes, like I'd say, 'Ladies and gentlemen, we're going to play "Hot House" and Ornette is going to play "Night in Tunisia" at the same time.' But now I realize he had something to build on.

"Miles has even more to build on. Not only has he got me and Yardbird and Freddie Webster and whoever else inspired him, he's also got himself, to reach back and get different things. The guy's a master, so I wouldn't come out and say that I don't like what he's doing now.

"Besides, it would be out of line. Could the King of England criticize the King of France?"

Gillespie's comments may subconsciously reflect an attitude that has been lucidly explained by Herbie Hancock.

"People become accustomed to a style that's been associated with a certain individual," he says, "so when they want to hear his music, they listen with these preconceptions. This is the wrong way to go about getting involved with anything. You're better off, listening to any music, not expecting anything, because the artist you listen to may be a completely different person when you confront him at a different time. Miles is a perfect case in point. There might be a particular area of his development that you prefer, but if you walk in looking for it, you'll be disappointed. If you just go in saying, 'Let me near what's going to happen,' then you can be objective and dig what the man's output is for its own self."

Other Davis-watchers take the position that his change in direction has been at least partially pragmatic.

"I can understand exactly why he's doing these things," says Clark Terry. "Miles is the kind of man who has always wanted to stay abreast of the times. He's smart enough to realize that this is what people are buying, and if this is what they're buying, why shouldn't he sell some of it?

"Maybe he's doing it sincerely, but I do know that it's a much more lucrative direction for him. I happen to know that there was a period when in spite of all his many possessions—investments, home, car—there was a period when he needed to bolster these; he really needed to get into a higher financial bracket. And there was an opportunity for him to get into this kind of thing, so he took the opportunity to jump out and do it.

"I don't know whether or not I'm musically mature enough to understand it. I do know that there are people in that area who are incompetent, and it's an avenue where they can parallel people like Miles who have studied and worked hard. Others can reach this point through a short-cut method. Nobody could do that when Miles was playing more lyrically. I loved him much more at that time, when he was more in depth as far as chord structures and progressions. Ain't nobody around can play more melodically than Miles when he wants to. In a sense it's a waste to see him not using all his knowledge."

I asked Terry, "What do you think people hear in it that is making him so successful in widening his audience?"

"What they hear in it is less significant than what they don't hear. What they don't hear, because it's not there, is the real balls of jazz, the chord progressions, the structures, and so forth. They are not musically mature enough to cope with this and Miles is smart enough to put something where they can reach it on their own level. If they're not hip enough to know what's happening—say, the way Miles was playing with Bird years ago, with swinging groups—if they're not hip enough to grasp that type of thing, they're going to grasp whatever is simple enough for them to cop. And the simple thing for them to cop happens to be that one-chord modal bag that is so fashionable."

Other trumpeters of Terry's generation share his viewpoint. "I guess he's trying to change with the times," says Harry "Sweets" Edison, "but personally I liked the way he sounded when he had Philly Joe Jones, Cannonball, Wynton Kelly, and Paul Chambers, around 1956—that was a magnificent bunch of musicians.

"I listened to him on *Bitches' Brew* and there was just too much going on for me to really enjoy his playing. I don't think a man of his distinctive ability needs to do that kind of thing. Also, Miles is such a good writer, but what he's doing now doesn't sound like he's putting into it all that he's capable of.

"I'm not going to underestimate him; I'm sure he's true to his own convictions, but I feel he could still play the way he played years ago, with the same feeling, and people would appreciate it."

Quincy Jones, the composer and former trumpeter, who has known Davis for twenty years, has made a close analytical study of Miles's progress. "When we were kids," he says, "we all ran around with a notebook copying off all the Miles and Bird solos. Most of us didn't jump on Dizzy, though, because he was just too much to try to emulate, so we'd try to grab hold of Miles.

"Miles has always been concerned with growth, with perfecting one thing and then taking on a new challenge. That's what keeps you feeling young, man. Nobody wants to stay the same."

Asked whether he felt that to retain one's basic image was less important for an artist than the continual development of new identities as in Davis' case, Jones replied: "I think you have to trust that same mojo that led you into the first style, and go from there. It's fortunate that Miles is flexible enough to have given us the kind of contrast that separates *Miles Ahead* from *Jack Johnson*. I think he's blessed, to have that scope, that range."

Recently, as Jones points out, there has been a curious shift of focal points in the thrust of the new jazz. "A decade or two back, the velocity and animation were usually carried by the melodic instruments on top, while the rhythm section laid down the bass like a canvas, remaining essentially a time-keeping device. But in the last few years that has been reversed. Any record you hear now, the horns almost have to play time, because the complexity has moved to the basement now, and you can't take that kind of complexity on top with what the fender bass players are doing nowadays. Too many passing notes. If you play too many alterations in the top, it cancels out the freedom in the bottom.

"With this change of roles, I think Miles is trying to see what his same lyrical and innovative mind can do. We know it's the same guy, so we have to trust our group leader. He's putting himself on a different menu, and I dig it. Every step he has made, he's always been right, and always ahead of his time, so I think we'll end up in good shape.

"I think we can expect further changes. At some point he may decide, 'Hey, the rhythm section I used on *Bitches' Brew* and *Jack Johnson* was too loud,' and he'll use his wah-wah pedal and amplifier on the trumpet to match it; or he might say, 'What if we dropped the volume of everything down,' and he might bring more lyricism in. Anything can happen."

Herbie Hancock concurs. "The music of the past is not necessarily old hat, but I can understand how Miles feels, because people come up to me and ask me to play 'Watermelon Man' and that's not where I'm at now, I don't want to play it. Miles isn't up there to please everybody, or anybody. He's there to be honest, that's all; and he has to be taken for what he is."

Miles Davis remains seemingly impervious to the controversy that surrounds him. He has often been quoted as indifferent to criticism and has claimed he never reads anything that is written about him, yet there have been many cracks in the wall he has built around himself. One review (of a record made during his appearance at a rock festival on the Isle of Wight) clearly got through to him. From Milan he called the *Melody Maker* in London: "What kind of man can call me arrogant? I know where you're at. You shouldn't be a critic. You are a white man looking for white excitement, but there are more subtle forms of excitement." He went on to express contempt for the entire rock scene.

Obsessed with what seems to him to be a necessity to analyze everything in racial terms, he once told Don DeMichael, in a *Rolling Stone* interview: "Rock is social music. There's two kinds—white and black—and those bourgeois spades are trying to sing white and the whites are trying to sound colored. It's embarrassing. It's like me wearing a dress." One wonders to what extent his rebellion against the "bourgeois spade" background (that is, his own parentage) is conscious. One wonders too how he explains the fact that many of the early rock groups to which he gave serious attention (Jimi Hendrix, Sly & The Family Stone) were racially integrated.

Whatever his true feelings about the rock of whites and bourgeois blacks, he has made a palpable and self-admitted attempt to compete with the rock musicians on their own level. On listening to a record by Cream, he said: "They sure play loud. If they're gonna play loud, I'm gonna plug into an amplifier too." It was one more psychological step toward the Fillmore and the Isle of Wight.

The reception of Davis by rock fans has varied quite conspicuously from job to job. At the Hollywood Bowl in 1970 his group was the supporting attraction in a program starring The Band. The latter was wildly received; Miles, opening the show, played continuously for forty-five minutes and walked off to tepid applause.

His own analysis of the stage at which his music had arrived around the turn of the decade is essentially that it does not call for analysis.

See, Leonard, what you're missing, I'm not doing anything, it doesn't need an explanation. I'm reacting to what's been done and what's supposed to be happening today. Everything you've ever heard, all that shit is condensed, you know? All the clichés are so condensed that you can play "Body and Soul" in two bars.

If some musicians don't understand it, they just don't have that kind of an ear. Everybody I get is special. If I wanted to play songs that have a definite beginning and an ending, all that calls for is an ordinary working musician. Keith Jarrett, Jack De Johnette, all the guys I've used have changed the whole style of music today. You should know that.

You ought to try playing some of the things we do. I could show you how. The other day I wrote down some chords and stuff for George Wein to play, and I had him playing like Keith!

You know what I don't like? It's the playing between solos. They don't blend or nothing . . . In my group we play a lot of polyrhythms and everything, you know, a lot of different keys off of keys and scales off of scales. You ought to study it.

I know you wrote that my group is loud. Well, that's just the times we live in. Everything is loud; everything gets higher. You take a symphony orchestra. You cannot write for two violins. You can't hear that shit. How many do they use? Dozens. They don't use one bass fiddle—they use twelve. It's the same thing. Anyhow, I still play way down sometimes, but you can hear it—every note.

One of the things you learn in my group is, you leave drummers alone, 'cause drummers have their own inside thing. And do like I did Herbie Hancock, take out all those fat chords and shit. And Keith—I just put him at the piano and let him go. Keith wasn't playing like that before he joined me.

A lot of what we have in the group has been developed in clubs. I love the possibility of just freaking off on your horn in a nightclub. In Shelly's I really found out something. Actually it was a learning period in there, when I played everything and made the band play everything they could possibly play.

That's what's good about working clubs. You play a first set, OK; second set, OK; third set, OK—and they're playing what they know, right? Then the last set they start playing what they don't know; which is out of sight! They start thinking, which is worth all the money in the world to me. Thrills me.

I worked Shelly's just to help keep the place open. I lost about ten pounds in that motherfucker. I made $4,000 a week there, but I went in weighing 139 and came out weighing 129. Then I was asked to play Boston and I said to myself, if I go to Boston I'll weigh 121. I haven't worked since. That was three, four months ago.

LF: What was all the talk in the press about your retiring?

MD: What I meant was, I got a tour in Europe. I'll make about $300,000 on it. Then I won't work again until the spring and I'll make a spring tour. No more week here and three weeks off and a week there. I'm through with that shit.

LF: How about festivals?

MD: I don't care. They're all such bullshit. Just one-job things.

LF: How are you going to keep your men together?

MD: I can always get a group. The men I need, I can keep on salary while I'm laying off.

LF: Will you ever again do anything like you did with Gil Evans? Or have you put all that behind you?

MD: I can't get with that. But we have a new instrumentation for a big band that's outa sight.

LF: What does it consist of?

MD: *If I tell you that, every motherfucker will be copying it. Quincy would be the first one. Quincy's always trying to pick my mind.*

The slighting reference to Jones is indicative of Davis' attitude toward an overwhelming majority of musicians in every field. In judging others he cannot overcome the temptation to expect them to measure up to his own levels of originality, proficiency, and sophistication. This leaves him with very little outside the purlieus of his own music that he can enjoy and respect without reservation.

His assessment of pop and rock stars vacillates according to his moods. He has often pointed out that rock musicians are limited by their lack of harmonic knowledge and generally poor technical musicianship. He has made mildly complimentary remarks about Crosby, Stills, Nash & Young, and The Who. Concerning Blood, Sweat & Tears he has blown hot and cold. On one occasion he called the group "a pretentious imitation of me and Gil Evans," but at another point he declared that B S & T was "the only group I know that really gives people [at the Fillmore] something musically." Asked to name his preferences in the field of pop composing, he said: "Elton John and James Taylor write good songs. Valerie Simpson writes good songs."

In the fall of 1971 Miles was in Los Angeles for several weeks. As he does wherever he goes, he spent much of his time in a local gym. He has been on a serious health kick for several years, has his own personal trainer, and a white terry cloth robe with his name emblazoned on the back. Proud of his physique, he thinks nothing of working out with a heavy speed bag, sparring for several rounds, skipping rope, then doing as many as a hundred or more pushups and situps.

In his spare time he might be found watching ball games on a small black-and-white television set in his room at the Chateau Marmont, overlooking Sunset Boulevard. This fading relic of the old Hollywood is his home whenever he visits the West Coast. One afternoon, after dispatching his lissome girl friend on a shopping tour, he was in the mood to talk about his contemporaries, his social attitudes, and his plans, such as they were, for the future.

LF: What live music have you heard lately that impressed you?

MD: *I never go out to nightclubs any more. When I go, I know what to expect. It's what I can hear in my head without going.*

LF: Are you going to hear Herbie Hancock's group at Donte's?

MD: *I don't want to hear it. I can't even listen to that, as much as I love to hear Herbie play. I can't stand the trombone . . . and Eddie Henderson—I just don't like to hear trumpet players that keep playing like Freddie Hubbard. You know, it's the way you look at something happen that enables you to be your own self, if you're not lazy. It's easy to play a cliché. A cliché should be your musical foundation, but it shouldn't be what you do.*

LF: What do you think of Tony Williams' group?

MD: *Tony needs somebody to solo, other than himself. Larry, the organist, he's all right, but you know, you shouldn't bother a soloist. Like, I never bother Keith. Sooner or later Tony will get tired of not hearing what he wants to hear.*

LF: What does the music of Pharoah Sanders say to you?

MD: *It doesn't say anything to me, because Pharoah's not doing anything.*

LF: How about Ornette Coleman?

MD: *If you hear a guy, he has to be with someone that's right for him. Like, I heard a white guy with Buddy Miles, and the way Buddy plays, the white boy was playing out of sight. Now if he was playing with another white boy playing drums, he wouldn't sound like that. When Ornette was playing with Leroy Vinnegar and Billy Higgins everybody was together. But I don't know what he's doing now.*
    You know, the horn doesn't sound like it's supposed to sound. To me it's not the right background. So I check him out, and if he doesn't have the right background he's a sad motherfucker. And he's not a trumpet player. That's something that takes years to develop. As for his violin playing, he's not going to scare Ray Nance.

LF: Have you listened to the Joe Henderson combo?

MD: *Joe Henderson can play his ass off. He used to play with me. But in general there ain't much happening that I want to hear. All the groups are trying to play like somebody I know. I don't want to hear clichés: I don't want to get back into the past. What's important is what's happening now, the new music and the music of the future. I don't even want to think about what I was doing myself last year.*

LF: Haven't you heard any rock groups that interested you?

MD: *I haven't heard anything coming from the white kids with the long hair and shit. I like to hear the Motown sound and James Brown, them funky singers.*

LF: You put it on a racial basis, yet some of your most rewarding associations have been interracial.

MD: *You don't understand. What I want to hear doesn't come from a white musician.*

LF: Including Gil Evans, Bill Evans, Dave Holland?

MD: *No, I don't mean like that. What I want to hear, like rhythm and blues, it comes from black musicians all the time.*
   When you get guys that aren't prejudiced, like Joe Zawinul and John McLaughlin, I hardly ever look at their skin; they don't make me look at their skin. But when I hear a rhythm section with Tony or Jack on drums, or Buddy Miles, they do some shit that you just don't find in a white drummer.
   A choreographer I know went to Africa with Harry Belafonte; he tried to copy some of the dances to bring them back to teach, and he said he just couldn't break it down. And he's a hell of a choreographer. It's something they have that you just can't figure out, it's a natural thing.

LF: Do you think you can tell from listening to a record whether a musician is black or white?

MD: *I think you could. I still can.*

LF: Would you like to do a blindfold test to prove it?

MD: *If I happen to be driving along some place and I hear something— not something that you put on—if I hear something, if I say he's white, he's white; you can bet your money on it.*

LF: Suppose it's a mixed group?

MD: *What difference does it make anyway?*

LF: You said you could tell the difference.

MD: *It's because I'm black, Leonard. I'm not white. I wouldn't turn on Al Hirt, but a white guy would.*

LF: I wouldn't turn on Al Hirt's show, and it's not because I'm white or black. On the other hand, if it were the Bobby Hackett show you'd turn it on.

MD: *Not necessarily. . . . If Herbie Hancock was on television at the same time as Al Hirt, who do you think I'd turn on?*

LF: Who do you think *I'd* turn on?

MD: *You'd turn on Herbie.*

LF: Damn right I would, and not because of black or white, because he's a better musician.

MD: *Why do you say Herbie's a better musician than Al Hirt?*

LF: A musician who appeals to me more. Beg your pardon. (It had slipped my mind that a few years ago, Miles had told me: "Al Hirt is a very good trumpet player; and he's a nice guy. It's a shame they made him into a television personality—fat and jolly and bearded and funny. I guess if he was thin he wouldn't have to do it. Harry James is a good trumpet player, and he never did no shit like that." Still respectful of Hirt's musicianship, Miles was taking exception to my simplistic "better musician" explanation.)

MD: *Herbie Hancock would be good for a TV program. He's the most patient guy I've ever seen. He plays all kinds of styles; and he's a nice-looking guy too, you know? Why shouldn't he have his own show?*
    What I'm saying is, it's not just Al Hirt, I mean because a guy is white, white people will follow him. You understand?

LF: Some white people will follow him.

MD: *I'm not saying all this to be the great black father. I'm just say-*
ing that our roots are black and that's where they'll remain, and I
can't help it.
   When I hear a white guy, or when I look at a white girl that's sup-
posed to be attractive, I don't feel the same thing that a white person
would feel. I can understand a white girl seeing a white guy, and her
screaming because she's white. But if I see a black girl screaming over a
white guy . . . I'm just saying their roots won't let 'em do certain things.
   There are mixed marriages that work. I'm not talking about that
shit. I'm just saying that white people cater to white people and black
people cater to black people. It's just a normal thing. One dog will fuck
another dog.

LF: Don't you nevertheless believe that integration is the ultimate
solution?

MD: *I don't know whether it is or not. I think things will just come. If*
they work, fine. If they don't work, we just gotta accept it. You see
black kids and white kids playing together, and they don't get fucked up
until older people come in. Interracial couples, when they dig each
other, they dig each other; it's just that outside pressure.

LF: Your ideal world basically is still an integrated world, isn't it?

MD: *Right. But I think it won't work . . . Most black people would like*
to see everybody integrated, you know? A lot of black people want to
be like white people; they think there's a level that they should be on,
that white people have a level that they want to try to reach. That's sad,
you know?
   People can live together, but all that old shit hasn't stopped. As
long as they keep on showing Army films with an all-white Army, it's
not going to stop. That's a joke.
   They fucked my son Gregory around, man; he went into the Army.
He had to knock out a couple of white guys in St. Louis. He said,
"Father, I'm going in the Army, and when I come back, if they start any
shit, I'm not responsible."

LF: The Army gave him a very bad time?

MD: Shit yes, they Jim Crowed him in Germany. He's a fighter, you know, he won four titles. He brought back all those trophies. He can break your fucking neck and not even think nothing of it. He's not afraid of nothing. He would say it was supposed to be broken. He's a Muslim. He just wants to learn black things.

I can understand how he feels. If a white man bothers me, man, I don't want to touch him because I don't know what I might do. I might kill him.

Davis' need to keep his cool was never more frighteningly illustrated than in an incident that took place on a hot summer night in 1959, when his group was playing Birdland. After escorting a young white girl out of the club to a taxi, he was standing on the sidewalk when a patrolman came by and asked him to move on. When Miles said, "I'm not going nowhere—I'm just getting a breath of fresh air," the patrolman threatened to arrest him. Miles said, "Go ahead, lock me up." When the patrolman seized his arm, a scuffle ensued during which a plainclothes detective passing by began hitting Miles with a blackjack. With blood dripping all over his clothes, he was taken, to the police station where, with his distraught wife, Frances, at his side, he was booked on charges of disorderly conduct and assault. At a hospital, ten stitches were taken in his scalp. After a lengthy series of legal maneuvers, a three-judge panel ruled that the Davis arrest had been illegal and the charge against him was erased. Miles decided to sue the city, but eventually dropped the whole matter in disgust. At the time of the incident he commented that it might never have happened if the girl he was escorting to the cab had been black.

LF: Have you been practicing while you've been out here?

MD: Uh-uh.

LF: Aren't you afraid your chops won't be up when you start again?

MD: Hell, I've been playing since I was thirteen. The older I get, the stronger I get. I still have the same mouthpiece I had when I was thirteen.

LF: Do you still have the urge to play, to be creating right now?

MD: *I never have the urge to play; just sometimes when I hear something, I want to play with it.*

LF: That's liable to continue as long as you live.

MD: *That's what I'm saying.*

LF: As long as there's something around that you can hear and want to be part of, then, you're not going to be just doing nothing.

MD: *Right.*

LF: The big difference between you and someone like Diz is that he will sit in with any kind of a band, Dixieland or whatever, but you still have your own thing that you want to play with.

MD: *Diz may do that, but he won't stay there a long time.*

LF: No, he just likes the change of pace.

MD: *Right.*

LF: With your children gone and no wife, don't you miss having a family around you?

MD: *I don't believe in families. Like, if I die, my money ain't going to go to people just because they're close relatives. The people that are closest to me are the ones that helped me be able to do what I do, not just because somebody's my brother. If I had a lot of money, I wouldn't leave everything to my brother or sister just because they're related to me.*

LF: Don't you feel close to your daughter or your grandson?

MD: *No, I don't. Do you?*

LF: I have no grandson, but I feel close to my daughter. I think most people feel a closeness because of family ties.

MD: *Family ties are a lot of bullshit. That's what's fucking up this world. Sitting down at tea and all that shit. It doesn't go that way. In the first place, who wants to eat that much?*

LF: That's not your nature, Miles, come on! If your daughter were sick and needed you, you'd go out and help her.

MD: *Help her do what? No, man, that ain't nothing. If you said, "Miles, I need $500," and I had it, I'd send it to you, because that's the way I am. Money ain't shit, if it helps you and I don't need it for anything else, why shouldn't I send it to you?*

LF: I don't see how I would deserve it.

MD: *I mean I don't have anything for my family. I don't live for my family, I live for myself.*

LF: But logically that should apply to your marriages too. Why did you get married if you don't believe in families?

MD: *Because they asked me. Every woman I ever married asked me.*

LF: Why didn't you have the strength of will to say no?

MD: *Because I figured it'd make them happy.*

LF: You just made an admission. You're willing to do something to make somebody happy.

MD: *Of course!*

LF: That's the same thing I was asking about your daughter.

MD: *That's not what I'm saying, Leonard. I didn't say I wouldn't go out there. If she had any trouble I'd go out there to see what was wrong with her. I still don't have any family ties. If one of them would die or anything, I don't know how I would act; you wouldn't see me acting like they do on television. When my mother was sick I went to see her in the hospital; I knew she was dying of cancer. But when she died I didn't go to the funeral.*

LF: What do you want to be doing ten years from now?

MD: *Nothing. If I don't have a deal that is lined up like I want it, ten years from now, I'd give up.*

LF: What does doing nothing mean to you? Sitting watching television? Going to the gym?

MD: *Right now I want to find out where I want to live.*

LF: You're thinking of moving out of New York?

MD: *I don't know where I want to live. But the best time I ever had in my life, other than playing trumpet, was when I was out in the country riding horses.*

LF: Do you still have a feeling for the country?

MD: *Yeah, I like space, man.*

LF: You should probably buy some more land.

MD: *I don't want to have to search. I don't know where to buy.*

LF: It sounds to me as though you're not that interested any more, or not deeply concerned, about continuing in music.

MD: *I didn't say that.*

LF: That's what you said in effect when I asked you what you wanted to be doing ten years from now.

MD: *If I started thinking about music—now—then I'll have to play the trumpet. But the minute I don't think about it, I can be contented doing nothing.*

Although the possibility seems remote, it is not inconceivable at this stage of his life that Miles Davis may extend his present policy of semi-retire-ment into almost total inactivity. For a quarter of a century he has to some extent controlled the direction of jazz, expanding the minds of his listeners along with the scope of his music. How long he can continue to grow, and take his audience along with him, is a secret as inscrutable as Miles himself seems to the young music student observing him at a distance.

For the present, though, his music remains as pervasive a force as ever, more challenging than yesterday when it seemed incomparably more complex than the day before. Now, as always, it mirrors the personality of the man, of his words and his actions. Although, as our conversation revealed, he is emotionally vulnerable, he prefers to keep his defenses up and cultivate the image that had led *Jet* to refer to him as "Terrible-tempered Miles." For all his displays of anger, cynicism, arrogance, and heavy sarcasm, he is no less capable of tenderness, generosity, and idealism. The psychological convolutions through which he moves toward these emotions are no easier to figure out than the processes involved in the creation of one of his uncompromisingly innovative solos or compositions.

In the light of Miles's life as an avocational boxer, a comment by Clark Terry seems singularly apposite: "I have a feeling that Miles is rather like Sugar Ray Robinson on the ropes, when he wants to psych out his opponent. Ray had a way of leaning on the ropes and faking, to the point where the opponent would say, 'I've got this cat now,' and then Ray would grab one hand with the rope and whale like hell with the other hand, and in most instances he'd floor the other guy. Miles uses all kinds of psychology in dealing with people, and he has found it to be lucrative."

As Quincy Jones once observed, "Miles is always trying to hide all that warmth, beauty, and romanticism; it's a tough job for him, and it shows through when he plays." And Dizzy affirms: "Basically Miles is very shy; that's the whole thing. You know, I know him probably better than he knows himself. I was talking to his daughter Cheryl in St. Louis, and I said, 'Did you know that your father is really a very bashful man?' and she said, 'Yeah, I've always known that, but nobody else can dig it; he puts up that front to cover up the shyness.'

"But what I really respect about him is he won't be a phony for anyone. He was the first one that came along in our business and figured he didn't have to smile at everyone, didn't have to tell no jokes or make no announcements, didn't have to say thank you or even bow. He figured he could just let the music speak for him, and for itself. He succeeeded in doing this, and you can't fight success. I say more power to him."

An ironic aspect of this phenomenon to which Gillespie did not draw attention is the extent to which Miles' personality has built a mystique around him and has contributed to the hold he has on the public. The irony lies in the fact that three or four decades ago Louis Armstrong, whose attitudes were antithetical to Davis' in almost every conceivable way, also owed his commercial achievements in large measure to his personality.

Armstrong, accepted first by musicians as the supreme instrumental catalyst of his day, later reached the masses by being, onstage, exactly what they wanted him to be. Davis, after gaining similar in-group acceptance, went on to acquire his material luxuries, and massive income-tax problems, by doing precisely the opposite: defying the public to like him, insisting that he be accepted solely for the intrinsic value of his music.

That he has attained this objective is a measure of the distance traversed by pure jazz in barely half a century, from the level of entertainment and comedy, "happy music" aimed primarily at the lowest common intellectual denominator, to its present eminence as a musical idiom admired and dissected by serious students all over the world. It is an accomplishment never before registered by any of the lively arts. The jazz world may well take pride in the role played by Miles Davis—black, volatile, rebellious, and resilient as jazz itself—in bringing about this phenomenon in the twentieth-century music scene.

—Hollywood, 1972

MY EGO ONLY NEEDS A GOOD RHYTHM SECTION
STEPHEN DAVIS

Stephen Davis, former reporter for *Rolling Stone* and the author of many books on rock music, was asked by Columbia Records in the winter of 1973 to interview Miles Davis at his Manhattan home. The result of their meeting is the following, most of which was published in the Cambridge alternative weekly *The Real Paper* on March 21, 1973.

Although more than twenty years have passed since this article was first published, Stephen Davis's piece still stands out as one of the few works to document Davis's lifestyle of the early 1970s. The author first explains the circumstances surrounding Miles Davis's legal tangles at the time. Then, he works in his provocative interview material in which the two converse about the trumpeter's music, wardrobe, atheism, townhouse decor, irritation with Columbia Records, and aggravation at being eclipsed in the press by former band members, such as Wayne Shorter and Joe Zawinul, who were running with Davis's musical innovations.

As with most Davis interviews, important new facts emerge, even about well-known aspects of Davis's life. For the names of famous and obscure trumpeters that influenced Davis's playing yet slipped his mind at the time of the interview, however, see *Miles: The Autobiography.*

Miles Davis, the jazz trumpeter, was fined $1000 in Manhattan Criminal Court yesterday after pleading guilty to a weapons and possession charge. He was arrested Feb. 23 in an apartment house he owns on Manhattan's upper west side.

—New York Times, March 2 1973

"Look," Miles's bearded manager says, "the whole thing is finished and we got him off for only a thousand. I think he'd rather just forget about it. What happened? I'll tell you two stories; here's the one you can't print. Miles and his girlfriend L. get back to his house around one in the morning, both really fucked up, at least Miles is. He can't find his keys, he's pissed off, he starts punching the door to his house. BAM BAM BAM. He empties his pockets looking for the keys and a bag of coke falls out and spills on the floor. Miles owns the building, but one of his upstairs tenants is drunk all the time, and he hears Miles trying to break down this heavy door and figures the place is getting ripped off. The drunk calls the precinct and a couple of cops come over, a sergeant and a patrolman. As soon as she sees the cops L. throws her handbag in a corner. The cops come in. The sergeant knows Miles, knows he owns the house, and at that point the search should have legally stopped. There were no longer any grounds for the cops being in the building.

"The cops see L.'s bag laying in the corner and asks who it belongs to. Miles and L. tell the cops they never saw the bag before. Which legally gave the cops the right to pick up the bag and search it as abandoned property. So they open the bag, find some more coke and a loaded .22 automatic, and they immediately bust the two of them.

"So at three in the morning I get a call from some Irish desk sergeant. 'We have Miles Davis down here and he's using you as his one phone call.' Miles gets on the phone and says, 'Neil, get me outta here. They're treating me like a nigger.' The cop grabs the phone away from Miles and tells me he can't allow anyone to talk like that over the phone. I hang up and call the lawyer and everybody else and go back to sleep. And somehow, being Miles, he gets them to let him make a second phone call at five in the morning. 'Neil, get me outta here! Wake up a fuckin' judge or something.'

"That morning I talked to the district attorney about dropping the charges because of the bogus arrest, and he tells me it's impossible to drop the gun charge on a black man in New York City when cops are getting shot on the streets every day. Have you ever heard such bullshit in your life?"

This narrative is related by Neil Reshen, Miles Davis's recently hired manager, in the vestibule of Miles's building on West 77th Street. Neil rang the bell five minutes before but there was no response. Also in attendance is Waylon Jennings, a client of Reshen's who is tagging along in hopes of meeting the reclusive trumpeter. Reshen rings again. Silence. "Anyway, its over," he continues patiently. "We got him off. Miles is in a good mood today. Ask him whatever you want. Getting busted doesn't bother him for too long. He's been harassed by these fuckers for so long he probably doesn't think about it anymore."

There's a huge gash in the door where an enraged Miles tried to kick it in the night of his bust. Reshen rings again. A woman's voice over the intercom asks who's there. She lets us in—light complexion, green scarf covering her hair—and shows us into a vestibule without a word and vanishes. The room is a Moroccan grotto, all arches and dark grey dripping plaster. One wall is a waterfall. It's so dark we can hardly see the massive gong hanging from the ceiling. On the coffee table are a broken trumpet, a broken wah-wah pedal and a paperback copy of *Jonathan Livingston Seagull*. From the gloomy interior of the house emerges the legendary Finny, Miles's valet and hairdresser, who had seen much action with the late Jimi Hendrix. Finny has large, half-closed eyes and hair wound into tight little pigtails hanging from his head. At two in the afternoon it's evident that the establishment is just waking up. Finny tells Neil Reshen to go upstairs and tells Waylon Jennings and me to wait down here.

What am I doing here? I'm here because Miles Davis is jealous. Miles Dewey Davis, 47 years old, the richest and most successful jazz musician in the world, a musical innovator who has been creating new modes of music approximately every four or five years since his breakthrough cool tonalities in 1949, is envious. Most of the young musicians who have played with him over the past few years have formed successful bands of their own. John McLaughlin's Mahavishnu Orchestra, The Tony Williams Lifetime, Wayne Shorter and Joe Zawinul's Weather Report, Jack DeJohnette's Compost, and Keith Jarrett's many albums as a leader and soloist compete with Miles's recent albums and in many cases outsell them. Miles doesn't like these musicians reaping the rewards and accolades that he feels responsible for. (Miles's two most recent albums, *On*

The Corner and *In Concert,* heavy with the dense electro-funk of guitarists Pete Cosey and Reggie Lucas, both got less-than-rave notices from everyone save San Francisco critic Ralph J. Gleason.)

So Miles fired his manager of 17 years and hired Neil Reshen, who specializes in artists deemed "difficult" by their record companies. Miles demanded Reshen hire a press agent. Reshen called Columbia Records and told them that Miles was pissed off. Columbia's publicity office called me and several other writers. I had approached them about interviewing Miles a year earlier, and had been told that Miles wasn't talking to anybody. Now here was another chance and I jumped at it, hopeful that Miles wouldn't go through one of the last-moment changes of temperament for which he was so famous. To say that Miles Davis had the reputation of being sullen was to pay him a compliment. He was said to be a violent and malevolent son of a bitch with a cinder for a heart and a cash register for a mind. All one had to do was listen to him play his horn to know that couldn't be true.

Waylon is talking. He's nervous. He's wearing a black cowboy hat and boots. He's an Outlaw, a big country music hero. He's in awe just to be in Miles Davis's lair. Neil Reshen comes back down, looking relieved. "Miles is gonna talk to you," he whispers. A pair of bright red patent leather Italian loafers begins to descend the staircase, followed by sockless black ankles and legs in tailored dungarees. Miles Davis negotiates the stairs gingerly, taking each step in half time. A few weeks ago he totaled his white Ferrari Dino on the West Side Highway, breaking both legs and landing him in the hospital for ten days. Miles makes it to the bottom landing, looks at the three of us and rasps in his blown-out croak of a voice, "Where's the cat from Nashville?" Waylon strides over and shakes hands. Neil introduces me. Miles looks carefully and pantomimes a fearful mock cringe at what he sees: longhaired rock journalist in denim shirt and uncool sweater. Hiking boots. Tape recorder. He's quaking with bogus trepidation, putting on a show. But wait, he's smiling, and we shake hands, his grip firm and dry. I'm in heaven.

Miles leads us through the ground-floor dining area to a glassed-in conservatory overlooking the enclosed courtyard in the back of the house, with bare ailanthus trees and lawn furniture. Egyptian hieroglyphics and mystical rune frescos adorn the outside walls. On a sofa surrounded by greenery are the drawings for the cover of the forthcoming *Big Fun* album, drawn by artist Corky McCoy in the streetwise style of *On The Corner:* jivey dudes popping fingers and talking trash, sinuous black goddesses whose buttocks bulge out of tight skirts, whose nipples pop out of giant African tits. One of them avidly fellates a trumpet ten times her size. Miles picks up the rendering and gasps to Neil, "Here, man, sell these mother-fuckers to Columbia."

Neil looks surprised. "I thought they already had the artwork for the cover."

"That's right," Miles croaks. "These are the ones we're not gonna use. Sell 'em to Columbia anyway." He snorts a laugh out through his nose. Miles hasn't had a voice in years, I've been told, but he's less reticent about it now than he used to be. Back in the fifties he had an operation to remove polyps from his vocal cords. One story has the surgeon slicing through the vocal chords. Another has Miles screaming at an errant club owner while he was recuperating. He speaks in a horse whisper that occasionally breaks into a high-pitched voice when he says yes or no to a question.

Neil and Waylon are ready to split. Miles hands Neil a thick sheaf of his mail to look over. Miles refuses to read his mail. Neil handles everything.

Now we're ready to talk. I've been primed with tapes of new music—a cassette of bluesy, percussive mixes dated 2/14/73 with Miles playing organ. (These tapes, which have never been on a record, are similar to "Rated X" and "Billy Preston," which appeared on *Get Up With It* in 1974.) We're in this glass-enclosed porch with a hospital bed that Miles bought after the accident, a hospital serving table and a wheelchair. Miles seats me in the wheelchair, propping up the leg supports and lifting my legs into horizontal position. "Now you can see how I've been living for two months." Miles pours himself a Heineken, lights a Marlboro with a silver lighter and settles back into the folds of the hospital bed, smiling, ready.

How are your legs feeling today?

"They're OK. Gettin' better all the time." Miles sits up, pulls up the legs of his jeans and shows the vivid scars around both ankles. Then he looks up, apprehensive. "Did you listen to my tapes?" His huge eyes bore into mine.

Yes, of course, talk about what you're doing.

Well we got that long blues thing with drums and different times and shit. On that I tried to show my piano player what was happening, and it wound up sounding so good with me playing on it that Teo Macero wanted to keep it that way. I was playing the same way on the organ that I would on the trumpet, playing in the same spaces. So I just told him to lay out. I thought the thing would wake up that way and it did.

Do you structure your sounds to affect your audience a certain way?

I'm not thinking about anybody but myself when we play. [Miles laughs ruefully.] I mean, how is my audience gonna move me? I know that if I don't move myself, then it's no good. I don't ever think about that audience shit. Man, I play with fuckin' blinders on. The way that we play now, its too hard for me to think about stuff like that. In Detroit the other night we played for two hours and fifteen minutes without stopping. I lose about five pounds, six pounds. I'm fuckin' wringin' wet.

I can hear the ghost of Jimi Hendrix in some of this music——

When I say "like" Hendrix or James Brown, I mean that I tell the guitar player that if he likes Hendrix or Sly, and I like Hendrix and Sly, to play something like that, just to open it up. It can't sound exactly like them because it'll have a little more music and shit in it. What we play on top wouldn't be like what Hendrix'll play on top. What Sly and them need is a good soloist. What Jimi needs—needed—was good rhythm, which he never had until he got Buddy Miles, you know, the Band of Gypsies.
   You don't look for any kind of particular sound. Its already there. All that shit is out there for you to pick up on.

The critics who don't like your new band say you're trying too hard to appeal to the Rock market.

I ain't thinking like that, man, about no fuckin' market. Shee-it. [Miles scowls, doesn't like the observation.]

Listen to what I say. Hendrix had no knowledge of modal music;
he was just a natural musician, you know, he wasn't studied, he wasn't
into no market, and neither am I. Columbia tries to get me into that
shit but I don't let 'em do it. They wanted to put some of my music on
some kind of sample record of some of their black music, and I said
fuck that shit, man. Leave my music alone.

Aren't you satisfied with Columbia?

Uh uh, man, by no means. I ain't satisfied. They don't do anything for
you unless you're white or Jewish. Except maybe when I got out a new
album or something. By now I don't even talk to them anymore. For
instance: when I showed 'em the new cover by Corky McCoy, they told
me it won't help sell any albums. And I told 'em how to merchandise
nigger music, man. Put Chinese on the covers. Put niggers on the cov-
ers, put brothers and sisters on 'em, whatever they're gonna call us next,
that's what you put on the covers to sell us.

   Corky McCoy's my best friend. I just called him up and told him
what to do. In fact, he was afraid to do it, and I . . . you know, look at
those covers, man. He just lives it. Black life! It's different from white
life, Chinese life, whatever. My life's different from yours.

How come [bassist] Michael Henderson is the only musician from your
last band to be in your present lineup?

What about Mtume? He stayed in too. Uh . . . Michael had a funky
sound, you know, and I been teaching him for awhile. [Henderson was
hired by Miles out of Stevie Wonder's touring band. James Mtume
Foreman played percussion.] Like if he's in E Flat and I play an A chord
or maybe a C or a D he doesn't get ruffled anymore, like he used to. He
sticks where he is. He's used to all my stuff by now.

   But I got to change bands, you know. You're not gonna use guys
like Keith [Jarrett] or Jack [DeJohnette] forever. I mean they're all capa-
ble, but after awhile, you know, they're gonna lose it. It gets to be all
the same. You hear Keith now, man, he lost it.

Do you ever listen to what the musicians who used to work with you—
John McLaughlin, Weather Report—are doing now?

Never.

Do you ever feel like you have your own school?

Yeah, all the time. But you know, when they're playing real good, I also feel like I'm in a school. It works both ways. You might show a guy something and he takes it and learns. I just don't listen to what the guys are playing now because I already know what they're gonna do. Like John [McLaughlin]: I got him his drummer. I got him his manager. I know what he's gonna do. He's got two sides to him: a lotta sides actually. I know how soft John is, or can be. That's the way he plays when he plays with me. That's what I like about him.

What about the influences your musicians have on you. Joe Zawinul, for instance, is credited with being responsible for some of your recent directions, beginning with *In A Silent Way*.

Let them [the critics] say it. I don't care what they say. As long as I been playing they never say I done anything. They always say that some white guy did it. I just let 'em say it. Shit, whenever Joe or somebody would bring in something that they wrote, I'd have to cut it all up because these guys get so hung up on what they write. They think its complete the way they write it. Like the way he wanted that In A Silent Way *was completely different. I put it in a mode, no chords or anything. I don't know what he was looking for when he wrote that tune, but it wasn't gonna be on my record.*

So now they all play the tune the way I had it. Even Joe's own group [Weather Report]. Shit, a little melody like that, why make it so important? It's just a little sound—let it go.

Miles, are you at all religious?

Um um. By no means. You mean God, and stuff like that? It's a big joke to me.

What do you think of musicians like Pharoah Sanders and Alice Coltrane, who seem to play their music in a religious context?

I never think of 'em. Religion just don't come into it. You've got to study music. You can't just be religious and the stuff just pops out like that. They're giving people the wrong impression. I mean, there's music that comes out of being in a religious group, like the Staple Singers, or

James Cleveland. Billy Preston and stuff like that. That's one way you can learn, in church.

Were you brought up in church?

No. If you ask me, that's just shit the white man uses to con black folks. All forms of religion are a big con. People are just scared to die, man. Everybody dies.

Are you afraid to die?

No. [Miles laughs out loud.] All these lectures—"Protecting Your Inner Karma," and all that shit. How many people even know they have one? I mean, think of all the guys that go to the [Vietnam] war: they go for no reason and kill somebody that they don't even know, and then you come back and a guy calls you a black motherfucker or something, and you have a reason to smash his head in and you do it and you're a criminal and you have to go to court, but you don't have to go to court for going in the army and killing fifty people that you don't know.

    It's easy to do . . . kill somebody. I mean the police do it all the time and nobody says a fuckin' thing. They don't go to church and say, "I'm sorry I killed that guy."

Miles stops talking for awhile and stares at a little group of three trophies that stand next to his bed. Each is an Army boxing trophy, a little gold-plated fighter brazenly leading with his right. Miles resumes:

They're trained like my son was trained—to kill. These trophies . . . my son's. He was a champion boxer in the Army. In Germany. He comes back, a white guy pokes fun at him because of his color, and the first thing my son does is try to break his neck. You know? And I tried to tell him about that shit.

    But he's a Black Muslim, and he says, "What do you think I'm supposed to do, father, let that guy stand up and say that to me? They sent me into the Army to kill somebody I don't even know, then they won't give me a job, they make fun of me." I mean, it takes all the spirit out of him.

Miles looks down and closes those huge eyes for a moment, revealing a poignancy I couldn't have envisioned in his features after studying them closely during the dozen of times I've seen him on a bandstand. Then his face quickly resumes its scornful, noncommittal mien.

Once I saw a mark on his arm, and I said, "What you wanna do that shit for?" And he said he just did it once, for his girlfriend.
    He's in jail now.

Where?

In St. Louis. I got to get him out, fast. So I never think about that religion shit. And when I do, it makes me mad, you know? People have to respect me. I know they respect me, there's no doubt about it, because they can't do it themselves. Otherwise there'd be five On The Corners *out.*
    Columbia. Shit. I got guys like Motown offering me five hundred thousand a year and shit like that. Atlantic Records wants me. Columbia don't pay me shit.

Why do you continue to record for them?

Because I can't get out of that contract. I mean, they don't even try to go into the black neighborhoods and sell records. They tell me, "We want to introduce you to a new audience," but that audience is always white! Sheeit! It'd be a sad fuckin' day if there were no Sly Stone, wouldn't it?

You've never had a problem finding your audience, have you?

They find me. It makes me mad when Columbia says, "We want these [new] people to hear you." I don't audition for no white man, and for no black man either for that matter. I don't give a fuck if they like it or not. All I tell 'em to do is sell the music black, not to put no white girls on the cover with no pants on and stuff like that. Sell it black. Like I like Sly, man, James Brown, James Cleveland. I like to look at black people—Jim Brown, Ray Robinson, people you never even heard of. I don't listen to the Rolling Stones and any of that shit. [Miles looks at me reproachfully.]

Well, do you listen to R&B?

I'm from St. Louis, man. That's all we played in St. Louis. The only reason my records sound the way they do is because I studied music. It's my background. We always played the blues in St. Louis. Bands came up on the boats from New Orleans, guys came from Kansas City and Oklahoma City, all playing the blues. I mean there's some funky shit in St. Louis even today. You can still go to any little town in Kentucky that has a black nightclub and hear a real good band that nobody ever heard of, musicians that can't get out of town and just lay around. They can't all go to New York or San Francisco because there ain't enough there for all of 'em.

Why did you come to New York in 1944?

To go to Juilliard. To get out of St. Louis. To find Charlie Parker. See, we were working in a club in St. Louis and right around the corner was a hospital for the heart and no black people could go in there. One day I finally said I have to get the fuck out of this town.

How long did you stay at Juilliard?

Till I found out that nothin' was happening. All that shit I had already learned in St. Louis. And outside of school I was with Charlie Parker, and I met guys like Gil Evans, and George Russell, John Lewis, Dizzy . . .

How did you meet Charlie Parker?

I sat in with him one night in St. Louis when he came through with Billy Eckstine's band. They had a trumpet player I really liked named Buddy Anderson and he had to stop playing because he started to hemorrhage and they called me to play. [He smiles fondly.] Actually, they didn't have to call me because I was already there. I knew his part and just started to play.

Who was your main teacher?

Buchanan. Elwood Buchanan. Then I had a teacher here in New York, who was with the Philharmonic, named Vachiano. He always used to tell me to play for him and I said man, I'm paying you for the lessons, show me *something. Then I had a teacher named Gosta who was really something, man. He could run the chromatic scale seventeen times in one breath, all the way up the horn and all the way down.*

You never seem to play with any vibrato. Did that come from one of these teachers?

Buchanan. He didn't believe in it. He said that all the white guys used it and the best guys were the black guys that just played straight sounds.

Who were your other influences when you were coming up?

There're a dozen of 'em. A whole lot. The main one must have been Clark Terry. My teacher played like him. There was a guy from New Orleans named Capeheart. There was another one but I can't remember his name. Ray Nance. Buck Clayton. You listened to everybody and took the parts you liked. You watch how they hold the horn, how they walk. I mean, you're 15 and looking at them like this. [Miles makes his eyes nearly pop out of his head.]

Would you say that Charlie Parker taught you to play a certain way?

He never said nothing. He just told me to play.

I think you made your first record with him in 1945. You were nineteen years old.

Yeah. It felt like this. [Miles quakes with fear.] I was nervous, man. But I had to get over being nervous fast because he was never there and I had to rehearse the band. Which I was used to doing in St. Louis. I was the musical director of the band in St. Louis when I was 15. We played shows and shit. Eddie Randall and the Blue Devils, we were called.

How did the famous *Birth of the Cool* sessions happen?

I wrote John Lewis a letter, he was in Paris, and I told him that I had an idea and that he should come back. Everybody just wrote something and we did it.

Did you have a name for that music? People called it cool jazz, or chamber jazz.

No, man, its the white folks that need those labels. I mean they named Dizzy's music "Bebop." [Miles frowns.] I can't believe this shit sometimes. They always turn it around. They always put some white guy, make him the top, say it was his idea and all that shit. Like you can see what Weather Report is doing even today. I don't see how they can sound bad, *you know? But I know they're limited because I know how both Wayne and Joe play.*

Here's my secret, man: I don't tell no one my secrets. Nobody knows all the instrumentation I had in On The Corner. *They're just guessing. I want to make the fuckin' critics think. Not even Teo [Macero] knows all the stuff that's on that record.*

I'm confused about when you made what you consider the first "Miles Davis" records.

They were on Savoy, around '46. But I made records when you weren't supposed to make them because they had a war on and were trying to save rubber. They're releasing that shit from those days, you know— "Take One! Take Two!" and that shit.

When you look back on those days now . . .

I don't look back on them. Never. I don't have any place in my head for that stuff. I only look ahead.

We talked for about three hours. Invited back the next afternoon, I returned to the house on West 77th Street with photographer David Doubilet to finish the interview and make some photographs for my article. Miles again sat me in his wheelchair and spread himself on a sofa to answer more questions.

You seemed bitter yesterday when you were discussing Weather Report.

I don't mind people imitating me. If they're kind of polite, they say where the shit comes from. You take Weather Report and people say they got a style all their own, and they don't. *They took the* Silent Way *shit, you know? But I guess they gotta do that on account of their wives get after them. I mean I've let a lotta guys go on account of their wives.*

Are you married now?

[His faces breaks into a grin.] Who the fuck am I gonna marry? I wouldn't marry somebody if they had a gun at my head and about five million dollars here on the fuckin' table. First place, I'm too difficult to live with and I know it. Second place, women just go off into them-selves . . . Some girls you can get along with, no questions, no headaches, they don't wanna change you.

Like when I was in the hospital for ten days I had a girlfriend call me up, and she said who's with you now and I said a couple of girls and she said I'll be over when you get rid of them. I said you must be jokin', I'm not gonna put any of these people out on account of one bitch. You know what I mean? It wasn't as if I'm layin' in the bed fuckin' 'em. They just come to see me because I'm fucked up. I ran my car into a pole on the highway.

There was talk that someone broke your legs for you . . .

[Miles frowned, looked at me sharply, and laughed, but it was more a derisive snort.] Why should they break my legs? If they wanted to really hurt me, all they'd have to do is hit me on the mouth.

[Miles is silent for a minute. He purses his lips.]

Here, give me your hand. [He took my extended forefinger and placed it on his upper lip, which was pursed tightly as if its owner was spitting into the mouthpiece of an imaginary horn. I felt a large, circular muscle spring up under my fingertip, a huge protuberance. I had to blink with disbelief as I considered the space I was being allowed into. I took my hand away. Miles smiled.] That comes after thirty years of playing the horn.

While Doubilet was getting in close to photograph Miles's lip, I asked him what he thought of the current music scene.

White people have their own white gods who they worship. I don't know who they are because I don't follow the scene that carefully any

*more. But I seen some of those shows, you know, where the boys look
and dress like girls. [This is a reference to David Bowie, the New York
Dolls and the then-fashionable Glam or Trash style.] I mean, I can see
whites digging Country & Western and that shit, but now it's just like
the guy's ass, and see how he moves. It's not music, man, its entertainment. So they should sell it as that. Burlesque, only with boys. Ha.
Which is all right, you know. When I go to Paris I go to all those shows
because they really do it right.*

Do you ever get tired of playing music?

*No man, I don't. Music is like a curse for me, and I feel like I have to
go through with it. What I don't like is being hustled. I mean, I put out
good music: why should I be hustled? Like the other day—I'm supposed to do an encore and I don't want to do it and my road manager
says, "Get back on the stage, motherfucker." But this wasn't like any
"motherfucker" I'd ever heard before. It was a white "motherfucker"
with too many Rs in it.*

    *I said to him, Man what the fuck are you talkin' about? But I had
to cool it because I knew I might break his jaw and I'd be right back in
court. Right? I had to tell Neil [Reshen] about it. I said, You talk to him
because I'd break his neck or something. I'd just take his head and
smash it against the wall. Shit. I just wanted to play the job, make
everybody satisfied, and* leave. *Which I did.*

    *I know. Everybody says I'm a violent guy, but nobody talks to me
like that, not even my mother, man. Now she understood me, and we
got to be the best of friends. I mean, me studying music at the age of 14
meant to her that I wasn't no idiot. She knew she couldn't just say anything to me and expect me to believe it because she was older than me.*

Did she give you a bad time when you left home and went to New
York?

*No. What could she say? My father—he was a dentist, an oral surgeon—
said to her, "Leave him alone." When I left he told me, "You need anything, let me know. I'll send you $50 a week allowance." But I was
already making $85 a week when I was 15. My parents got a divorce
when I was young and I helped send my sister through school. My parents
. . . [He smiles again.] Mothers and fathers are something else, man.*

We took a break and Miles told us to follow him up to his bedroom, where Finny was busily steam-curling the hair of an extremely attractive young woman. Miles turned on two large color TVs to two different newscasts and told us to look around. "You should have a fuckin' notebook," he cackled. He lay back on the large circular bed in what looked like Miles Davis's bedroom as conceived by the Playboy Advisor. Miles switched to an old movie and became absorbed. I walked into the big closet. The massive wardrobe spilled off racks and shelves onto the floor in a phantasmagoria of cloth and color—cool Italian silk suits from the Blackhawk days, beautiful tweeds, luxurious gray and charcoal gray flannel suits, more recent denim ensembles, chamois shirts, buckskin pants, an array of high heeled silver boots.

Miles motioned for the photographer to check out his bathroom. I asked what for and Miles crossly replied, "I don't know. Tell him he can jerk off if he wants." We walked into the bathroom to find Miles's immense ten-foot bathtub, big enough for three, all blue-tiled and surrounded by mirrors. I asked if we could photograph him and his friends in the tub and he looked at me like I was stupid. "Sheeiitttt," he said.

He asks to see the camera, and starts to talk photography. "I got lots of pictures of naked bitches I took in here, man. They all dug it, you know? I got pictures of them doing funky things to each other and everything.

"I mean, I ain't no *collector*. I don't look at 'em or anything. I just *got* 'em." Miles muses on women. "There's a lot of women comin' around here lookin' to give away pussy and sex but I don't fuck 'em, at least not all of 'em. I don't fuck bitches that want to fuck me. It doesn't appeal to me. I have to fight off that shit all the time."

So now that this police business is settled, are you going back to work?

Shit. There's always too much policin' going' on, 'specially policin' of kids. If I were a judge and they busted Sly, I'd say to the police that brought him in, "What the fuck are you doin'? Let that motherfucker out so he can make some more music to keep those black folks happy so they won't really start a fuckin' riot." I mean they're so stupid. Why should they bust Sly. He ain't sellin' no dope. He ain't sellin' shit. All he has to do is write two notes and that'd be enough.

Do you think drugs can help you at all? Or is it poison?

Certain drugs might help you make up your mind, you know? They don't help you to play, because you've got to study to do that. But if you're hesitating about playin' something, sometimes it can help you to go ahead and do it without any hesitation, 'cause you'll be concentrating on the music.

I like your attitude.

Well, I can see where, say, a writer like you might take a drug and it might help you make up your mind if you had five or six choices and it could help you settle for one. But there's no telling what happens with drugs. When you take drugs and you got nothin' to do, that's when you get into trouble. If you don't put all your energy in something, you get paralyzed. Like this. [Miles freezes, seizure-like.] Who wants to be like that?

Do you listen to records?

No man, they're all in here. [Miles taps his head.] Everything. I got a place for Lightin' Hopkins. I got a place for Stravinsky. And right here [Miles taps his frontal lobe in the middle of his foreheard] I got a place for SSSlllyyyyy.

How come you're not stuck in 20 years ago like most of your generation of jazz musicians?

I figure it like this. I never look down or talk down to any musician because he's 19 or something. I don't sell anybody short. I'm always listening. Yesterday's dead, man.

What do you see in the future?

Tomorrow.

Why wouldn't you appear at the Newport Jazz Festival last summer?

Well, I didn't wanna be no Newport Nigger. I mean that shit is just a big party, like a reunion. They don't do anything or try to play anything

new. I'm not like that. I want the new stuff all the time. I'm not into
myself that way. I don't listen to my old records. I'm not into gold
records and trophies and awards and being on the covers of no maga-
zines. My ego doesn't run like that.

What does your ego run on?

My ego only needs a good rhythm section. I mean, my band now, man,
they have so much fuckin energy, and I got to bring it out of them, or it
doesn't work.

Time to go. I shut off the recorder and David Doubilet packed up his cam-
eras. I asked Miles if he ever read anything about him that he liked.
"Ralph Gleason," he rasped. "He understands me." I asked him if he read
a recent article in *The Saturday Review* titled "Miles Davis—The Man
Behind the Mask." Miles smiled and began pulling at his handsome face,
stretching the skin, tugging at the combed-back hair, pulling his new
moustache. "This ain't no mask," he said.

MILES DOWN THE ROAD
ERIC NISENSON

Eric Nisenson's account of Miles Davis's 1975–1981 period of seclusion is invaluable because so little has been written about that part
of Davis's life. As Nisenson points out in his book *'Round About
Midnight: A Portrait of Miles Davis,* Davis's poor health in the
1970s made concertizing increasingly more difficult. After his June
1975 New York concert at Lincoln Center (with Sam Morrison on
reeds), Davis again had to withstand hip surgery, for which he was
hospitalized for quite some time. After his release and lengthy con-
valescence, Davis found himself uninterested in playing the trumpet
or leading a band, which he had done virtually nonstop for almost
thirty years. Instead, Davis turned his attention to playing the piano
and other pursuits.

Ultimately, the desire to play his horn, assemble a touring band,
and put an end to the rumors that were swirling about in the press
impelled him to return to the concert stage. But before ceasing his
layoff, a series of medical procedures—throat and gallstone surgery,
another operation on his hip, and treatment for a peptic ulcer—had
to be endured.

Nisenson mentions that Davis's favorite music of this period was
that of James Brown and Stockhausen and Puccini's opera *Tosca.*
These three, the author maintains, are indicative of the rhythmic,
complex, and lyrical sides of Davis's musicianship. Although Davis

had hoped to record selected arias from *Tosca* with orchestrations by Gil Evans, as of 1982 the collaboration had not been recorded. Jan Lohmann's Miles Davis discography makes no mention of the project whatsoever.

For many years Miles had talked about retiring from performing, but in 1975, when he finally did stop playing and recording, it was not really a matter of choice. His deteriorating health made performing out of the question. After a particularly long stay in the hospital in 1975, Miles explained, "It's like Gil Evans was, just about the time of the *Birth of the Cool* sessions. After them, he went to the hospital and just gave up arranging for a while, he just lost his feel. Well, I just gave up my feel for the horn."

Miles rarely left his house, and even the strong pain relievers prescribed for him helped very little. In addition, Miles hated these drugs because they made him drowsy. "If I can't stay up for five days at a time," he said, "I just might as well forget about it." However, he managed to hide his constant pain from most of his friends, since he had always hated people who whined about their ailments. On one very rare occasion he confided, "If only you knew how much this hurt. It's a motherfucker, man."

Despite his illness—and unknown to most in the outside world—Miles remained unceasingly creative. For nights on end he would sit at his piano, composing. When friends came over he would play thick chords, saying, "Listen to this, isn't that beautiful?" He would also spend time composing with close friends, such as the songwriter Elena Steinberg. However, he rarely, very rarely, touched his trumpets. When a friend suggested that the horns be fixed, since they were in disrepair, Miles bristled and said, "When I'm ready to play again, I'll fix them myself." He was also constantly irritated by those well-intentioned friends and relatives who would call him and ask when he would play again. He would tell them, "When I *feel* like it; nobody has to tell me when I should play again. I'll know." But privately he would express doubts about his ability to pick up the horn again: "I don't know," he said after he had been in retirement for a long while. "I might have to start all over again, learning the basics, just like I did when I first started playing the horn."

He occasionally enjoyed his position as mentor to young players. One time a cornetist came to the house and was asked to demonstrate his style. After only a few notes, Miles grabbed the cornet out of the younger man's hands, picked up a nearby hammer, and acted as if he were going to smash the horn while croaking, "Learn how to play this damned thing." The cornetist was shocked, but Miles was trying to shake him up, to psychically slap him into becoming a better musician. Then relenting, Miles smiled and said, "Look, you've got a nice approach to the horn, but you don't have your sound right. You play with too much vibrato, and as my teacher told me when I was a kid, some day when you're old you'll be shaking and have a vibrato anyway. You need to find your sound, because that sound is the whole thing. Musical ideas are easy, but it's developing your sound—that's at the heart of it."

Columbia's president, Bruce Lundvall, regretted Miles's retirement. Although none of his subsequent records sold as well as *Bitches Brew*, all his records were steady sellers. Every record that Miles had made for the company, beginning with *'Round About Midnight*, remained in print and in demand. However, although he had made many recordings in the early seventies when he was virtually living in Columbia's studios, he had agreed to only a few releases of old material. One record, *Water Babies*, which consisted of performances by the mid-sixties quintet, was released as a favor to Tony Williams, who had composed much of the material. But Lundvall was persistent with Miles: please, he begged him, just come into the studio and record *anything*. Miles told him that he didn't know how to run a record company. "Well," Lundvall asked, "what should I do?"

"Why don't you take up jogging or something, instead?"

Finally Lundvall did something that record company presidents rarely do: he went to the house of one of his artists. While he was there, Miles played him a recording of some fascinating, hypnotic electric music he had made. "Wow, that's great," exclaimed Columbia's president. "Bruce," said Miles, "that was from *Jack Johnson*, which was released over six years ago. Now get the hell out of my house." This incident did not deter Lundvall from releasing new Miles Davis albums. Along with Teo Macero, he went to the Columbia vaults, and while Miles was in retirement, released two albums of material that ranged from the very first sessions of the quintet in 1955 to Miles's early-seventies music.

Although Miles enjoyed seeing friends, he was inhospitable to people who thought they had some right to meet him. Once, Mick Jagger dropped by his house. Miles did not know Jagger and when he opened the door, he said to the rock star, "What do you want?"

Jagger responded, "I'm Mick Jagger, and I've always wanted to . . ."

"Get the fuck out of here. I don't care who you are."

When a friend asked Miles why he sent away such a celebrity, he replied, "I didn't care that he was Mick Jagger, no one comes here unless they're invited. I wouldn't go to his house unless he invited me. And I even like the way the guy sings!"

Nevertheless, Miles would often get depressed when former associates failed to keep in touch with him. "Why don't guys like Thad Jones or Percy Heath ever call me?" he would often wonder out loud. One Christmas he was especially upset. "After all the musicians I trained," he said, "the only one who sent me a Christmas card was Joe Zawinul." When Sonny Rollins called him one morning, Miles was delighted—he still retained tremendous affection for the tenor man.

Dizzy Gillespie got in touch with Miles for a surprising reason: he wanted Miles to teach him how to improve his tone when he played ballads. Miles laughed when he remembered this incident: "After all the shit I learned from Dizzy, he comes to *me* in order to learn! I told him that he was too set in his ways to change now. But I also told him that all that air that puffed up his cheeks when he played wouldn't do his tone any good unless it went through his horn."

One person who stayed in constant contact with Miles was Cicely Tyson, who would call regularly and try to lift his sometimes waning spirits. His trainer, Bobby McQuillen, paid frequent visits, encouraging him to keep in shape, telling him, "You're still a young man, Miles. You've got plenty left to give to the world."

Usually his pungent humor outweighed his depressions. Once a friend mentioned an orgy. Miles shook his head and said, "I don't like orgies. I'm not putting these million-dollar lips on no two-dollar pussy."

In 1978 Miles's friend Elena Steinberg invited him for a stay at her house in Connecticut. Miles appreciated the peace of the country and began seriously considering buying a house in New England. While he was there, Larry and Julie Coryell, good friends of Elena's, encouraged Miles to record some of his newly composed music in their own studio, with Larry on guitar, as well as a bassist and drummer. Miles only played piano at these sessions, but the music displayed his personal musical approach. He decided, though, that the tapes were too unsatisfactory to be released, and told Larry that he could keep them as a gift.

As much as he liked the quiet of the country, he found that he needed the discordant rhythms of New York City. "New York is great," he would say. "It's got so much noise. Subways, horns, I can't stand quiet. I go nuts." Upon returning to New York, he turned to several projects he had long been thinking about. One of the most intriguing was a new collaboration with Gil Evans, this time recording *Tosca,* with Miles playing the arias on trumpet. *Tosca* was one of his favorite pieces of music. Miles has often said, "My favorite music is Stockhausen, *Tosca,* and James Brown." These represent the three essential aspects of music that are most important to him: the complex, constantly changing electronic textures of Stockhausen (to whom he often compared Gil Evans), the lyricism of *Tosca,* and the eternal rhythms of James Brown. The *Tosca* project, to date, has not been recorded, but Miles keeps the score of the opera at home and still pores over it.

All during his retirement, Miles continued to keep active. He hated rehashing his past. When somebody asked him about an incident involving Charlie Parker, he grimaced and said, "That was so damned long ago. Who cares about that shit?" Indeed, to Miles, living in the past is destructive for an artist. One night, after several days of staying up and writing at the piano, he lost track of what day it was. "It's Thursday," claimed his girlfriend of the moment. Miles made a face and growled, "You're a lying motherfucker." When a friend showed him a newspaper with the date, which was indeed Thursday, he stood up and pointed to the awards which were hung behind the piano. "Do you see those awards?" he said quietly. "I got them because my memory is so damn bad."

As time passed Miles became increasingly restless—composing at the piano was simply not as exciting as playing with a band. And he was becoming tired of public speculation about activity in retirement. Rumors circulated that he was dead, that he was back on drugs, that he was embarrassed because he could no longer play. In 1979 Miles granted a short interview to a friend's friend who worked for *Oui* magazine. When the reporter asked Miles if he was using cocaine, Miles laughed and said, "Isn't that stuff expensive?" He had little patience for such snooping into his private life, and he began to be called "the Howard Hughes of jazz." Not that Miles cared. *He* knew that he was going to return to music, when he felt he was ready. "Everybody thinks I'm dying or on drugs or something," he would tell friends, "but I'm going to surprise the world."

His return was delayed by further operations, including the removal of gallstones, another hip operation, treatment of a stomach ulcer, and an operation intended to improve his speaking voice (it helped only slightly).

In late 1980 Miles began seriously playing the trumpet again, something he found far easier to do than he had initially feared. His nephew, Vincent Wilburn, son of his sister Dorothy, started a punk band, and Miles began working in private with it, recording music with little relationship to any of his previous work. Then, with encouragement from his manager and friend, Mark Rothbaum, Miles began to put together a working band of his own and to plan a new recording. In March 1981 he recorded three albums for Columbia, which released *The Man With the Horn*, one record from the sessions. It would be criticized as being one of the least ambitious in Miles's career. And indeed, it lacks the complexities of his electric music of the early seventies. The band was composed of young, mostly unknown players (with the exception of the superb Al Foster, who had played with Miles in the previous decade).

In its simplicity the music embraced Miles's entire career, since the young musicians played straight 4/4 swing rhythms in addition to funk. Many critics failed to perceive this band's resemblance to the early sixties band with Wynton Kelly and Hank Mobley: it served as an ideal vehicle for Miles to make beautiful musical statements without distraction. And he surprised his audiences at Lincoln Center, the Savoy, the Beacon, and other places by playing ballads like "My Man's Gone Now" as well as funk and even quasi-reggae pieces. He was still playing brilliantly, using a portable-miked horn but no wah-wah pedal, playing melodically and with a sometimes fiery rhythmic attack. He seemed more relaxed than ever, sometimes joking with the musicians onstage, or offering them drinks of water. Miles was coming back with full strength.

In November 1981 Miles married Cicely Tyson at the home of their mutual friend Bill Cosby. Cicely had remained friendly and concerned about Miles throughout his six years of retirement, and the two had grown close again in the months before his return to playing.

Although he continued to have physical problems, Miles felt strong enough to announce that with the help of his new wife, he would continue playing until he died. He had always maintained that his fate remained in his own hands:

"If I want something, it just seems to happen, or I make it happen. You know, I live in my mind, that's all I need. They can come and take away my arms, my legs, my dick, whatever, as long as they leave me my brain. As long as I have my mind, I'll always figure out a way to get it all back."

HANGIN' OUT WITH DAFFY DAVIS
ERIC NISENSON

For the 1996 republication of *'Round About Midnight: A Portrait of Miles Davis,* Eric Nisenson was given an opportunity to elaborate on his experience as Davis's first biographical collaborator. Nisenson's reflection, written thirteen years after the biography's publication, explains how his project (originally intended as Davis's autobiography) came to be, as well as the wild course of their relationship.

Nisenson met with Davis during the trumpeter's "retirement," a period in which Davis was overwhelmed by the effects of arthritis, sickle cell anemia, and the basic degeneration of his body, particularly in his ankles and hips. Although Davis spent a considerable amount of time with Nisenson, it's surprising that he wasn't mentioned a decade later—even in passing—in *Miles: The Autobiography.*

What follows (with the author's consent) is an edited version of Nisenson's Preface to the 1996 edition. As you will see, the author's experience with Davis remains one of the greatest experiences of *his* life.

I have idolized Miles Davis since I was about fifteen years old. I idolized him in the same way other kids worshipped Mickey Mantle or Elvis, or the Beatles a little later. I tried to get as many of his albums as I could afford back then, read everything I could get my hands on, and continually told Miles stories to my friends, most of whom couldn't have cared less. I do not think that even my imagination at its most febrile could then have conjured what would come years later: that when my phone would ring, especially late at night, I would groan, "Oh no, it's that damned Miles again. Why can't he leave me alone?" And I would pick up my phone to hear that famous whispered growl demand, "Bring your white ass down here, Eric. Now."

Back when I was a teenager, even the idea of meeting Miles Davis seemed preposterous. His reclusiveness was part of his legend, as was his supposed hostility to white people. Yet I always had the weird feeling that if we met we could be friends. Maybe it was because I felt as alienated as he did. And I understood why he did the things he was always being criticized for—not announcing tunes or introducing the members of his band, turning his back to the audience when he played, refusing to compromise no matter what. I found it wonderful that Miles refused to cooperate with *Time* magazine when they were planning to do a cover story on him. Who else would have the guts to turn his back (excuse the pun) to a cover on *Time?* Only Miles, who kicked their photographers out of the Village Vanguard when he was performing there (instead *Time* put Thelonious Monk on its cover). This was my kind of guy.

In the late seventies I moved into an apartment on New York's Upper West Side after having lived in San Francisco for several years. Although I had a day job working as a college textbook editor, I spent a lot of my time at the nearby home of my friend, the great bassist Walter Booker. Bookie had converted part of his huge apartment into a recording studio, and when he wasn't touring with Sarah Vaughan or Nat Adderley, he recorded sessions with some of the finest musicians in jazz. Bookie looked at me as a kind of "historian" for his studio, someone who would record the unique musical events and the interplay of the musicians, many of them jazz legends, who constantly passed through. Needless to say, I was often enthralled and amazed by the music and musicians who went in and out of Bookie's home and studio. His place had become kind of a jazz salon where virtually every great jazz musician came by at one time or another. And one night Miles Davis dropped by.

I was actually scared of meeting him—afraid that he would make a nasty insult or simply be rude to me. But he was wonderful—talkative, funny, warm, and friendly. He walked up to me to shake my hand and acted as if he knew me. I had this strange sense—as if we had known each other in some previous life. He was much shorter here than he had seemed when I had seen him perform, and his intensely intelligent, probing, wary eyes pulled you in as if they were bright embers at the center of his pitch black face. The controlled muscularity of his movements were like those of the large wild cats, cheetahs and tigers, that he enjoyed watching fight on film. But there was no doubt—none—that he attracted attention whether or not you knew who he was: he was a walking definition of "charisma."

I knew enough not to say something like, "Gee, Miles, I really like that *Sketches of Spain* album." I knew Miles hated that sort of crap. I just shook his hand and said I was glad to meet him, wondering if he could tell how awed I was just to be in his presence.

But Miles and I hit it off immediately, which in some ways astonished me but in other ways seemed obvious and natural. We were both shy, basically loners. (Miles immediately picked this up—he had developed the perception of a fighter in that he was able to suss out somebody's character very quickly. Once I introduced him to a guy who wanted to be my agent. Miles shook his hand, the guy said a few words, and Miles turned to me and said, "He's a liar." He turned out to be—unfortunately—quite right.)

Miles knew how to use his voice—that famous whispered growl—to his advantage, as a way of pulling in those around him. He obviously knew that he was hard to understand unless one listened carefully, so he made everyone focus on what he was saying.

Miles invited me to see his home and a couple of days later I took him up on his offer. I called before I left and Miles repeated his invitation and asked if I could pick up a six-pack of Heineken when I came over. That seemed innocent enough, but I didn't know at the time that this was the beginning of a kind of indentured servitude. When I came to Miles's 77th Street house (it had been converted from a church) he was in the outer entranceway, a disgusted look on his face. "The Con Edison guy came here and asked me if he could talk to the owner of the house. He thought I was the janitor! I told him, 'You're looking at the owner, you white motherfucker.'" It was obvious that Miles had never become inured to such casual racism, that running into it was still shocking and profoundly upsetting. Later on, whenever Miles came to visit me, I had to go back to the street with him in order to hail a cab. Even Miles Davis could not get a New York City cabdriver to stop and pick up a black man, especially at night. I, of course, had no problem.

This took place during the late seventies, the period of Miles's so-called "retirement." In the early seventies Miles had been at a creative peak, breaking away from the post-bop which he had played for most of his career and creating perhaps his most revolutionary music. He valiantly toured and recorded, despite several overlapping physical ailments, often performing on crutches. But in 1975, Miles gave in to the toll on his body and entered into a period of supposed retirement. He was ostensibly healing mind and body, but he was really on a self-destructive roller coaster, staying up for days at a time on cocaine and then crashing with barbiturates. "If I can't stay up for three days at a time, hell, I might as well forget about it," he used to say.

Miles's 77th Street house was a five-story building; Miles lived in the first three stories, and the top story was rented to a homosexual couple. The floor right above Miles's top floor was empty mainly because Miles was so sensitive to sound that just hearing footsteps or loud conversation bothered him. Later on in our friendship Miles offered me the apartment at a reasonable rate, but I was warned by someone who knew a previous tenant that living right above Miles was a very bad idea; I would have had to make all my guests take off their shoes before they entered, and if I watched TV or listened to my stereo I would have *had* to listen through earphones. Otherwise Miles would raise hell about the "disturbance."

The interior of the house itself seemed to be a reflection of Miles's state at that time. It was like a *Playboy* pad gone to seed. For instance, there was a large projection television—but a couple of the bulbs were burnt out and so it was like watching a 3-D movie without the glasses. In the bathroom was a tub big enough for two, but with a huge crack. There were boxes all around the house, almost as if Miles had just moved in (although he had been living there since the sixties). Even Miles's piano, on which he worked out ideas and composed new pieces, was in sorry shape—terribly out of tune with a few keys totally unplayable. Overall, the house did not look so bad inside because Miles kept it dark all day long.

Miles and I hit it off right away, perhaps because I immediately caught on to the fact that what some called "rude" or "insulting" was really his way of testing people, playing with them to see if they were hip enough to be trusted. With me that meant a continual series of mock anti-Semitic jibes. It was obvious to me that Miles was actually completely unprejudiced, and he looked on racism, of any kind, as inherently ridiculous. His nickname for me was "Jewish bastard," and he used to say things like "I'm having a party this weekend and you're invited, Eric. Yassir Arafat is the guest of honor." Of course, the funniest part of that crack was the idea of Miles putting on any sort of party during this reclusive period. Once Miles said to me, "Okay you Jewish bastard, call me nigger, go ahead. I've been called that a million times."

I replied, "Well, Miles, if you've been called that a million times, I better call you 'wop.' That's it, you little wop." Miles was stymied at his own game. This kind of playful jousting was one of his favorite activities, and I was able to hold my own most of the time. However, Miles often tried to get me to box with him, throwing light punches which I refused to return (Miles was, of course, a trained amateur boxer). I was at least a foot taller than him and he continually wanted to show how somebody his size could physically deal with someone like me. I conceded to him that he undoubtedly could, but he kept on trying to get me into a little back-and-forth anyway.

Almost from the beginning Miles confided things to me that few knew, particularly the extent of his physical problems. He was in intense pain frequently and was often emotionally discouraged. Our jousts seemed to cheer him up, and I felt glad to be of aid. Once we became friends it became hard for me to think of him as I once had, as a musical legend. He was my friend Miles now, amazingly enough.

I soon found myself in the position of being his errand boy. He would call me up (he seemed to know the moment I got home from work) and invite me—actually, command me—to come over and bring groceries or pick up a package at the pharmacy or cash a check, or any other errand that needed doing. And a few times he had me pick up little packages from one of his coke dealers who lived a block away from me. I hated doing that.

I always turned Miles down when he offered me some (he made it a practice of insisting that if someone did some of his cocaine, that they do the same huge amount at one time as he did). My main concern was for Miles's health, not my own safety. But he would explain to me in great, and quite poignant, detail the reason for his use of coke. It distracted him from the pain better than anything else, he told me, and it elevated his spirit. Without it he sank deeply into depression over his physical state; without it, he told me quite earnestly, he had no reason to continue living. "I've done everything, been everywhere, done so much shit, there's nothing to look forward to." Except, he made clear, the coke. I tried to get him to see psychiatrists, get some treatment for his depression. But he would hear nothing of it. He knew exactly what he wanted out of life. Yes, I should have been stronger, but I suppose I still looked at Miles, even in this state, as an idol, a god. And I did what this god wanted me to do. What can I say?—he got to me. I never made a nickel from delivering anything to him (if anything, I lost money for bus and late-night cab rides), including the coke, which I only had to deal with when he couldn't get his dealers to deliver.

Much of the time, however, Miles just wanted company—desperately. Although a lovely young girl was living with him at the time—whom I will call "Daisy"—she did not provide much intellectual fodder for a mind as brilliant as Miles's. He had also discovered that I was virtually a walking and breathing encyclopedia of his life and career. He was proud of the fact that he had forgotten so much—to him, that was the mark of a true artist and innovator, for if you cannot remember the past you are forced to continually create something new. But he did need to retrieve information from time to time that he had forgotten.

Soon, visiting Miles often became deeply depressing. He was so jaded, so world-weary and cynical, he almost seemed to be living at the heart of the void. A friend of mind begged me to bring him to meet Miles. But after we left Miles's home, my friend said, "I don't ever want to see him again. I'll just stick to listening to his music." I understood how he felt, but I also had deep compassion for Miles.

I don't remember how we first started talking about collaborating on Miles's autobiography. It seemed as much his idea as mine, although such a project had been a fantasy of mine long before I met him. At first Miles was not too sure. "If we do this book," he told me, "I'll have to say in it that——— ———(a famous black entertainer) is a flaming faggot." (Incidentally, Miles was not at all homophobic—he was friendly with several homosexuals, including those who rented the top apartment in his building.)

"No, Miles, you don't have to talk about him. Talk about those you respected like Charlie Parker."

"Charlie Parker," Miles declared, "was a hog." He then told me the story about the cornbread that is in the book.

"Well, okay, what about Coltrane?"

"Coltrane," Miles declared, "was a hog. You see, a genius like that, he has to be selfish. That's just the way geniuses are." As Miles said this, he was putting about half a gram of cocaine up his left nostril, deftly illustrating his point.

Finally, Miles agreed to do it, if the advance was sufficient. Thus began our "interviews," which were more like discussions, and, for me, like pulling teeth. Miles would start talking about Bird or the 52nd Street scene of the "Birth of the Cool" band ("Why," Miles asked rhetorically "am I called anti-white when my first band was almost all white?"), but then he would say, "That was so long ago, who cares what happened that long ago?" I tried to convince him as well as I could, telling him that lots of people did. He would not let me use a tape recorder for some reason. When someone asked him how I was supposed to remember all that he had said, Miles replied, "Eric will remember it. He doesn't need a tape recorder"—which was partially true. However, it certainly would have been easier with one. If I hid one in my briefcase or put a small one in my pocket, Miles was always able to ferret the damn thing out.

Miles had a very ambivalent attitude toward his past. At times, he was proud of his accomplishments; at other times his illustrious past almost seemed like a weight around his neck. For example, I knew Jimmy Cobb, Miles's former drummer (and, incidentally, a greatly underrated player) pretty well. Jimmy had found a tape of Miles's group with Coltrane from its 1960 world tour, the group's last. But when he tried to give it to his old boss, whom he had not seen for a while, Miles wouldn't even open his door, telling Jimmy through the intercom just to slide it under. Jimmy, who used to be close to Miles and is a very sensitive person, simply left. He did give it to me, however. The music, particularly Coltrane's, was really extraordinary, so I invited Miles over, telling him I had something I wanted him to listen to. Several days later, returning from a trip to Connecticut, Miles dropped over. I asked him if he wanted to hear the tape; at first he said no. I told him who it was and he said he still did not want to hear it. Then a little later, in the middle of a conversation that had nothing to do with music, Miles said, "Put it on, Eric."

The first tune was "So What." Miles groaned. At the beginning of the trumpet solo, Miles acted as if he were on the bandstand, grumbling to the bassist Paul Chambers, "Play the right fucking notes, Paul." He turned to Daisy and said, "Hey that's some pretty good trumpet playing, don't you think, Daisy? I wonder who that is." I doubt if even Daisy was unaware who was playing the trumpet.

But when Coltrane came on, Miles really got sucked into the music, exclaiming when Trane played a brilliant series of ideas or a particularly roiling arpeggio. Miles moved his body to Coltrane's solo, more caught up in this music than I had ever seen him. When it was over, Miles stood up to go, indicating to Daisy that it was time to leave. I said, "Wait, Miles, there's a lot more on the tape."

Miles looked at me with more sadness in his eyes than I had ever seen and said, "How could you do that to me, Eric? I thought we were friends." Needless to say, I was devastated.

Miles now had great leverage with me. If he wanted me to do something, and I was hesitant, all he had to do was threaten to pull out of the book. Eventually I began to ease the amount of control he had over me. If he said, "I want you to pick up a six-pack of Heineken and get over here now," and I told him "absolutely not," he would usually reply, "Well, that's it, Eric. Just forget about the book. It's all over." But I knew that he would call back an hour later, a day later, or sometimes two days later, and once more make a demand, as if nothing had happened.

Sometimes Miles's imagination worked overtime in figuring out a ploy to get me to run him an errand or to come over and keep him company. Here is a particularly bizarre example. It was late—after one in the morning—and I was at my girlfriend's place. We were just going to bed when the phone rang—somehow, Miles had obtained my girlfriend's phone number—and he wanted me to pick up some coke for him, because none of his dealers would deliver. I hated that particular errand, especially late at night. I was dog tired to boot and had the beginnings of a flu. Miles went through his usual threats, but I would not budge. "All right," he muttered, "this is the end, Eric," and hung up.

A few minutes later the phone rang. It was Daisy this time wanting to talk to me. "Eric," she said in a virtual monotone, "Miles says that unless you get over here now he's going to kick your white Jewish ass." I could clearly hear Miles's whisper in the background telling Daisy exactly what to say. "Well, Daisy," I replied, "you tell Miles that I'll see him tomorrow so he can kick my white ass then. It's cold outside and there is no way I'm going to run around, especially for Miles's poison. And tell him that I'm coming down with the flu, Daisy." I got the feeling that, as was often the case, Miles did not need coke as much as company. How deeply saddening—one of the great geniuses of this century truly desperate for a little company at one-thirty in the morning. "Okay," said Daisy, obviously embarrassed.

A few minutes later Miles called again. This time he talked to my girlfriend. He told her he knew exactly how to give me a treatment for my flu that would get me well in a matter of hours. But of course I had to come down there for the treatment (which had something to do with soaking in a bathtub with some special salts). I told my girlfriend to tell Miles, "No dice."

Finally I crawled into bed, thinking—foolishly—that Miles had certainly given up for the night. But a few minutes later the phone rang yet again. I told my girlfriend not to bother answering it, but she did anyway.

What a surprise—it was Daisy with a terrible emergency—Miles had fallen down his stairway! I have to come over right away!

"Oh my God, Daisy, that's terrible. Listen, call 911 immediately. Do you want me to? I'll call them for you." I heard that whisper in the background. "No, uh, Miles wants you to pick up something for him and to come right away." Another whisper. "This is an emergency."

"Sounds pretty bad, Daisy. But you have to call 911 right now, I can't help him. Understand? Miles has to get treated as soon as possible."

Hesitation. "Uh, okay." And she hung up.

And yes, a few minutes later the phone rang yet again. I answered it this time. "Eric," said Daisy—I could hear Miles's whisper in the background—"Miles wants you to know that he did not really fall down his stairway."

"Oh, really?"

"No, Miles says that he just doesn't like bullshit."

"Tell him, neither do I, Daisy, neither do I."

If all this seems like a game, of course it was, at least to a degree. On a number of occasions Miles would have me come over, supposedly just to discuss the book, and then after five minutes or so say, "Okay, Eric, I want to be alone. Get the fuck out of here." I did not find this particular ploy very amusing.

I cannot say that Miles did not return my favors. One time I went to his house right after a horrific haircut. Miles insisted on recutting my hair, telling me that I was the first white guy whose hair he had cut. And when he had the straight razor against my neck he cracked, "Now I've got you where I want you, white boy." Real funny stuff, Miles.

Another night Miles and I had a lengthy argument about the book. I wanted his old friend Bobby, his long-time boxing trainer, to help with the book, since he had known Miles for so long. But Miles was adamant, furious that I would even broach the idea. "He's just a boxing trainer. He doesn't know about any other shit." I thought that was very unfair to Bobby, who was not only highly intelligent but who had been close to Miles over a period of many years. He had even toured with him on several occasions, so I thought he would be helpful in jarring Miles's stubborn memory. But Miles insisted that if Bobby was part of the project, he would pull out.

As I was leaving that night, Miles told me to wait for a minute. He went into his bedroom and came back with a pair of his boxing gloves and an old jock-strap. I knew it was his way of saying, "Okay, I'll allow you in the same ring with me." I was being accepted on existential terms by Miles.

Miles constantly surprised me. For instance, he was a superb chef. One night he invited me over for what he claimed was "the best fried chicken you will ever eat." He was right. And he was knowledgeable on a wealth of subjects. He discussed literature with me, comparing the great writers to the great jazz masters. Although I had never seen Miles read, he knew who the important American writers were—he mentioned as "the masters" Hemingway, Steinbeck, Fitzgerald, and Faulkner. He told me that there was one writer he simply could not stand—Hermann Hesse. He once had a girl living with him who loved Hesse and had all his books. Miles gave her an ultimatum—get rid of the Hesse books or leave. I was not sure whether Miles hated Hesse because of his pretentious style or just because he was German (although he never mentioned Thomas Mann or any other German writer). But he had the same low regard for Hesse as a writer that he did for such musicians as Stanley Turrentine and Oscar Peterson ("Oscar had to be taught how to play the blues" was his dead-on comment).

Sometimes Miles's generosity took strange twists. Somehow he heard that I had had a big fight with my girlfriend and he invited me over to talk about it. As soon as I walked in he told poor Daisy to give me a blow job "to cheer Eric up." Daisy—who until recently had been living a relatively sheltered life in the Midwest—was horribly embarrassed by this sort of thing. "Not tonight," I told Miles, "we've got a headache." I was pretty sure that if I had been unhinged enough to take Miles up on his offer, he would have caused me great bodily harm.

By the way, I have heard many rumors about Miles's supposed bisexuality. I never witnessed anything that made me think he was anything other than heterosexual—he certainly never hit on me—but he thought of himself as being beyond sex. He told me a story about a brief affair that he had with a woman in Chicago. According to Miles, right in the middle of lovemaking, he realized that sex completely bored him—so, as Miles told me, he withdrew from the situation, explaining to this poor woman that he simply had no more interest in this sort of thing. I wonder if she ever recovered.

I am not so humble that I am not able to repeat what Miles said about me to my girlfriend. Early one afternoon he came over to visit, which he rarely did. He was having problems with Daisy, he told me, and he wanted my advice. While I was out of the room he said to my girlfriend, "I love your old man. He reminds me of Gil Evans, a white guy with no prejudice." Being compared to Gil Evans by Miles Davis—I could have died with a smile on my face when my girlfriend reported it. (He would never, of course, say something like that directly to my face.)

Miles seemed facetious about most matters, and he could be very funny. His sense of humor could be downright silly. One time I started a sentence, "Miles, I . . . " and he interrupted me, saying, "Eric, I'm really sick of being called Miles. Call me Daffy from now on. Daffy Davis."

But there were dark moments too. His jaded outlook on life often made me depressed, and many times he sank into deep blue funks. And the darkest moments concerned his treatment of Daisy. One night he called me up and asked me to come over. I had not heard from him in a few days and I could tell from Miles's voice that there was a problem. When I got there, he was by himself. He had broken Daisy's jaw, he explained, and she was hospitalized. "So, what do you think, Eric. Am I an asshole?"

I was furious; Daisy was one of the sweetest, most innocent creatures on earth; she cared deeply about Miles although she was about thirty years his junior and did not really know who he was. "Yes," I said, "you're a damned asshole, Miles. How could you do such a thing?"

"I meant to pull my punch. I know how to pull my punch."

This was Daisy's crime: a few nights previously, one of Miles's dope dealers came to the house with his girlfriend. Miles gave the girlfriend a red hat of his. After they left Daisy said to Miles that he had never given *her* a red hat. And that's what did it.

Miles had had a private telephone line put in her hospital room. Although it was after midnight, he decided to call her, despite my protest. When she answered, Miles asked what she was doing. Well, she was trying to sleep, of course, despite the pain in her jaw.

It was obvious that Miles felt bad about this incident, just as he probably felt bad all the times he had beaten and abused women throughout his life. But it amazed me how Miles can scream about the evils of racism—rightly so—and abuse women. What utter hypocrisy.

This incident deeply troubled me, and in many ways our relationship was never the same. Daisy moved right back in with Miles when she was released, which I could not understand. One day I said to Daisy that she seemed a bit depressed. "What's she got to be depressed about?" growled Miles. "She's in her early twenties and I'm fifty-two." I thought, "She's got plenty to be depressed about, Miles."

Eventually I put together enough materials from our "interviews" to create a proposal. I talked with several publishers, but they all wanted to know the same thing—would Miles participate in publicizing the book? Miles had been very explicit about this, so I had to tell the truth: he was so reclusive during this point of his life that he could not even come to the publisher's office to sign a contract. Most publishers had no interest without Miles's participation in the publicity. I was offered a relatively small advance, but Miles refused—he knew that he deserved at least six figures since, in his words, "I've got a million dollars worth of information." So the publisher offered me a deal to write an unauthorized biography. I told Miles about this and he expressed no problem with my doing such a book. He even let me continue, from time to time, to ask him questions about his career.

Several years later when Miles did get a large advance to do his autobiography, he was well out of the reclusive mode of his supposed "retirement" and he agreed to publicize the book; he even did that incredible *Sixty Minutes* interview with Harry Reasoner, something I cannot imagine him even considering during his "retirement."

I stopped seeing Miles, for the most part, when Cicely Tyson came back into his life. I was a little surprised about that—Miles used to do nothing but complain about her. I was equally surprised to see him hanging out with Bill Cosby when I had seen him get livid at Cicely for giving Cosby his phone number. But I believe that the part of Miles that still wanted to survive saw in Cicely a strong woman who could push him to actively turn things around in his life—which is exactly what she did. However, she insisted that Miles drop his old friends, completely change his environment. Naturally, there were those such as myself who felt that we had been good friends, that we had tried to discourage Miles's self-destructiveness. But maybe she was right, as painful as it is to admit it. Maybe Miles had to be cut off from everyone who "enabled" him to get high, no matter how unwillingly. And she did save his life, inarguably. Later, Miles would explain that she wanted complete control over him and did not want him to have his own friends. I do not know whether or not that was true. But even if it was, Miles owed her a tremendous debt.

Miles cut me off very sharply and I, like a number of other friends, was hurt. I was told by many who had long been on the jazz scene that Miles did this all the time, often for not much reason at all—Jimmy Cobb is an excellent example. One person told me that sooner or later Miles did this to almost everybody close to him; for some reason I thought that I was an exception.

But the bottom line is that I owe Miles an enormous debt. He went out of his way to try to teach me how to think at the highest level of creativity. Miles was trying to show me the *way* of the artist—his attitude was definitely that of master and student. He was not teaching me any specific technical points about the work of an artist, but rather the existential terms—the stance and consciousness of the artist (although many of his lessons I had to suss out for myself—such as the gift of the boxing gloves and jock strap).

Despite his inexcusable treatment of women, despite the way he treated me at the end, despite even those final years of his life when he seemed to turn his back on most of the things he had once believed in, Miles changed my life for the better. Knowing Miles Davis was without doubt one of the highlights of my life and I have no doubt it will remain so until my dying day.

Interviewer Ben Sidran has a rare gift for creating settings in which his guests can relax and be themselves. Part of Sidran's success lies in his engaging personality and unthreatening manner. The fact that he's a jazz singer and pianist gives him added credibility. But equally important is Sidran's marvelous interview technique in which informed questions and well-timed compliments respectfully honor his subjects.

Notice how Sidran riffs on the word "genius," compares Miles Davis to Duke Ellington, mentions Davis's "pretty notes" and unique sound, and commends the trumpeter on a particularly interesting point. Such things establish a close rapport, which inevitably leads to the surrender of important new information. In the interview that follows, which Sidran conducted on January 30, 1986, and included in his book *Talking Jazz,* Miles Davis speaks of his fondness for drawing. This is probably the only time Davis discussed this aspect of his creative work to such an extent.

Sidran's interview with Miles Davis is but one of 300 that Sidran has done with jazz musicians since 1969. Hopefully his large body of work, full of untold surprises, will soon be made available, either in print, on CD-ROM, or on cassette, at selected sites around the world.

The following interview was held on a warm January afternoon on the terrace of Miles Davis's beach house in Malibu, California. I had gone to the house with Miles's record producer, Tommy LiPuma, who had told me that Miles's reputation for being a difficult man to talk to was not necessarily accurate. From the minute Miles opened the large wooden front door to his house and invited us inside, it was obvious that this was the case. In fact, when Tommy introduced us, Miles inexplicably gave me a hug. Throughout the interview, which took place during the afternoon and, informally, continued well into the evening, Miles was gracious, humorous and extremely generous with himself and his time. The interview began with us sitting across from each other at a table, with a bowl of potato chips in between. Miles had a sketch pad in his lap and was drawing with a large magenta felt-tip pen.

Ben: As we're talking, you're starting to do some drawing. I know that drawing has been a big part of how you've been spending your time for the last several years. Have you always been involved in drawing?

Miles: Yeah, my father taught me and my brother. Actually, I showed my brother how to sketch. My brother can see anything and draw it right off, you know. But he doesn't have any imagination like I have.

Ben: So imagination is. . . .

Miles: That's it. In everything. Imagination.

Ben: My impression is that your drawings are related to your playing in some ways, the gestures . . .

Miles: What it is is balance. If you make a drawing on a page, you have to balance it, you know. And that's the way most everything is. Art, music, composition, solos, clothes, you know, when you dress up . . .

Ben: Balance.

Miles: Yeah, a little over here, a little there, a little there.

Ben: I first noticed your sketches on the cover of one of your record albums a few years ago. Is drawing something you've always done, has

it always been part of your artistic process, or did you become interested in it again later in life?

*Miles: Yeah, you know, I stopped for a while. I really started to sketch
again after I married Cicely [Tyson]. Because she takes so long. You
know how actresses are. They take so long to get ready for anything,
you know. Rather than scream at her, I just started sketching. Especially
on planes. After we had a close call going to Peru for the Miss Universe
contest. The plane dropped about 2,500 feet and then dropped another
1,000 feet. And, you know, everybody was . . . some people were cry-
ing. A lot of celebrities were on that flight. And then I started sketching,
you know, cause it really scared me. That's really a trip to do that, to go
through that.*

*So now when I fly from New York to California, sometimes I
sketch. Most all the time I sketch. If I don't go to sleep, I'm sketching.
And I've done sketches that took me five hours, you know, to finish.
But it relaxes you, you know?*

Ben: Are you spending most of your time in California these days?

*Miles: Most of the time. I try to. I try to stay here because of my circu-
lation. It's good for my circulation. The cold weather really does a number on my skin in New York, and the air's dirty, the streets are dirty.
But that pace in New York. I love that pace. I would never like it out
here all seasons. Just in the wintertime. Either here or the south of
France.*

Ben: You really are part of the greater art community, not just the music
community. You're one of the few American jazz musicians to have
made that transition.

Miles: From what to what?

Ben: From being thought of as a *player* to being thought of as an *artist*.

*Miles: Oh, yeah. Well, you know, if I was thought of any way else than
that I wouldn't want to be here. If I couldn't contribute. You know, I
was telling some friends in Sweden if I couldn't do anything to help,
even if I was in some other form of art, if I couldn't discover something
or help the art, or find a new way to do it, you know. I wouldn't want*

to be here. I would just want to be dead. If I couldn't create. There would be nothing for me to live for. If I couldn't maybe write a composition that I like—not somebody else, that I would like, and my friends would like. And they say, "Yeah, Miles, that sounds good." If I couldn't do that, I wouldn't want to be here. It's selfish, I know. But geniuses are selfish. [Laughs.]

Ben: Part of your genius, it seems, has been to take groups of musicians and put them in challenging situations. Looking back over the output of your recorded work, the "newness" a lot of times stands out as much as anything. You're creating situations that force musicians to rely on their instincts rather than their habits.

Miles: *That's right. It's the groups of people that you associate with, you know. It's not all me. It's them. People like Herbie Hancock, Chick Corea, those people that I work with. They're talented people. Especially when they get in their creative period. People have creative periods, periods where they [snaps his fingers three times], like that, you know? And then if they could just wait on that, or recognize it when it's there. I recognize it in other people. I recognized it in Wayne Shorter and Herbie and Chick, Keith Jarrett, Sonny Rollins, different people, you know. Philly Joe, Red Garland. George Duke. He is something else, man. See, I saw that. I heard that. You know, he reminds me so much of Herbie. If Herbie would just slow down a little bit. George has great talent. Have a potato chip.*

Ben: Thanks. Again, part of the message of your music seems to be "be yourself," and you use minimalism to achieve this. Like those pretty notes you play, as opposed to a lot of notes.

Miles: *Pretty notes! If you play a sound you have to pick out . . . it's like the eye of the hurricane, you know? You have to pick out the most important note that fertilizes the sound. You know what I mean? It makes the sound grow, and then it makes it definite so your other colleagues can hear and react to it. You know what I mean? If you play what's already there, they know it's there. The thing is to bring it out. It's like putting lemon on fish. Or vegetables. You know, it brings out the flavor. That's what they call pretty notes. Just major notes that should be played.*

And rhythms, I used to, a lot of times, I would tell Herbie to lay out. He wrote a couple of pieces that were up in tempo, and rather than have him play the sound for me, I played the sound for him to listen to, you know? The sound of the composition he wrote. Because if you have too much background, you can't play an up tempo and really do what the composer tries to give . . . to me. And I try to give to the fans and music lovers.

Ben: You talk about the "sound" of the composition as if a song has a central "sound" to it, a sound source.

Miles: *I try to get his sound, whoever is writing the composition. If I'm going to play something against that, I have to get the sound that he wants in there, without destroying and blowing over it, so as not to bury it. You know what I mean? So it takes a lot . . . it really takes a long time to do that, you know. But if you're leaning that way, it doesn't. But if you aren't and somebody tells you?*

When I was about fifteen, a drummer I was playing a number with at the Castle Ballroom in Saint Louis—we had a ten-piece band, three trumpets, four saxophones, you know—and he asked me, "Little Davis, why don't you play what you played last night?" I said, "What, what do you mean?" He said, "You don't know what it is?" I said, "No, what is it?" He said, "You were playing something coming out of the middle of the tune, and play it again." I said, "I don't know what I played." He said, "If you don't know what you're playing, then you ain't doing nothing."

Well that hit me. Like bammm. *So I went and got every thing, every book that I could get. To learn about theory. To this day, I know what he's talking about. I know what note he was talking about.*

Ben: What note was it?

Miles: *It was a raised ninth. I mean a flatted ninth. [Laughs.]*

Ben: This conversation about the "sound" of the composition brings to mind the recording *Kind of Blue.* As you know, *Kind of Blue* is probably the number one jazz record on virtually all the jazz critics' lists.

Miles: *Isn't that something?*

Ben: Does the success of that record surprise you, Miles? It seems to have been such a simple record in a lot of ways.

Miles: *Not back then. Because Bill Evans, his approach to the piano brought that piece out. He used to bring me pieces by Ravel. Like the Concerto for Left Hand and Orchestra. Have you heard that? It's a piece Ravel wrote for his friend who went into the army. He came back, but he was a pianist, and he had lost his right hand. So Ravel wrote a piece for left hand and orchestra, for piano.*

And Bill used to tell me about different modes, which I already knew. And we just agreed on something and that's the way that album went. We were just leaning toward—like Ravel, playing a sound with only the white keys—and it just came out. It was like the thing to do. You know what I mean? Like an architect, all of a sudden all of the architects in the world start making circles, you know, like Frank Lloyd Wright. All his colleagues are leaning the same way at the same time, you know?

So it was Bill, and it was made for Coltrane, you know, that kind of thing. Because I used to give him a lot of chords. I would give him five chords to play in one chord, and I would tell him he could play either way. He was the only one who could do that. But I got it from Rachmaninoff, modulating from key to key. Bill and I used to listen to Bartók and, ah, what's his name, who wrote "The Fire Dance"?

Ben: Khachaturian?

Miles: *Yeah, Khachaturian, I would give Coltrane little chords like that to play, you know, against one "sound." You know, instead of saying like "D dominant seventh," or something like that, you could play under the chord, over the chord, or a minor third up from the fifth of the chord, you know?*

But it has to be a dramatic player, like Trane was, who can just turn you on with the sound of one note, and a group of notes. The only two people I ever heard doing that was Charlie Parker and Coltrane. You know, that's the only two that I ever heard in my life do that.

Ben: You mean the rhythmic freedom in the way they run changes?

Miles: *Coltrane didn't start playing like that until . . . A girlfriend of mine in France, one day she said. "Miles, these guys want to talk to* *you, they want to give you a trumpet or something." So I said, "I don't want to talk to anybody." She said, "They just want to talk to you and maybe you can pick out a couple of trumpets that you want." So I said, "OK." So I also got a soprano sax for Trane. And he never put it down. It was on a tour with Norman Granz. He played soprano sax in the bus, in the hotel, every day, all day, twenty-four hours a day. And he got that "sound." And then I gave him those chords and he just went, you know? Because he wasn't playing like that before. Sometimes a player plays so loud that it locks in with the sound that he left. You know, like bammm. It blocks out everything else. So I gave him all these options. I mean, it sounds technical, but you have to think like that if you're an artist, you know. You have to know how to do different things.*

Ben: Hearing you talk about this session I am struck by the fact that like Duke Ellington you would prepare music for your players, rather than bring music to them and say "play this." Your music really does come out of the people you are hanging out with and recording with.

Miles: Yeah, that's right. Duke is one of my favorite composers. Just lately, I have been hearing in my head "Rain Check," that he wrote.

Ben: You mentioned Coltrane's sound on the soprano saxophone. At one point, Coltrane said that he had been hearing a higher sound in his head, but that it wasn't until he got his hands on the soprano that he was actually able to realize what he had been hearing internally all along.

Miles: Right. See, it takes a long time for guys to develop. You know what I mean?

Ben: How come nobody else can get *your* sound? It's a simple thing, a gesture almost, but it is very difficult.

Miles: I have my own sound, because when I was like this [gestures with his hand low to the floor] my trumpet instructor, I loved the way he sounded. He was black and he used to play with Andy Kirk, and the low register like Harold Baker. And, you know, I just leaned toward that cornet sound, you know, like Nat Adderley plays cornet? But it's just a "sound." And it's popular. [Laughs.] You know, like years ago, composers . . . the reason you read about Beethoven was because he was the one they could understand. The other ones, you know, that they couldn't understand, they didn't get mentioned. So my tone must be the easiest for somebody to hear. You know, like Louis Armstrong, that kind of sound.

But, you see, your sound is like, it's like your sweat. You know, it's your "sound." Lester Young had his sound. Coleman Hawkins, Clifford Brown. Fats. You know, there's no more "sound" today. Freddie (Hubbard) has a sound but it's . . . during those days when you didn't hear anybody to copy, guys got their own sound. But now that you have so many records and cassettes, it's not about sound, you know what I mean? That's the reason they can put the sound in a keyboard [a digital sampling device]. But it's the white sound in the keyboard. It's the white trumpet player's sound in the keyboard.

Ben: You can't put the black sound in a digital sampling keyboard?

Miles: Nobody's done it yet.

Ben: That's an interesting point, that before there was such wide recording distribution people were forced to develop their own sounds.

Miles: Forced to play without—they didn't have anything to listen to, you know? But you would watch guys play an instrument and you would like the attitude, the concept, the way it looks, the way they hold it, the way they dress. But nowadays, they have . . . I saw maybe three trumpet players in Lionel Hampton's band, and they were white, right? They all sound alike. Wynton [Marsalis]. He doesn't have a distinctive sound. But Freddie almost has. Woody Shaw is a real creative trumpet player. He's like Dizzy. They might do anything. I mean you can still get a good solo out of Dizzy 'cause he's—he really turned my brain. And Charlie Parker. You know, those guys, they did a number on my head. As far as me learning.

Ben: How did they do it?

Miles: They just opened it up.

Ben: You mean just hearing and watching them?

Miles: See, what they were thinking, it put a stamp on what I was thinking, that it was OK to go like that.

Ben: You mentioned people getting excited just watching a player. I remember you said one time that we could know everything there was to know about your playing by watching how you stand.

Miles: It's a certain way, like when I play, sometimes if I play about that high from the floor [holds his hand out three feet above the floor] it's another sound that you can get . . . there might be one over there [raises his hand higher], maybe one up there, but I never go any higher than that. Standing straight up maybe.

But I found out in Juilliard that if I stayed any longer, you know, I was going to have to play like a white man. I was going to have to act like a white man toward music. The direction, you know what I mean, so I left. Because there was certain things you had to do, or a certain way you had to play to get in there, to be with them. And I didn't come all the way from St. Louis just to be with a white orchestra. You know, I turned down a lot of those.

But I found that I could go my own way. I said to my friend Freddie Webster, I said, "Freddie, I'm going back to St. Louis," and he was one of those who said, "Man, you know if you go to St. Louis, back to St. Louis and them hooges and crackers there, you're going to get mad and blah blah blah . . . you know, you might get killed." So I said, "No, I have to go tell my father that I'm gonna leave Juilliard." He said, "Why don't you call him up?" I said, "Uh uh, not my father. I can't call him up and say I'm going with Bird and they do this and Dizzy is this." You know, my father was a professional man. He was a surgeon. So I caught the train. I went in his office, he looked up and said, "What the fuck are you doing here?" I said, "As soon as you get through." He was working on a patient. He's a dentist. So when he got through I said, "This music is happening, Juilliard isn't, and I'm down on the street where everything is happening. I'm learning more down there, what I want to do, than at Juilliard." My trumpet instructor at Juilliard is still in the Philharmonic Orchestra, New York. But I couldn't do that, you know? So he said, "OK." So I said, "Save your money." So that was it. But I couldn't stay. I couldn't stay.

[He looks at the sketch he's making.] Damn, am I messing up something right now?

I couldn't phone my father from New York and tell him that. Duke Ellington he knew, but not Dizzy and Bird and Monk and Coleman Hawkins. Although we did have a record of Body and Soul. *And Art Tatum. That's the only records we had in our house.*

Ben: Those two records?

Miles: Art Tatum and Duke with Jimmy Blanton. Blanton is from St. Louis, from my hometown. Oh yeah, I had Bird with Jay McShann, Hootie Blues. And Basie. Yeah, we had a few, but that was after I knew what I wanted to hear. 'Cause those bands, those days, Earl Hines and Jimmie Lunceford . . . Sonny Stitt was with the McKinney Cotton Pickers, and they heard about me in St. Louis and they wanted me to go with them, and my mother wouldn't let me go. And I said "Aw, shit!"

Ben: You got there by going to Juilliard instead.

Miles: Right.

Ben: These days you're talking about seem so far away from today. The times, the way the music was treated by players . . .

Miles: Yeah, I know. Something else gets in your mind, in my head, but those are good memories for me, you know.

Ben: It seems people today, even musicians, do have difficulty keeping interested in the music, when in the past it was everything.

Miles: You know, it's because they don't take time out to learn different things. They wouldn't take time out to do that. A jazz musician that you call a jazz musician . . . I was reading this damn thing in The Times *about jazz legends. These legends shouldn't have to call people and ask them can we play here and stuff like that. I don't do that. I would never do that, you know. I didn't get into music just to make money. If I wanted to make money, I know what to do.*

Ben: It seems a major thing has happened to all music, not just jazz, and that is it's moved from music that was *captured* in a recording studio to music that was *manufactured* in a recording studio. It's a whole different premise now the way music is being made. How was recording your latest album, which is done with drum machines and sequencers, different from the way you used to make a record, where you came in with some tunes, did them and left? Do you approach it a lot differently or does it feel the same to you?

Miles: It's easier.

Ben: Really?

Miles: Uh huh. Because I show the guys I'm working with what I want. I write it out or play it. And then by the time I get to the studio, it's all on tape. You feed it right into the board. And all I have to do is play over it. It's easier like that. I went crazy trying to make Decoy. *I mean I threw everything out. Now, I just take a studio, we use a drum machine to keep it in, 'cause I tried to put things together in "Decoy," and they, you know, the ones that didn't have a drum machine, the tempo was doing this and doing that. Musicians feel sad, they have personalities. Like Al Foster, and like some of them want to play and there's no part for them anymore. I can see they don't feel it. But rather than wait for two and three sessions for them to feel like it and learn the composition, to add to the composition, rather than playing over it. Like a lot of guys do, they play too many fucking notes. Like Mike Stern. I tell him all the time. I said, "Mike, you need to go to Notes Anonymous." You know, like Alcoholics Anonymous? I mean, it's much easier now for me.*

Because, you know, like a guy like George Duke, he writes a composition, it's all there, all you have to do is play on it, and respect that man's composition. But you have to pick the people that you want.

You see, my voice is changing because this is very touchy with me. I don't want to fire him. I don't want to fire these guys. But I do want, when a person writes a composition, you have to let that composition soak in. You know what I mean? You have to try to see or hear what the composer wanted, you know, and you have to play that style. Not that you're just gonna play your style in somebody else's music. If they composed it, they didn't want that kind of thing in there. And you gonna do it on every number?

So we don't need that. Or if you're in the rhythm section and the tempo drops, you get mad 'cause somebody tells you the tempo dropped. We don't need that. We have time and it's right there. As long as electricity is on, the tempo is like that. And you don't have to use an excuse like "I can't play with the drum machine," you know, there's no excuse. If you're a musician, if you love music, you would want "Body and Soul" to sound like "Body and Soul."

Ben: Well, what about "Body and Soul," and what about those classic songs?

Miles: *Those songs to me don't exist, you know? I'm not gonna play that shit. We don't have time for "Body and Soul" and "I Got Rhythm," you know? Or "So What" or Kind of Blue. Those things are there. They were done in that era, the right hour, the right day, and it happened. It's over, it's on the record. People ask me why don't you play this? Go buy the record. It's still there. What you like is on the record. You don't like me, and I don't want you to like me because of "Kind of Blue." Like me for what we're doing now, you know?*

I was put here to play music, and interpret music. That's what I do. No attitude, nothing. That's all I want to do. And I do it good. 'Cause my colleagues say "Yeah," you know what I mean, and that's enough for me to keep doing what I do.

I stopped playing the trumpet. Dizzy came over to my house, he said, "What the fuck is wrong with you? Are you crazy or something?" I say, "Man, you better get out of here." He said, "No, I'm not either." He's like my brother, you know? But that's it for me. All the rest, people think I do this, I do that. Yeah, I do that and this I might do a lot of things, but the main thing that I love, that comes before everything, even breathing, is music. That's it, you know. Nothing. I buy Ferraris, yeah, but music is always there. Right here.

Ben: And that means that you're going to have to keep hanging out with musicians.

Miles: *That's right.*

Ben: And you're going to have to keep your ear tuned to the radio, and you're going to have to plug in all the latest equipment?

Miles: *Right.*

Ben: Because you can't go back.

Miles: Uh uh. I can't.

Ben: As we've been sitting here talking, you've been drawing. And it's almost been one gesture, drawing and talking . . .

Miles: Right, it's the same thing.

Ben: I got one more question for you. The song "Nardis." How did you happen to name it "Nardis"?

Miles: I can't remember. It might have had something to do with nuclear power. I wrote it for Cannonball [Adderley]. I think I just liked the name. What does it mean?

Ben: I don't know, but it's my last name backwards.

Miles: No kidding? No kidding. I don't know, but that's a nice name, man.

THE DANISH CONNECTION
GARY GIDDINS

Gary Giddins's review of *Aura* was first published in his November 14, 1989, "Weather Bird" column in the *Village Voice*. Palle Mikkelborg wrote this ambitious ten-movement feature for Miles Davis, Giddins points out, in honor of Davis capturing the 1984 Sonning Music Award, Denmark's highest honor for lifetime achievement in the arts. Previously, the Sonning prize had been given only to composers and soloists of European extraction: Copland, Bernstein, Messiaen, Stravinsky, Isaac Stern. In his memoir Miles Davis said, "I was the first jazz musician and the first black ever to win it. . . . I was happy and honored that they gave me that award."

A few months after the Sonning was announced, Davis traveled to Copenhagen to record *Aura*. It was Davis's first recording with a large orchestra since his work with Gil Evans in the early 1960s and quite a departure from the cut-and-paste jobs Davis had done for the past fifteen years in the studios with Teo Macero and Marcus Miller.

Giddins's piece discusses the various parallels between *Aura* and Davis's past work: the two-note riff reminiscent of "So What," brass voicings similar to Gil Evans's, a bass and piano section that sounds like *Miles in the Sky.* But despite the mélange of musical references, funky rhythms, and a ten-note tone row spelling Miles

Davis, *Aura* is a primarily a vehicle for Davis's "wounded sound." That alone makes it an important constituent of Davis's recorded oeuvre.

About Mikkelborg's composition, Davis said in *Miles: The Autobiography,* "I think it's a masterpiece. I really do." Giddins is inclined to agree: "For me, it was Davis's best recording in at least six years since the release of *Star People.*"

Miles Davis's new Columbia release, *Aura,* not to be confused with his tepid new Warners release, *Amandla,* is his most satisfying recorded work in several years—perhaps since the 1983 *Star People,* with which it has some continuity. There's no surprise in that: *Aura* was recorded in early 1985. Thus its belated appearance, just in time to partake of the publicity surrounding the publication of *Miles: the Autobiography,* evinces no signs of renewal; but it does solve a puzzle in the Davis discography. *Aura* is no mere compilation of live performances or studio outtakes, but a singular and ambitious suite by the Danish composer and trumpeter Palle Mikkelborg, who considers it one of his finest compositions. For his part, Miles, sounding rather like Holden Caulfield, says, in *Miles,* "I think it's a masterpiece, I really do." What's more, he blames Columbia's handling of it for his departure from the company.

In November 1984 Davis was awarded the Sonning Music Award, a Danish prize previously reserved for musicians in the, ahem, educated European tradition (Stravinsky, Messiaen, Bernstein, and Copland are a few recipients). In honor of the occasion, Mikkelborg composed *Aura,* which was recorded the following February when Davis returned to Denmark. A large Danish orchestra—more than 30 participants, though not at the same time—was augmented for the sessions by percussionists Vince Wilburn (Davis's nephew) and Marilyn Mazur (who later joined his band), and guitarist John McLaughlin, who had played so pivotal a role at the dawn of Davis's fusion conversion 20 years ago. Davis isn't precise about what happened next, but apparently Columbia withheld funds midway through the project and Davis had to get an NEA grant to finish it. For five years it lay in the CBS vaults. Now that they have put it out, they've done something less than a fastidious job: insufficient information (no dates), incorrect banding of two movements ("Red" and "Green"), and the absence of any clue on the cover as to what this album is all about. You have to hunt the small print of the liner notes to find the odd credit: "All songs by Palle Mikkelborg."

It doubtless salves Davis's Promethean ego to have the cover to himself, and some justification can be adduced in the inspirational motive behind the work, not to mention the fact that the composer could never have gotten his music distributed here without the fronting of a celebrity soloist. Other than Gil Evans, Davis has refused to share his covers with anyone, and at least once he failed to credit even Evans in small print or large. For that matter, the Warners albums are essentially star vehicles for Davis engineered by Marcus Miller. That's the way it's done in America: in the '30s and '40s composers and arrangers were the invisible men of big band music; before and after the Swing Era, name performers occasionally forced songwriters to share credits and royalties. Beyond that socially condoned blackmail, there is the competitive nature of show biz itself, which favors the perception of solitary genius. I once asked Howlin' Wolf why he never listed the names of his musicians on his album jackets and he retorted, "Why should I? They're my records." Still, throughout *Miles,* Davis rightly and often eloquently bemoans the lack of seriousness accorded jazz. Surely he can recognize that releasing the present album as "*Aura:* Miles Davis" is like putting out an album of piano concertos as "*Emperor:* Mauricio Pollini," with inner-sleeve acknowledgment of a conductor and orchestra and a tiny production credit reading, "All songs by Beethoven."

In other words, although *Aura* is as much about Davis and his music as it is a vehicle for him, it is a long and complicated semiserial suite that stands out among his recent recordings precisely because the setting focuses and underscores his strengths with fierce compositional urgency. Mikkelborg's Nordic sensibility is like a slab of ice in the midnight sun, imbued with Ivesian fog and Messiaenic twitterings, and wholly congruent with Davis's electric and rhythmic seasonings, his contemplative vanity, and tenacious reveries. Davis's piquant sound humanizes the brew, but it's Mikkelborg's brew—Davis doesn't even appear on two of the 10 movements.

The piece's overall structure is audacious, eclectic, and loose, yet it aligns the most durable modes and postures of Davis's post-'69 music, thus making a case for them while adding to the oeuvre. Occasionally, the composer adds sly references to earlier Davis periods too, as when the orchestra's two-note riff echoes "So What" during "Blue," or when the Gil Evans connection to both soloist and composer is made manifest in the brass voicings of "Green," or when Thomas Clausen's piano and Niels-Henning Orsted Pedersen's bass (Miles is absent) recall in "Indigo" the complexity of rhythmic interaction that had peaked in Davis's last acoustic milestone, *Miles in the Sky.* For the most part, however, *Aura* is a bewitching affirmation of the deluge that followed his seemingly incidental discovery of the Fender Rhodes. Like the rousing and largely ignored *Tribute to Jack Johnson* in 1970, it smacks of the optimism that the initial jazz-rock alliance promised. That it proceeds from a Schoenbergian gimmick, a 10-note row corresponding to the letters spelling *Miles Davis,* shows how evenhanded consolidations have become.

Mikkelborg is probably best-known in this country for the rich orchestrations of his 1975 collaboration with Dexter Gordon, *More Than You Know,* on Steeple-Chase. From 1964, when he was 23, he was associated with the Danish Radio Jazz Group and Big Band for more than a decade, often as leader. Highly regarded as a trumpet player, he worked with all the major visiting players, and led various ensembles, including a trio with the talented Bill Evans-inspired Clausen and the phenomenal Niels-Henning. For a while he toured with a band that included the Norwegian guitarist Terje Rypdal, and it's impossible to listen to parts of *Aura* without thinking of Rypdal's ECM sessions and his glacial chords, hanging ominously in the wintry night. Inspired by Davis as a player and composer, he has fashioned for him a montage of blackbeat rhythms and modes, held together by the signature row; Davis's wounded sound is contrasted with the full weight of an orchestra for the first time since he worked with Evans in the early '60s, and his response is largely kinetic and piping.

Davis's solos here haven't the level, midregister, plaintive lyricism that practically invited lyrics, but they are animated by an unequivocal intensity, which keeps him leaping into the high end and chewing on the relentless rhythmic figures (tersely accentuated by Wilburn's electric drums) like a cat just let out of the house. Some of his finest moments are pockets of low pitches, but they are intermittent and brief—he soon skyrockets away from them. The "Intro" emerges from the ether as slowly as *Daphne and Chloe:* McLaughlin states the serial theme and exchanges solos with Davis. In "White," Davis plays the most lyrical figure in the work, but almost immediately recedes from it for a strangely dejected overdubbed duet (conversation with himself); the effect is not unlike the march-and-meditation of his and Evans's "Saeta." "Yellow," without Miles, is an orchestration of "White" with key parts assigned to harp, oboe, and bells.

"Orange" and "Red" are among Davis's strongest performances of the '80s, the former a succession of coherent solos by McLaughlin and Davis, first muted and then open, punctuated by brief transitions, and the latter a torrid trumpet solo paced with characteristic deliberation over a fixed mode and nervy rhythmic vamp. Apparently "Red" is misbanded on the

CD, clocking at 9:52 instead of the correct 6:00; its second half, a shroud of synthesized chords that reverberate like Gregorian chant plus a Bo Stief bass solo, is actually the first half of "Green." The second half of "Green" is another highlight, Davis actually responding to another soloist of comparable faculty, Niels-Henning, in a setting embellished by the wordless choir of a singer, Eva Thaysen, overdubbed 16 times. *Aura* loses some of its direction in the next three movements, though Davis plays with sunny élan in the reggae-buoyed "Blue," followed by another version of "Red," this one muted, and "Indigo," something of a non sequitur for piano and bass. The closing "Violet," a still-water blues, pulls it back on track, with McLaughlin filling in Davis's rests, and both men soloing with patient finesse over a dense organ chord. As Davis records of the past decade go, *masterpiece* is probably not too strong a claim. As for Mikkelborg, *Aura* should recommend him to a wider audience, and to other soloists who long to hear themselves in a richly textured setting.

In Francis Davis's view, Miles Davis's career can be viewed as one continuous reaction to bebop—that "impossible combination of the breakneck and the Byzantine" that so captivated the trumpeter when he was coming up. Perhaps as an overcompensation for the vagaries of his hard-driving lifestyle, Davis's less-is-more sensibility can be seen in all phases of his work: in his nonet's taming of bebop; in his downhome small group work of the '50s; in his rejection of chord structures and his embrace of modal jazz; in his incorporation of dance rhythms and spacy, background dreamscapes; even in the repackaging of chunks of his recorded work by studio technicians.

Miles Davis's desire to pare down and simplify things was a constant in his life. But, as Gary Tomlinson has argued, Davis's mediation of extremes strikes to the very heart of his being. Most obvious is Davis's "insider's lifestyle and outsider's stance," as Francis Davis has put it, situated between bourgeois privilege and the marginalized place afforded Davis by the dominant white culture. Less obvious is Davis's bisexuality, a wedding of difference that was hidden from public view.

Already a jazz improviser and fierce individualist, in 1944 Davis attended the Juilliard School of Music, an institution for whites that encouraged instrumental uniformity. On the street, with his allowance and preppy clothes, he drank malts and ate pastries while his colleagues poured shots and did drugs. Davis's trumpet sound was introspective; his English brash and laden with obscenities. His ballads were breathtakingly exquisite; his exquisite women were smacked breathless.

Over the years, Davis's bands celebrated extremes by incorporating black and white musicians of varying styles. As Miles Davis told Amiri Baraka in 1985, "White musicians are overtrained and black musicians are undertrained. You got to mix the two . . . you got more to work with." Ultimately, as this excerpt from Francis Davis's book *Bebop and Nothingness* points out, the trendsetter becomes the trend follower.

In *Miles: The Autobiography,* the trumpeter Miles Davis remembers his excitement at hearing the Billy Eckstine Orchestra, with Charlie Parker and Dizzy Gillespie, in a St. Louis nightclub in 1944. "It was a motherfucker," Davis writes of his first in-person exposure to bebop, and also his baptism by fire as a musician. "The way that band was playing music— that was *all* I wanted to hear."

Davis's reaction was typical of that of most young musicians in the 1940s. What thrilled them about bebop was its impossible combination of the breakneck and the Byzantine. It was all they wanted to hear and all that they wanted to play. But an early mark of Davis's singularity was that soon after becoming Gillespie's protégé and Parker's sideman, he also became their loyal opposition. "Diz and Bird played a lot of real fast notes and chord changes because that's the way they heard everything; that's the way their voices were: fast, up in the upper register," Davis observes in *Miles,* which was written in collaboration with the poet and journalist Quincy Troupe. "Their concept of music was *more* rather than less. I personally wanted to cut the notes down."

Davis's entire career can be seen as an ongoing critique of bop: the origins of "cool" jazz (his collaborations with Gil Evans in the late 1940s), hard bop or "funky" (his 1954 recording of "Walkin'"), modal improvisation (the track "Milestones" in 1958 and the 1959 album *Kind of Blue*), and jazz-rock fusion (*In a Silent Way* and *Bitches Brew,* both recorded in 1969) can be traced to his efforts to pare bop to its essentials. His decision, in 1969, to court a younger audience by playing rock venues, adding amplified instruments to his ensemble, and cranking up both the volume and the beat, also amounted to a critique of modern jazz, which he felt had become tired and inbred. So, in effect, did his withdrawal from recording studios and public performance from 1975 to 1980, years in which "sex and drugs took the place that music had occupied in my life until then, and I did both of them around the clock." He barely touched his horn in these years, but he haunted jazz with his silence.

Two generations of listeners now feel that Davis has sold them out: jazz fans of a certain age who have never forgiven him for going electric, and the rock audience that discovered him with *Bitches Brew* and—try as it might—can't get with the slick, techno-funk he's been recording since *The Man with the Horn*, in 1981. The audience he has his sights on now, though he's unlikely to reach it without a hit single, is the audience that grooves to Prince and Michael Jackson. And commercial survival doesn't seem to be his only motivation. Ego, racial identity, and a desire for eternal youth (or continuing relevance) all seem to be mixed up in it.

For many of his more worshipful fans, of all ages and races, Davis's music has always been just one component of a mystique that also involves his beautiful women, his up-to-the-minute wardrobe, his expensive taste in sports cars, and his scowling black anger: his celebrity boils down to an insider's lifestyle and an outsider's stance. (Or as Ornette Coleman once put it, Miles is a black man who lives like a white man.) His magnetism is so powerful that fans who haven't liked anything he's done in years continue to buy his records and attend his concerts, irrationally hoping for a reversal of form.

On stage he remains an electrifying presence, though you wonder (as you do with Dizzy Gillespie, but for a different reason) not how well he'll play, but how *much*. He's become a kind of roving conductor, walking from sideman to sideman, describing what he wants from them with a pump of his shoulders or a wiggle of his hips, blowing riffs into their faces and letting them pick it up from there. He still turns his back on the audience for much of a show, as he was infamous for doing in the fifties and sixties. The difference is that now he has a wireless microphone on his horn that allows him to be heard clearly with his back turned—and that audiences would be disappointed, at this point, if he failed to strike his iconic pose. Though his shows are never boring, you're not quite sure how you feel about them afterwards. Is Davis admirable, as his apologists would have it, for refusing to rest on his laurels—for keeping up with the latest black musical and sartorial fashions? Or is there something pathetic about the sight of a sixty-three-year-old man in clogs, parachute pants, and jheri curls shaking his fanny to a younger generation's beat?

"When I hear jazz musicians today playing all those same licks we used to play so long ago, I feel sad for them," he writes.

> Most people my age like old, stuffy furniture. I like the new Memphis style of sleek high-tech stuff . . . Bold colors and long, sleek, spare lines. I don't like a lot of clutter or a lot of furniture either. I like the contemporary stuff. I have to always be on the cutting edge of things because that's just the way I am and have always been.

Anyone this vigilant about staying on "the cutting edge" is chasing trends—not starting them, as Davis did in jazz from the late forties to the early seventies (*Bitches Brew* and most of the double albums that followed it, though turbid in retrospect, were undeniably influential at the time).

Davis has two new releases in the stores, one of which is so shockingly good that you're slightly disappointed in it for not being perfect. *Aura* (Columbia C2X 45332), recorded in 1985, is a ten-part orchestral work by the Danish composer Palle Mikkelborg (who is also a Davis-influenced trumpeter, though he doesn't solo here); it bears the influence of certain pieces from the early seventies by George Russell, an American composer who was then living in Denmark. More boldly than Russell's works of that period, *Aura* attempts to reconcile electronically generated and acoustically produced sonorities, advanced harmonies and a big, crunching beat. The work sags in places: a duet between Davis and the bassist Niels-Henning Orsted Pedersen has too much New Age gloss surrounding it, as do the passages dominated by woodwinds. But a number of the ten sections cagily evoke Davis's landmark collaborations with Gil Evans, and three sections—subtitled "Red," "Blue," and "Electric Red"—are spectacular in their endless permutations of the work's initial ten-note theme and static but oddly compelling 7/8 rhythm. On these three sections in particular, Davis responds to the orchestra with ecstatic, sustained improvisations that give an idea of what he's still capable of when challenged.

Amandla (Warner Brothers 25873-1) is more current and more typical of Davis's 1980s output. It has its virtues, not least among them its yeasty rhythms; Davis and his producer, the multi-instrumentalist Marcus Miller (who wrote most of the tunes) have obviously been listening to zouk and other African dance music. But too much of *Amandla* sounds like generic instrumental funk, with Davis playing sound stylist rather than improviser—in contrast to the alto saxophonist Kenny Garrett, whose brief solos inventively harmonize the signature attributes of two of his predecessors in Davis's group: Wayne Shorter's ascetic spatial sense and Cannonball Adderley's preacherly bonhomie. Davis, in a rare act of noblesse oblige, guest-stars on two tracks of Garrett's *Prisoner of Love* (Atlantic), a disappointing exercise in saxophone smooch-and-groove à la Grover Washington, Jr. Even without consulting the personnel, you'd recognize Miles by that hornetlike middle-register buzz of his. He exudes presence, but he puts so little of himself into his solos that he sounds like he's being sampled.

Aura notwithstanding, Davis's major accomplishment of recent years is *Miles,* which enjoys an obvious advantage over the Davis biographies by Ian Carr, Jack Chambers, Eric Nisenson, and Bill Cole. Without the full involvement of their subject, these were essentially turntable companions—critical guides to Davis's work within a biographical framework. But with *Miles,* Davis proves to be his own most perceptive critic (at least about his music before 1969), and the book is so successful in capturing Davis's voice (including his incessant, if tonally varied, use of profanity) that the odd line that sounds like the doing of Troupe (as when, for example, Davis supposedly resorts to quoting a jazz critic to describe the dramatic contrast between his style and that of his former sideman John Coltrane) calls for a double take.

"The challenge . . . is to see how melodically inventive you can become," Davis writes, giving the most succinct explanation I've ever read of the advantages of improvising on modes or scales rather than chord changes. "It's not like when you base stuff on chords, and you know at the end of thirty-two bars that the chords have run out and there's nothing to do but repeat what you've done with variations." *Kind of Blue,* which popularized modal improvisation, was the most influential jazz album of its period, but it was a disappointment of sorts for Davis, he writes. The sound he wanted on *Kind of Blue,* and feels he didn't quite achieve, was that of the "finger piano" (probably an African thumb piano) that accompanied a performance he saw by an African ballet troupe. Though Davis himself doesn't make the connection, what an unexpected rationale this provides for the three electric pianos that phase in and out behind the horns on *In a Silent Way!*

He writes about fellow musicians with an eye for detail that brings them into photograph-like focus. On Gil Evans, for example:

When I first met him, he used to come to listen to Bird when I was in the band. He come in with a whole bag of "horseradishes"—that's what we used to call radishes—that he'd be eating with salt. Here was this tall, thin, white guy from Canada who was hipper than hip . . . But bringing "horseradishes" to nightclubs and eating them out of a bag with salt, and a white boy? Here was Gil on fast 52nd Street with all these super hip black musicians wearing peg legs and zoot suits, and here he was dressed in a cap. Man, he was something else.

Though acknowledging Charlie Parker's genius, Davis characterizes him as "a greedy motherfucker" who "was always trying to con or beat you out of something to support his drug habit."

Bird always said he hated the idea of being thought of as just an entertainer, but . . . he was becoming a spectacle. I didn't like whites walking into the club where we were playing just to see Bird act a fool, thinking he might do something stupid.

Miles's considerable value as jazz history isn't what makes it such a page-turner. Autobiography is a problematical literary form, because it's never clear which is being submitted for the reader's approval, a book or its author. Davis writes that he loved Parker as a musician, but "maybe not as a person," and the Miles Davis who emerges from *Miles*—as complex as any character in recent fiction—elicits a similar ambivalence from the reader.

His treatment of women is contemptible: it seems like he's slugging another one every twenty pages or so. It isn't bad enough that he talks with unconvincing remorse of hitting his own women; a story intended to establish Billy Eckstine's tough-guy credentials has Eckstine slapping a would-be girlfriend while Davis looks on admiringly. He's spiteful toward the actress Cicely Tyson, the most recent of his ex-wives, for whom he professes not to have felt "the sex thing" after their marriage.

Cicely has done movie and TV roles where she played an activist or something like that, a person who cared a lot about black people. Well, she ain't nothing like that. She loves to sit up with white people, loves to listen to their advice about everything and believes everything they tell her.

Davis's fame and his relatively privileged upbringing haven't spared him from injustice, such as being clubbed over the head by a white policeman after he was ordered to move on from the entrance of a New York City nightclub in which he was performing in 1959. But much of what Davis interprets as racism is his own hubris, as when he accuses white jazz critics of having written in the mid-sixties of such black avant-gardists as Ornette Coleman, Cecil Taylor, and Archie Shepp in an effort to deflect attention from *him*. (Never mind that the critics most identified with what was then called "The New Thing" were Amiri Baraka and A.B. Spellman, both of whom are black.) He's peacock vain. He tells of admiring himself in a mirror in 1956, when his star was on the rise. He wasn't yet making as much money as he thought he should be, but he was looking "clean" in Brooks Brothers and custom-made Italian suits. "I felt so good that I walked to the door and forgot my trumpet."

He writes of getting together every so often with the late James Baldwin in France and "lying our asses off." You have to wonder, as you do with all autobiographies, how much lying is being done here. Probably not a lot, because for a man this caught up in his own mystique—a man fully aware that his art and life are already the stuff of legend—just telling the truth about himself as he sees it amounts to a form of self-aggrandizement.

Pearl Cleage may be the only woman to take umbrage with Miles Davis's battering of women and write about it. In her piece, Cleage begins by discussing her association with Davis's music, which began in the late '70s when a friend, A. B. Spellman, taped for her *Kind of Blue*. Davis's record became an important part of her mythology because it served as the soundtrack of choice when romance was at hand. "Miles was perfect," she writes. "Restrained, but hip. Passionate, but cool." It gave "the gentleman caller an immediate understanding of what kind of woman he was dealing with."

Yet years later Cleage had the unsettling experience of reading Miles Davis's memoir and at last learning what kind of a man accompanied her hours of lovemaking. Ironically, it was someone who hated women, or at least hated some of them some of the time. That was enough to make her contemplate throwing Davis's music out with the trash. In Cleage's mind, buying, even listening to, Davis's music was tantamount to condoning his contemptible way of life, which included repeated crimes against women without any sense of remorse.

I thought I wasn't going to be able to write this piece at all. I had been avoiding it for a month. Trying to think of something else to say. Something funny. After all, we are gathered here to celebrate our creative genius. Not to talk about men beating women and five-a-day domestic murders and all that "sexist shit."

That wasn't the reason I almost didn't do the piece, though. I almost didn't do the piece because I thought Miles Davis had put a hex on me. I thought somehow he had found out that I was writing a piece suggesting that *he is guilty of self-confessed violent crimes against women such that we should break his albums, burn his tapes and scratch up his CDs until he acknowledges and apologizes and rethinks his position on The Woman Question.*

That sounds terrible doesn't it? Breaking Miles Davis records? Because of a few mistakes in his personal life? Next thing you know, I'll be fussing about 2 Live Crew just because they don't know the difference between rape and reciprocity . . .

But I'm getting ahead of myself. I hadn't even written the piece yet. I was just thinking about it. Well, I was a little closer than that. I was sitting down to write it, but I needed to have the records. The albums in my own collection that would provide my personal connection to the subject. I needed to hear the music playing beside me in order to remember why I had been avoiding this question so energetically. And why I was so mad at Miles.

I remembered distinctly, one evening, several months ago when I was feeling particularly well organized, I pulled out the five Miles Davis records that I own and put them aside until it was time to write. But when I needed them back, I couldn't find them anywhere. I looked in all the places where they should have been. Nothing.

Finally on my third trip down to the basement for one last look, a thought popped into my mind that made my blood run cold. He knows! Miles Davis made my records disappear because somebody told him I was going to write a piece that said *he is guilty of self-confessed violent crimes against women such that we should break his albums, burn his tapes and scratch up his CDs until he acknowledges and apologizes and agrees to rethink his position on The Woman Question.*

Didn't sound quite as bad that time, did it? The idea of it, I mean. Just the idea that we could hold a black man responsible for crimes against black women. It's still a pretty heady thought, though, and not necessarily one I thought Miles would endorse, especially since he is the one I'm so mad at.

But there's a reason for that! He's the one who admitted to it. Almost bragged about it. He's the one who confessed in print and then proudly signed his name. Nobody was ever able to show me where David Ruffin admitted to hitting Tammi Terrell in the head with a hammer, even though on the West Side of Detroit where I grew up we had all heard it from somebody who said it like they had the inside line on such things.

Mad at Miles

And nobody was able to provide me with a quote from Bill Withers describing how he beat up Denise Nicholas when their marriage was grinding to a painfully public close although people tell me *Jet* covered the whole episode in great and gory detail.

But Miles . . . well, I'll let the brother speak for himself. This is an excerpt from *Miles: The Autobiography* by Miles Davis with Quincy Troupe:

Cicely was especially jealous of a woman taking her place in my life, but after a while she didn't have no place in my life, even though she turned down a lot of movie offers just to stay around me. Cicely's like two different women, one nice, the other one totally fucked up. For example, she used to bring her friends around anytime she wanted, but she didn't want my friends coming around. And she had some friends who I couldn't stand. One time we argued about one friend in particular, and I just slapped the shit out of her. She called the cops and went down into the basement and was hiding there. When the police came, they asked me where she was. I said, "She's around here someplace. Look down in the basement." The cop looked in the basement and came back and said, "Miles, nobody's down there but a woman, and she won't talk to me. She won't say nothing."

So I said, "That's her, and she's doing the greatest acting job ever." Then the cop said he understood—she didn't look like she was hurt or nothing. I said, "Well, she ain't hurt bad; I just slapped her once."

The cop said, "Well, Miles, you know when we get these calls we have to investigate."

"Well, if she's beating my ass you gonna come with your guns ready, too?" I asked him.

"They just laughed and left. Then I went down and told Cicely, "I told you to tell your friend not to call over here no more. Now if you don't tell him, I'm gonna tell him." She ran to the phone and called him up and told him, "Miles don't want me talking to you anymore." Before I knew it, I had slapped her again. So she never did pull that kind of shit on me again.

The truth is, this is all my friend A.B.'s fault. It was wintertime. My train got into D.C. early and I caught the Metro out to his house. By the time I got there, there was a fire in the fireplace, his wife Karen was up drinking coffee and the kids were wandering around in their nightgowns, demanding breakfast.

Karen and A.B.'s house used to be a nun's dormitory and they still have a built-in receptacle for Holy Water in the room where A.B. keeps his records, which is only fitting since A.B. has the most *divine* records of anybody I have ever known. Most of them are so rare and hard to find that you can't even think about stealing them because when he spots them at your house later, you'd have to say something lame and unconvincing like: "Yeah, man, I was really lucky to find that record of the Brazilian drummers. I know! Just like that one you used to have before you lost it." You wouldn't have a chance.

And A.B. doesn't just have a lot of records, he knows a lot about music, most especially about jazz. Which is why I asked him to suggest something that might help me understand about trumpets. I didn't make it any more specific than that because it wasn't any more specific than that. I wanted to understand as much about trumpets as I had learned about saxophones from talking to A.B. about John Coltrane.

I was an innocent. He could have given me anybody. But he gave me Miles Davis. *Kind of Blue.* And he didn't even warn me that *Miles was guilty of self-confessed violent crimes against women such that we ought to break his records, burn his tapes and scratch up his CDs until he acknowledges and apologizes and agrees to rethink his position on The Woman Question.*

(It gets easier to say the more you say it. It's starting to sound almost legitimate, isn't it?)

I know I was late, the album having been recorded in March of 1959 when I was only eleven years old and if Smokey Robinson wasn't singing it, there was no way I was going to hear it, and this being the late seventies and all, but I didn't care. I was amazed by the music. I loved it, listened to it, couldn't get enough. A.B. was pleased that his choice had been the right one and he taped the record for me before I left so I could listen to it on the train.

Which is, of course, what I did. I spent the night curled up in my tiny roomette watching America roll by outside my window and listening to Miles Davis play me into the next phase of my life.

The Bohemian Woman Phase. The single again after a decade of married phase. The last time I had a date I was eighteen and oh, god, now I'm thirty phase. The in need of a current vision of who and what and why I am phase. The cool me out quick cause I'm hanging by a thread phase.

For this frantic phase, Miles was perfect. Restrained, but hip. Passionate, but cool. He became a permanent part of the seduction ritual. Chill the wine. Light the candles. Put on a little early Miles. Give the gentleman caller an immediate understanding of what kind of woman he was dealing with. This was not a woman whose listening was confined to the vagaries of the Top 40. This was a woman with the *possibility* of an interesting past, and the *probability* of an interesting future.

This was the woman I was learning to be, and I will confess that I spent many memorable evenings sending messages of great personal passion through the intricate improvisations of *Kind of Blue* when blue was the furthest thing from my mind and Miles, like I said, was perfect.

But I didn't know then that *he was guilty of self-confessed violent crimes against women such that we ought to break his records, burn his tapes and scratch up his CDs until he acknowledges and apologizes and agrees to rethink his position on The Woman Question.*

Still sounds pretty scary, doesn't it? Scratching up CDs and burning cassettes. Pretty right-wing stuff, I know, but what are we going to do? Either we think it's a crime to hit us or we don't. Either we think our brothers have to take responsibility for stopping the war against us, or we don't.

And if we do, can we keep giving our money to Miles Davis so that he can buy a Malibu beach house and terrorize our sisters in it?

Can we make love to the rhythms of "a little early Miles" when he may have spent the morning of the day he recorded the music slapping one of our sisters in the mouth?

Can we continue to celebrate the genius in the face of the monster?

When I asked a musician friend of mine if he had read the letter in a national magazine from a woman who said Miles had settled out of court with her in a suit charging him with extreme physical and mental cruelty during the course of their lengthy professional friendship and subsequent love affair, my friend the musician said, *"Is that the one he beat up at the airport?"*

As opposed, I guess, to the one he beat up in her apartment, or in the backseat of his limo. Or, well, you can see how complicated the problem gets . . .

I tried to just forget about it. But that didn't work. I kept thinking about Cicely Tyson hiding in the basement of her house while the police were upstairs laughing with Miles. I wondered what she was thinking about, crouched down there in the darkness. I wondered if thinking about his genius made her less frightened and humiliated.

I wondered if his genius made it possible for her to forgive him for *self-confessed violent crimes against women such that we ought to break his records, burn his tapes and scratch up his CDs until he acknowledges and apologizes and agrees to rethink his position on The Woman Question.*

(Didn't sound bad at all that time, did it?)

I wondered if she tried to remember the last time she had known a brother whose genius was not in the way he played a horn, or made a living or ran a city, but in the way he loved her.

The danger is that we have gone so long without asking the question that we have forgotten the answer.

The danger is that we have gone so long taking what we can get that we have forgotten what we wanted.

But I can't stop thinking about it. I can't stop wondering what we would do if the violence was against black men instead of black women. Would we forgive the perpetrator so quickly and allow him into our private time; our spiritual moments; our sweet surrenders?

I can't stop wondering what our reaction would be if, say, Kenny G— a resourceful, crossover white male who is selling well enough in our community these days to tie with Anita Baker and Luther Vandross as the seduction music of choice for black urban professionals between the ages of twenty and forty-five . . .

. . . What if Kenny G was revealed to be kicking black men's asses all over the country in between concert appearances and recording sessions?

What if Kenny G wrote a book saying that sometimes he had to slap black men around a little just to make them cool out and leave him the fuck alone so he could get some peace and quiet?

What if Kenny G said this black man who saved his life and rescued his work and restored his mind pissed him off so bad one day he had to slap the shit out of him? *Twice.*

Would Kenny G be the music we would play to center and calm ourselves?

Would Kenny G be the music we would play to relax and focus the person we love on romance?

Would Kenny G be the music we would play when our black male friends came to call?

And if we did and they questioned us about it—and you know they would question us about it!—would we explain our continuing support of Kenny G's music by saying: "Yeah, I know he's beating black men and all that, but this white boy is a musical genius! I don't let personal stuff get

in the way of my appreciation of his music. After all, the brothers probably asked for it. You know how it is when y'all start naggin' and shit."

So the question is: How can they hit us and still be our heroes?

And the question is: How can they hit us and still be our leaders? Our
husbands?

Our lovers? Our geniuses? Our friends?

And the answer is . . . they can't.

Can they?

MEMORIES OF MILES
MARC CRAWFORD

Marc Crawford was a friend of Miles Davis for more than thirty years. Crawford first introduced Davis to Alex Haley, which ultimately led to the famous *Playboy* interview, as well as James Baldwin, which spawned a friendship of some twenty years.

Marc Crawford's touching obituary of Miles Davis, which originally appeared in the Brooklyn newspaper *Daily Challenge,* uses a paradigm devised by P. R. Sarkas to assess Davis's lifetime of accomplishments. Sarkas had written that most of humanity are members of one of four groups: warrior, laborer, acquisitor, and intellectual. (Although Crawford doesn't say so, it is implied that exceptional humans are members of two or more groups.) As Crawford sees it, Davis unquestionably belonged to all but the laborer category, and even with them he had a "loving rapport."

The warrior in Davis was best manifested by his overcoming heroin addiction. Davis the intellectual hated black middle-class pretentiousness and "the intellectual dishonesty of racist whites." Davis was also a quick learner and could explain complex music phenomena to the layman, the hallmark of a true educator.

As for being an acquisitor, Davis was a tough negotiator and made an unprecedented fortune in a marginal line of work. And despite his background and privileged status, Davis felt at home with black working folks and wanted them in his audience wherever he played. Late in life Davis would maintain that his music was written to reach all his people.

At some point it seems the late Miles Davis decided to get even with life for taking him through all those changes. In *Miles,* his 1989 autobiography, he wrote: "As long as I could get what I needed from the white world on my own terms, without selling myself out to all those people who love to exploit me, then I was going to go for what I know is real. When you're creating your own shit, man, even the sky ain't the limit."

At times, this legendary trumpeter/composer/bandleader was the world's most celebrated, highest paid and influential jazzman. On November 13, 1988 at the Alhambra Palace in Granada, Spain, he was knighted and inducted into the Knights of Malta, an order which grew out of the crusades in the 11th century. On July 18, 1991 the French government bestowed upon the 65 year-old musician its highest honor. Miles was made a Chevalier of The Legion of Honor. Minister of Culture Jacque Lang called him the "Picasso of jazz," and told Miles: "France has a very special kind of love for you." Lang continued: "With Miles Davis, you are in a constant musical adventure. . . . He has been able to cross all the eras while staying eternally avant garde."

On September 28, 1991, Miles Dewey Davis III, died at St. John's Hospital and Health Center in Santa Monica, Calif., from pneumonia, respiratory failure and stroke. His final resting place will be a mausoleum across from Duke Ellington in Woodlawn Cemetery.

The Rev. Jesse Jackson said at a recent Manhattan memorial service at St. Peter's Lutheran Church: "He was our music man, leaning back, blowing out of his horn, out of his soul, all the beauty and pain and sadness and determination and wishful longing of our lives. He would growl his independence and ours out of his horn. And sometimes by turning his back as he played a solitary song, he would only let us hear him talking to God."

Mayor David N. Dinkins called Miles's music "a profoundly African American form" and expressed the gratitude of eight million New Yorkers.

In an Oct. 1 editorial, titled "Miles Ahead," the *New York Times* wrote: ". . . Mr. Davis' genius emerged in his 20's, with the 'Birth of Cool' recordings. He recorded prolifically and changed constantly, breaking fresh ground with his revolutionary bands in the 1960's, then forging adventurously into the 70's and 80's—when, in sequins and enormous dark glasses, he looked and occasionally sounded like a rock star. His work spoke at once to old and young, though what the old relished as classic Miles, the young might consider square . . . One of his albums was called 'Miles Ahead.' And he was: an American original, as cool as they come."

Most people fit into only one of four social divisions which Indian scholar P.R. Sarkas identifies as warrior, intellectual, acquisitor and common laborer. But Miles Davis was a charter member of the first three and enjoyed a loving rapport with the last.

As a warrior, perhaps Miles' greatest victory was the conquest of his own heroin addiction in the early 1950s. "I made up my mind I was getting off dope," he told me more than 30 years ago. "I was sick and tired of it. You know you can get tired of anything. You can even get tired of being scared.

"I laid down and stared at the ceiling for 12 days and I cursed everybody I didn't like. I was kicking it the hard way. It was like having a bad case of flu only worse. I lay in a cold sweat, my nose and eyes ran. I threw up everything I tried to eat. My pores opened up and I smelled like chicken soup. Then it was over."

Resurrected and reinvented, Miles marched ever after to the beat of a different drummer: "Life is absurd," wrote the French writer Albert Camus, adding, "but it would be cowardly not to live it." Like one of Camus' characters, Miles asserted his humanity by rebelling against all that he could not abide.

"He's got a mean streak in him a mile wide," some said. Others called him an "evil genius."

"It had to put a hard crust on him," said Miles' father. "There was always somebody trying to get him back on dope again. He had an iron will that broke it and that will power applied to everything he did as a result. I'm proud of him."

James Baldwin, one of Miles' favorite people, used to say that "a writer lives by his private cunning and public cowardice." But Miles, the musician, became an in-your-face warrior who looked the world dead in the eye.

"I don't think nothing about death," he told me. "I should have been dead a long time ago. But it missed me when I was on dope. Some people accuse me of being mean and a racist because I don't bow and scrape. When they look in my eyes and don't see no fear they know it's a draw."

Miles did not suffer fools easily, turned his back on audiences, refused autograph seekers, performed few benefits, and as rule did as he pleased.

"I don't do nothing unless I want to. And if I do, they got to pay enough money so I can forget I didn't want to do it after it's all over. I don't think about critics. I'm the first critic and if I get past me it's alright and I'm too vain to play anything bad."

"So what?"

"That's your problem, you work it out!"

"You wouldn't need no NAACP if every Black man stood up straight and met situations head on."

Back in the 50s he underwent throat surgery and doctors ordered him not to use his voice for a week. But on the third day Miles cussed out a club owner who insulted his intelligence. His voice was reduced to a permanent raspy whisper ever after. He once kayoed a promoter with a right hand and left hook.

"Miles might have been a champion," Sugar Ray Robinson said, "had he chosen the ring instead of the bandstand." Still, in the 50s and 60s he worked out regularly in gyms across the country—Johnny Coulon's on the Chicago Southside and Gleason's in New York were among his favorites. At 5'7", he weighed in at 143.

When sons Gregory and Miles IV were teenagers Miles built them a gym in the basement of the Russian church he had converted into a home on Manhattan's 77th St. "I tell them never to be excited by the inflection or the way a man says a thing, just listen to what he's saying. Weigh it, I say, and then do whatever you think the situation requires. My kids don't have no fear."

"You're too soft," he once told this writer. "You need to tell more people to kiss your ass. Understand? Promise you'll do that."

At 4 a.m., some months later, Miles called, "You telling people to kiss your ass?"

"Yeah."

"Well how did it feel?"

"Feels great, Miles."

"Well, I ain't proud of you. Think of all them motherfuckers you missed!" Click.

Miles' father, the late Dr. Miles Davis, Jr., was a wealthy gentleman farmer who lived out his life in predominantly German Millstedt, Ill., as a breeder of Norwegian hogs, a practicing dentist and one of the first African American graduates of the dental school at Northwestern

University. He was also an admirer of Marcus Garvey. When Miles III was growing up they lived in a racially integrated upper middle class neighborhood in East St. Louis, Ill.

"My father didn't take no shit off nobody," Miles wrote. "(He) went looking for a white man who had chased me and called me a nigger. He went looking for him with a loaded shotgun. He didn't find him, but I hate to think of what would have happened if he had."

"By genetics and breeding Miles is always going to be ahead of his time," Dr. Davis said, adding, "and he's a much better man than most of his critics.

"Historically, way back into slavery days, the Davis' have been musicians and performed classical works in the homes of the plantation owners. My father, Miles I, was born six years after Emancipation and forbade me to play music because the only place a Negro could play then was in barrelhouses.

"My father was the most efficient double-entry column bookkeeper in Arkansas before the coming of the adding machine and white men came to his home under cover of night for him to fix their books." But eventually they turned mean and drove him out of the state after he added another 500 more acres to his holdings.

Miles was unquestionably an intellectual. And if as an adult he cursed like a sailor he was no less blessed with a beautiful intelligence. He entered New York's Juilliard School of Music at 19. Two things he could not stand were middle class Black people putting on airs and the intellectual dishonesty of racist whites.

"I don't buy polish. With all the diction and shit you have got to be saying something to me. Polished Negroes are acting the way they think white people want them to act, so they can be accepted."

"When he was in high school," Dr. Davis said, "he played trumpet. In school competitions he was always the best, but the blue-eyed boys always won first and second prizes. Miles had always to settle for third. The officials, Miles and everybody else knew he should have had first prize. You can't treat a kid like that and tell him to come out and say the water wasn't dirty." Still Miles wrote: "I might have lost but I didn't feel bad because I knew I was a bad motherfucker and so did the white boy."

It was to Miles' home on 77th Street that I brought James Baldwin to meet him for the first time in 1966. The living room was designed so that from anywhere on the first floor Miles could have an unobstructed view of his wife Frances' legs. Miles was standing by the kitchen counter when Baldwin and I entered. But as I began to make an introduction their eyes met in a violent clash and locked on to each other from a distance of six feet. They engaged in the longest most intense staring match I have ever witnessed. Jimmy's bulging eyes blazed with a terrible fire. Miles' smouldered like two searing coals. Neither would blink. There seemed a crackling electricity between them. At last, Miles turned to me. "There's beer in the box." He went out the kitchen door. "My God!" Jimmy whispered, "he's shyer than I am." Jimmy and I sat and talked. Miles stayed out in the garden. With no goodbye, Baldwin and I left an hour later.

Here is what Miles wrote about that: "Who I do remember meeting around this time was James Baldwin, the writer. Marc Crawford—who knew him well—brought him by. I remember being in awe of him because he was so goddam heavy, all those great books he was writing, and so I didn't know what to say to him. Later, I found out that he felt the same way about me. But I really liked him right off the bat and he liked me a lot, too. We had great respect for one another. He was a very shy person and I was, too. I thought we looked like brothers. When I say both of us have a shyness I mean an artistic kind of a shyness, where you are wary of people taking up your time. I saw this in him, saw that he was aware of it. But here I was with James Baldwin, in my motherfucking house. I had read his books and loved and respected what he had to say. As I got to know Jimmy we opened up to each other and became great friends. Every time I went to southern France to play Antibes, I would always spend a day or two out at Jimmy's house in St. Paul de Vence. We would just sit in that great big beautiful house of his telling all kinds of stories, lying our asses off. Then we would go out to that wine garden he had and do the same thing. I really miss seeing him now when I go to southern France. He was a great man."

To this writer, Miles was not only an intellectual but a great teacher who could demystify things so they could be seen for what they actually were. He would play records by Stravinsky, Rachmaninoff, Ravel, and the old masters and make me see them as just dues-paying musicians of an earlier time not much different from the virtuosos of today. He would sometimes stop the record, raise the arm and set it back to replay the passage, saying: "Now, listen to what that motherfucker did here." His explanations were always plain to see. He introduced me to the recordings of the Italian pianist Arturo Benedetti Michelangeli with Ravel's Piano Concerto in G Minor. "Listen to those trills," Miles ordered. The sound was sustained as though made by an electrified instrument and Miles sat there, his first and second fingers aflutter, demonstrating how the effect was created, and smiling.

His lawyer back then and best friend was the late Harold Lovett. They were about the same size physically and Harold was equally sharp and gutsy.

"Miles," Harold said, "is just a brand new Negro in his thinking. He knows what he wants and is getting it. He has prepared himself for it. He can direct his group from off-stage with his presence. He can go into a dressing room and they know he's listening. He's as much a composer as he is a bandleader and he doesn't write anything down. His group rehearses on the date and musically it is as well organized as the Modern Jazz Quartet. It isn't luck with Miles, it's training."

In his later years, Miles took up painting, working as much as six or seven hours a day. His house in Malibu is filled with paintings. To the surprise of no one who knew him his paintings were well received. He wrote: "I had a couple (one man shows) in New York in 1987, and I had several all over the world in 1988. I had a few in Germany, one in Madrid, Spain, and a couple in Japan. And people are buying paintings of mine that are selling for as much as $15,000. This show in Madrid sold out and the ones in Japan and Germany almost sold out."

Miles, the painter, seemed to have a Midas touch but he fingered many different pies. As a performer, composer for record and films and bandleader, his music made millions.

"What's wrong with getting paid for what you do and getting paid well?" Miles, the autobiographer, demanded to know. "I never saw nothing in poverty or hard times and the blues. I never wanted that for myself. I saw what it really was when I was strung out on heroin, and I didn't want to see it again."

His heaviest investments back in the 50's, he confided, were in blue chip stocks, mostly public utilities. In late 1960 he told me: "I pay my sidemen the highest prices because they're worth it and I've got the best rhythm section (pianist Wynton Kelly, bassist Paul Chambers and drummer Jimmy Cobb) in jazz. I'm retired now because I don't do nothing unless I want to. I just glance at the stock markets every now and then, because people have to stop using gas and lights and cars have to stop running before I'm hurt." And often he'd phone up trombonist J.J. Johnson who lived in Manhattan's George Washington Bridge apartments. "Hey J.J.," he'd say, "look out the window and tell me if the lights are burning in Jersey."

But Miles, apparently, did not believe money made men. Men make money. He could drive as hard a bargain as any and if there was a dollar to be made he could smell it, a must for any true acquisitor. Still, neither his heart nor principles seemed negotiable. On the road, the late alto sax-ophonist Julian "Cannonball" Adderley collected Miles's money and paid off sidemen back then. "There was this time we played Birdland after a hard won concession that no big bands play opposite us," Cannonball said. "Well, anyway, Maynard Ferguson calls Miles from Philadelphia and tells him he's got to have work for this big band of his. Miles goes back into the Birdland office where's he's just argued for the no-big-band deal and tells the guy, 'Give Maynard the gig.'

"This Brooklyn club owner tells Miles he'll give him $3,000 a week to come in, which Miles is not too particular about doing anyway. He tells Miles that Horace Silver will be playing opposite him for $1,000. Well, Miles hit the ceiling. 'A thousand dollars!' he roared. 'The man can't work for that. Why don't you pay him what he's worth?' To make a long story short," Cannonball said, "the club owner wouldn't bend, so Miles took $2,500 and Horace got $1,500 instead of $1,000 for the engagement.

"But the time Miles really floored me was when this white hotel owner friend of mine in Florida wanted to put on the largest jazz festival ever held in the South. He was willing to pay top dollar and felt it would be the beginning of a yearly thing. He wanted Miles in the worst way and even offered to put up Negro Musicians and their families in his hotel. He asked me to point out to Miles that by our pioneering we would be helping to open doors to the future. I layed the proposition before Miles and he looked at me funny and said: 'Man, we'd be jive to do something like that. I ain't interested in opening doors. The man ought to open his own doors now—just because it's right. If I wasn't Miles Davis, if I was just another guy in the street and went in his place they'd throw me out by the neck.'"

Dexter Gordon nicknamed Miles "Sweetcakes" soon after he arrived in New York in 1944, because of the reed-thin 19-years-old's passion for malted milks, pies, cakes and jelly beans. Then he neither drank nor smoked. But Sweetcakes was a quick learner. For a year at Juilliard he studied European music by day and Charlie Parker, Dizzy Gillespie and Thelonious Monk by night up at Minton's in Harlem. Miles wrote: "I was learning more from hanging out, so I just got bored with school after a while. Plus, they were so fucking white oriented and so racist. Shit, I could learn more in one session at Minton's than it would take me two years to learn at Juilliard . . . after it was all over, all I was going to know was a bunch of white styles; nothing new."

Miles hit the jackpot in night studies both as a player and composer. He quit Juilliard in 1945 to replace Dizzy Gillespie in Charlie Parker's quintet and soon became Bird's arranger and musical director as well. It was a struggle at first and Miles asked to quit every night. But Bird encouraged him to stay and said he loved the way Sweetcakes played. "I was 19 years old and playing with the baddest alto saxophone player in the history of music," Miles wrote.

Soon after, a tall lanky Canadian named Gil Evans, who in future years would arrange "Birth of the Cool," "Miles Ahead," "Porgy and Bess" and "Sketches of Spain," came into Miles' life and stayed for a long time.

"I first met Gil when I was with Bird, and he was asking for a release of my tune 'Donna Lee,'" Miles told me nearly 15 years after. "He wanted to make an arrangement for a government electrical transcription of it. I told him he could have it and asked him to teach me some chords and let me study some of the scores he was doing for Claude Thornhill." Ironically, Gil, a one-time big bandleader and veteran arranger, never played an instrument professionally until he took up the piano in 1952.

"He really flipped me on the arrangement of 'Robin's Nest' he did for Claude. See," said Miles, placing his left hand on the table that suddenly in his mind's eye had become a piano, "Gil had this cluster of chords and superimposed another cluster over it." Miles covered the left hand with his right so that the fingers on the hands above fitted between those on the bottom. "Now the chord ends," Miles said, suddenly taking his right hand away, "and now these three notes of the remaining cluster are gone," he went on, removing the thumb, first and second fingers of the left hand. "The overtone of the remaining two produced a note way up there," Miles swore, pointing at the far end of the piano. "I was puzzled. I had studied the score for days trying to find the note. But it didn't exist, not on paper at least. That's Gil for you."

"Gil's not only a composer and a hell of an orchestrator, he just knows instruments and what you can get out of them. He and Duke Ellington are the same way. They can use four instruments when others need eight. People always want to categorize music—jazz, classical. Put labels on it. But Gil says all music comes from the people and the people are folk. Therefore, all music is folk. I used to write and send Gil my scores for evaluation. Gil used to say they were good, but cluttered up with too many notes. Sometimes when I'm playing, I start a phrase and never complete it because it isn't necessary. I have communicated the idea. Let's suppose somebody tells you something that bugs you and then asks your opinion about it. You just might say 'Aw!' and from the way you said it, they get the message that you don't dig it.

"... what the classical guys don't know is what Gil knows. They don't know folks. Gil is always listening to Gypsy, South American and African music. He's always got some new record for me."

Miles' continuing growth added to his international reputation achieved by playing with Bird. At 22, he had become a figure in his own right. "After I had been around the music scene for a while," Miles wrote: "I saw what happened to other great musicians, like Bird. One of the basic things I understood was that success in this industry depends upon how many records you sell, how much money you make for people who control the industry. You could be a great musician, an innovative and important artist, but nobody cared if you didn't make the white people who were in control some money. The real money was in getting to the mainstream of America, and Columbia Records served the mainstream of this country."

Bebop, Miles soon realized, was light years away from the mainstream, from Columbia and from all that money just waiting to be made. Besides, by 1948, Miles was listening to a different music in his head that could only come out of his horn, a slower music, less intense than Bird's. He had talked to Gil about experimenting with more subtle voicings. The nine piece band that Miles, Gil Evans and Gerry Mulligan put together rehearsed for nearly a year before recording for Capitol in 1949. A year later they recorded the landmark "Birth of the Cool." Miles provided his horn, leadership, theory, musical interpretation and selections. The sidemen were all white. Miles used Capitol Records to get Columbia's attention. But it would take six more years for his Prestige Records contract to expire.

"Bird and Diz played this hip, real fast thing, and if you weren't a fast listener, you couldn't catch the humor or the feeling in their music," Miles wrote. "Their sound wasn't sweet, and it didn't have harmonic lines that you could easily hum. . . . 'Birth of the Cool' was different because you could hear everything and hum it also.

"Birth of the Cool' came from Black musical roots. It came from Duke Ellington. We were trying to sound like Claude Thornhill, but he had gotten his shit from Duke Ellington and Fletcher Henderson. . . . White people back then liked music they could understand, that they could hear without straining. Bebop didn't come out of them and so it was hard for many of them to hear what was going on in music. It was an all-Black thing. But 'Birth' was not only hummable but it had white people playing the music and serving in prominent roles. The white critics like that. They liked the fact that they seemed to have something to do with what was going on. It was just like somebody shaking your hand just a little extra. We shook people's ears a little softer than Bird or Diz did, took the music more mainstream.

"That's all it was.

"As a musician and as an artist, I have always wanted to reach as many people as I could through music," Miles wrote. "And I have never been ashamed of that . . . I've always thought that music had no boundaries, no limits to where it could grow and go, no restrictions on its creativity. Good music is good no matter what kind of music it is. And I always hated categories. Always."

Back in the early '60's vibraphonist Milt Jackson remarked: "A great musician has an extracurricular 'something' the ordinary musician does not have. I don't know how to define it, but whatever it is Miles has it." Dizzy Gillespie said: "He just gets the right note he wants, the one nobody else would think to get." But for drummer Chico Hamilton: "Miles is not an entertainer, he's not even a trumpeter, Miles is a sound!—the whole earth singing."

Throughout his career, by the time others were feeding off his latest offerings, Miles was well on his way into something else: bebop, cool, hard-bop, modal jazz, funk until he went into seclusion in 1975.

Miles appreciated life's finer things, good restaurants and wine, Leontyne Price and the theater. He set fashion trends, drove Mercedes Benzes, Ferraris, and Masseratis, but he also felt comfortable with working class Black folks and could cook up a mean pot of pinto beans and neckbones.

"In Frisco," Cannonball told me, "this friend of mine invited Jimmy Cobb and I to dinner at his home. Miles happened up and the man said: 'Mr. Davis would you honor me by coming to dinner?' 'Hell no!' Miles shot back, 'what do I want to get to your house for dinner for? I can buy my own.' Yet, in Minneapolis, when another friend invited Jimmy Cobb and I to dinner he told Miles: 'Look, Inky, I'm having some barbecue over to my pad and if you want some you can come and if you don't you can go to hell!' Miles came. Next night he went back, uninvited, too."

"I don't even like to play to an audience that ain't got Negroes in it," Miles said when that word was in vogue. "I think the average American Negro should look like me. Black is beautiful—if it's on the right frame." Later, "Black is beautiful" became a widely repeated phrase.

Miles and Black working class people who knew of him had a mutual admiration society. Middle class Blacks adored his music but many drew a line through his conduct and language. Even though some saw Miles' musical adventures as a violation of tradition, he remained a folk hero to those who didn't give a thinker's damn about a C major 7th or an augmented 13th. He was Miles. Where other Black public figures temporized, adulterated and spoke euphemistically, Miles told it like it was in no uncertain terms, whether at dinner in the White House or a pig foot stand in Kansas City.

Miles was fascinated by the Civil Rights movement of the 1950's and 60's. Evening TV news filled the screen with heroic working class Black people, young and old protesting segregation, boycotting, sitting in, marching, being swept down mean southern streets at the end of high powered fire hoses, beaten bloody by racist police or attacked by their dogs. He watched them fight for freedom armed only with non-violent passive resistance. He knew he could never be non-violent and marveled at their dedication, discipline and sacrifice. When little 14-year-old Elizabeth Eckord faced a jeering white mob of 20,000 all alone in front of Little Rock High School, Miles wept. Sometimes I think it affected his frame of mind when he went to work and that I could hear it in his music. Miles, himself, had been bloodied by police in New York. He empathized with those more easily victimized. He had been more fortunate. His suit against the police attack had been successful.

Artistically, Black folks were the first to confirm him. He was incubated as a jazz trumpeter at age 17 in St. Louis' Rhumboogie Club.

"It was in the Black community, so the place would be packed with Black people who really were into music. This was where Eddie Randle played. His band was also billed as the Rhumboogie Orchestra. I auditioned with another trumpet player and got the job," Miles wrote. That audience nurtured him, stayed with him, let him feed off its energy, encouraged, patted their feet to his music, amen-ed him when he was right, shouted when it got better and waved both hands over head when he found the lost chord. Those audiences were human, alive and hot in the blood."

Who can say what Miles might have been without his earliest trumpet influence, Clark Terry. "Clark Terry was the one who really opened up the St. Louis jazz scene for me, taking me with him when he would go sit in," Miles wrote. "All through this period I loved Clark—still do to this day—and I think he felt the same way about me."

In the early 50's, when Miles was strung out on heroin in New York, Clark put him up in his own hotel room before leaving for an out of town gig. Miles promptly sold everything of Clark's that wasn't nailed down to feed the monkey on his back.

"I avoided anyplace I thought Clark was going to be," Miles wrote. "When we did finally run into each other, I apologized and we went on like nothing had ever happened. Now that's a good friend. A long time after that every time he caught me in a bar drinking with my change on the counter, he'd take it for payment on what I'd stolen. Man, that was some funny shit."

For two weeks in September Miles lay in a coma at St. John's Hospital in Santa Monica. Back east on Long Island, Clark, now 70, had undergone surgery for a cracked spine at Jewish Medical Center two days before Miles regained consciousness. Miles came out of it with his hearing intact, but was unable to speak. Clark's hands were full wrestling with his own pain, problems and the sickening side effects of medication. Doctors said he would not be able to play or make a living for five months and would have to wear a body cast. But even as they transfered him to Helen Hayes Hospital in Rockland County Clark seemed more concerned about Miles.

Telephoning was a chore. But each day Clark called California with messages of love, support and encouragement to be whispered in Miles' ear. Clark held on until assured his message had been delivered. "Miles smiled," they told him. Then Clark prayed.

What memories those messages from Clark must have triggered in Miles. Perhaps Miles wrote what he most remembered about him:

"One of the most important things that happened for me in high school—besides studying under Mr. Buchanan—was when one time the band went to play in Carbondale, Illinois, and I met Clark Terry, the trumpet player. He became my idol on the instrument . . . I had on my school band uniform and Clark had on this hip coat and this bad, beautiful scarf around his neck. He was wearing hip butcher boy shoes and a bad hat cocked ace-deuce. I told him I could tell he was a trumpet player by the hip shit he was wearing. He kind of smiled at me. . . . "

And later, ". . . him telling me I was bad and could really play at that time did a lot of good. I already had confidence, but Clark telling me this just gave me more . . . I learned a lot from listening to him play . . . we hung out all over the St. Louis area, sitting in and going to jam sessions, and when people heard Clark and I were going to be sitting in on a particular night, the place would fill up quick. . . . He introduced me to the flügelhorn . . . he used to borrow my flügelhorn . . . that's how he started playing . . . he's still playing it today and is one of the best in the world, if not the best.

"Every time I got a new horn back in those days, I would go looking for Clark to fix up my horn and get the valves to working, and he would fix it up like nobody else could. Man, Clark had a way of twisting and lightening the spring action of the pumps of a trumpet, just by adjusting the springs around that would make your horn sound altogether different. It made your horn sound like magic, man. Clark was a magician with that shit. I use to love for Clark to fix my valves."

There was a terrible hurt in Clark's eye when I entered his hospital room that Saturday afternoon last month. The impossible had happened. Miles was gone—his eyes closed for keeps. Clark resembled nothing so much as a helpless child who had tried so hard but, somehow, couldn't make things alright. If Miles could die. . . .

Old friend and tenor saxophonist Red Hollaway flew in from California and stood at his bedside holding Clark's hand in both of his. "You're not going to die, Clark. You're going to get well." He might have been talking to a child.

"There was always somebody trying to get me to say mean things about Miles," Clark said to no one at all. "But I wouldn't even know how to fix my mouth to do that."

In his last message to our people Dr. W.E.B. Dubois admonished that we must "never despair because the way is hard and time long." In his book Miles left us a message too. He wrote: "Some white people—and Black people, too—will laugh at you one minute and then turn around and say they love you the next. They do it all the time, try to divide and conquer people with shit like that. But I've got a long memory of what has happened to us in this country. The Jewish people keep reminding the world of what happened to them in Germany. So Black people have to keep reminding the world of what happened in the United States, or as James Baldwin once told me, 'These yet-to-be United States.' We've got to watch out for those divide-and-conquer techniques that whites have used on us all these years, keeping us apart from our real inner selves and our real inner strength. I know people get tired of hearing it but Black people have got to keep saying it, throwing our conditions up into these people's faces.

We've just got to keep it in front of their eyes and ears like the Jews have done. We've got to make them know and understand just how evil the things are that they did to us over all these years and are still doing to us today. We've just got to let them know that we know what they are doing and that we're not going to lighten up until they stop."

SILENCE, EXILE, CUNNING
GREG TATE

Greg Tate's obituary below is reprinted from the October 15, 1991, issue of the *Village Voice*. For the author, Miles Davis was the quintessential African American, "the model and the measure for how *black* your shit really is." In Tate's view, Davis's essence— the way he spoke, dressed, conducted his business, controlled the media, led his bands, and played his instrument—was a kind of roving "I'm black and I'm proud" placard. Miles Davis exuded "intelligence, elegance, creativity, and funk," says Tate. He was "an objectified projection of our blackest desires, a model for any black artist who wants to thoroughly interpenetrate Western domains of power and knowledge with Africanizing authority." He was a complex figure and unquestionably a hero to black Americans.

Unfortunately, Davis's heroism is beginning to fade from memory as an awareness of his darker side becomes more widely known. In his 1989 autobiography, published two years before his death, Davis shamelessly trotted out the details of his mistreatment of women, such as his brutalization of Cicely Tyson. Davis's shocking disclosures—uttered with the same kind of brashness that helped build his reputation in the first place—have probably alienated his admirers to a greater degree than his use of electric instruments did twenty years before the book's publication. "Miles may have swung like a champion," says Tate, but "he went out like a roach."

Pronouncing the death of Miles Davis seems more sillyass than sad. Something on the order of saying you've clocked the demise of the blues, the theory of relativity, *Ulysses,* or any other definitive creation of this century. Miles is one of those works of art, science, and magic whose absence might have ripped a chunk out of the zeitgeist big enough to sink a dwarf star into. A friend of mine once said that you could not love being black and not love Miles Davis because Miles was the quintessential African American. African American, not as in two halves thrown together, but a recombinate entity born of sperm and egg to produce a third creature more expansive than either.

Quincy Jones has opined, if someone asks what jazz is, play them *Kind of Blue.* For some of us coming from the African-centric tip, Miles Davis *is* the black aesthetic. He doesn't just represent it, he defines it. Music, poetry, philosophy, fashion, sports, architecture, design, painting, scholarship, politics, film, physics, feminity, even if not feminism—it don't matter, Miles is the model and the measure for how *black* your shit really is. Miles rendered black a synonym for the best of everything. To the aristocratic mind of this East St. Louis scion of a pig farmer/dentist, it naturally followed that if you were playing the baadest music on the face of the earth with the baadest musicians living, then of course you were driving the baadest cars, wearing the baadest vines, and intimate with the most regal of women and celebrated of artists, thinkers, and athletes. What black also meant to Miles was supreme intelligence, elegance, creativity, and funk. Miles worked black culture encyclopedically—from the outhouse to the penthouse and back again, to paraphrase brother Stanley Crouch. He rolled up on symphony orchestras with greasy blues phrases and dropped Stockhausen over dopebeats. Like Bessie Smith, he wasn't ashamed to show his ass in high society, as to take his Issey Miyake gear to the toilet stool. (I'm proud to say I nearly bore witness to that shit.)

Accepting Clyde Taylor's definition of black music as "our mother tongue," no artist in history territorialized as many of its multi-accentuated language groups as Miles. And the way he worked those linguistic systems demands we interact as critically with his music as we do with the texts of Baldwin, Baraka, Morrison, or the slave narratives. The music of Miles Davis is the music of a deep thinker on African American experience.

The reason black music occupies a privileged and authoritative position in black aesthetic discourse is because it seems to croon and cry out to us from a postliberated world of unrepressed black pleasure and self-determination. Black music, like black basketball, represents an actualization of those black ideologies that articulate themselves as antithetical to

Eurocentrism. Music and 'ball both do this in ways that are counterhege-
monic if not countersupremacist—rooting black achievement in ancient
black cultural practices. In the face of the attempt to erase the African contribution to world knowledge, and the diminution of black intelligence
that came with it, the very fact of black talents without precedent or peers
in the white community demolishes racist precepts instantaneously. In this
war of signifying and countersigning, Miles Davis was a warrior king and
we were all enthralled.

Paying tribute to the courtly airs of Jean Michel Basquiat, Diego
Cortez compared Basquiat's noblesse oblige to Miles's, pointing out how
important it was for black culture to have its own aristocrats. George
Benson has spoken of how Miles made being a black jazz musician feel
like the most exalted honorific one could achieve on this earth. In the business of reinvesting the devalued human stock of chattel slavery with a
sense of self-worth, Miles was among the most bullish CEOs in the history of the company. Primarily because he's a blues people's genius.

Obviously, the notion of *black genius* is an oxymoron designed to send
Eurocentrists screaming to the mat. Though considered an absurdity by
academe, the artistry of a Miles or a Holiday or a Hendrix obliterates that
prejudice with a vengeance. That Miles Davis ranks beside Picasso in the
modernist pantheon has long been the stuff of journalistic cliché. All
things being equal, Miles and Pablo will probably end up sharing a room
together in a hell of mirrors being flogged by furies for all the women they
dogged. That Miles looms as large as Warhol as far as postmodern
thinkers go is an insight for which we can thank Arthur Jafa. Like Warhol,
Miles came to use his visual presence and celebrity to manipulate the interpretation of his work and eventually made that stuff a part of the work as
well, particularly in the '80s, when his cordial stage demeanor attracted
more attention than his band or his horn playing.

Befitting his status as black aesthetic signifier in the flesh, Miles cannot merely be read as a fascinating subject. He's also for many of us an
objectified projection of our blackest desires, a model for any black artist
who wants to thoroughly interpenetrate Western domains of power and
knowledge with Africanizing authority. For those who approach him as a
generator of musical systems, metaphors, metaphysics, and gossip, Miles
was the premiere black romantic artist of this century. It's difficult to say
at what point the legend of Miles enveloped his work. The mythologizing
process began as early as the mid '50s. You can't interpet Miles's work if
you don't acknowledge his syncretism of life and music. This has less to
do with trying to read his music through his clothes or his sex life or his

choice of pharmaceuticals than with him being, as his biographer Quincy Troupe says, "an unreconstructed black man," a Stagolee figure who makes the modern world deal with him on his terms if it's going to deal with him at all. Few black men receiving their pay from major white corporations could get away with saying they'd like to spend the last minutes of their life choking a white man and suffer no repercussions for it. No one else in jazz could have chucked a following built over a lifetime to pursue the wild and wacky musical course Miles took from *In a Silent Way* onward.

The funny thing is that as disorienting as that period was for his old fans, Miles stepped into the era of black power politics and hippie rebellion like he'd had a hand in creating it all along. He never seemed like the old jazz hand who was trying to get hip to the Youth and Soul movements of the day. Homeboy came off like he was redefining cool for that generation too. As in the '50s and '60s, in the '70s he emerged as chief prophet of musicality for the next 20 years. Punk, hip-hop, house, new jack swing, worldbeat, ambient music, and dub are all presaged in the records Miles cut between 1969 and 1975. There's no other figure whose work can be said to have laid the cornerstone for the advances of Brian Eno, Parliament-Funkadelic, Prince, Public Image Ltd., Talking Heads, Public Enemy, Living Colour, Marshall Jefferson, and Wynton Marsalis. Miles? Yeah, they named that one right. Only thing more to the point might have been Moebius.

On the other hand, the reason Miles was always so fresh was because he was so rooted. When I met Miles for an interview in 1986 it immediately struck me that the person he most reminded me of was my late maternal grandmother. Like her, a barber who spent her last years cutting heads at an Air Force base, Miles not only seemed to be a country person thoroughly wise in the ways of cosmopolitans but the type of country person who seems to become even more country the longer they stay among so-called sophisticates. Not as a ploy, like you'd find in folktales, playing dumb in order to get over on city slickers, but more like recognizing countryness as a state of grace. I imagine this sense of transcendence comes from knowing you are of ancient, enduring, and obdurate stock and that the rest will soon fade.

Lester Bowie once countered Wynton Marsalis's line on the tradition by saying that the tradition in jazz *is* innovation. Perhaps the median between these poles is that you become an innovator by working your way deeper into the tradition rather than by working out of it, recognizing that there's gold in them haunted hills. If the trick is to advance the tradition without refusing, abusing, or deifying it, then Miles wrote the book of love there. You could reduce everything Miles ever played to an obsession with four elements: deep bass, open space, circular time, and blues falsettos. In a mystical or metaphorical sense you could read these constants as earth, air, water, and fire. No matter how avant his music might have seemed to the rear guard, Miles held to those constants. Miles is a nomad, and nomads are famous for being able to recreate their way of life anywhere. I think it was his clarity about where he came from that gave him his urgency to keep moving on, a fugitive for life.

Baraka says black musical tradition implores us to sing and fight. I disagree. I think we'd do that anyway, just out of human necessity. What I do think it teaches us is more Joycean in tenor: silence, exile, and cunning. Miles's music makes you think of Nat Turner, proud without being loud because it was about plotting insurrection. In this sense Miles never changed. His agenda remained the same from day one: stay ahead.

Writers only have their style to leave behind, said Nabokov. Miles says he was always looking for musicians who had a style, a voice I think he meant, of their own. In a music built on celebrating democracy and the individual, Miles developed a voice that was not only singular, but critical of all who picked up the instrument afterwards. After Miles, you couldn't just be a good trumpet player. You had to sacrifice your soul and maybe give some blood in the process. Others might have played trumpet from the heart; Miles played it like he was having open heart surgery. At the same time, every note thanked God for putting Louis Armstrong on the planet. Miles's tight-lipped sound conveyed the gaiety of Armstrong's wide vibrato while conjuring up the calculating pockets of dark sarcasm and meanness that at times ruled his spirit.

These qualities were nowhere more apparent than in his treatment of women, if we take him at his word for the gloating accounts of physical and psychological abuse in the as-told-to Troupe biography. Much as I love Miles, I despised him after reading about those incidents. Not because I worshiped the ground he spit on, but because I'd loathe any muhfukuh who violated women the way he did and relished having the opportunity to tell the world about it. Miles may have swung like a champion but on that score he went out like a roach.

Selected Bibliography

The following are recommended sources on Miles Davis. For a listing of pre-1991 readings on Miles Davis from various book and scholarly materials in numerous languages, see my book *Jazz Performers: An Annotated Bibliography of Biographical Materials* (pages 69–73).

Albertson, Chris. "The Unmasking of Miles Davis," *Saturday Review*, November 27, 1971.

Avakian, George. Liner notes to *'Round About Midnight*.

Balliett, Whitney. "Miles," *The New Yorker*, December 4, 1989.

Baraka, Amiri. "Miles Davis," pp. 24, 43–45, 48, 50, *New York Times Magazine*, June 16, 1985.

Belden, Bob. "Making History." Mosaic Records brochure #14, 1995.

——— and John Ephland. "Miles . . . 'What Was That Note?'" *Down Beat*, December 1995.

Blumenthal, Bob. Liner notes to *The Complete Live at the Plugged Nickel*.

Breskin, David. "Searching for Miles: Theme and Variations on the Life of a Trumpeter," *Rolling Stone*, September 29, 1983.

Brofsky, Howard. "Miles Davis and 'My Funny Valentine': The Evolution of a Solo," *Black Music Research Journal*, 1983.

Brookmeyer, Bob. "Review of LP *Miles Ahead*," *The Jazz Review*, November 1958.

Budds, Michael. *Jazz in the Sixties*. Iowa City: U. of Iowa, 1978, pp. 38–40, 45–48, 93–94.

Carr, Ian. *Miles Davis: A Biography*. London: Quartet, 1982.

Chambers, Jack. *Milestones I: The Music and Times of Miles Davis to 1960*. Toronto: University of Toronto, 1983.

———. *Milestones II: The Music and Times of Miles Davis since 1960*. Toronto: University of Toronto, 1985.

Charters, Samuel B. and Leonard Kunstadt. *Jazz: A History of the New York Scene*. New York: Doubleday, 1962, pp. 329–334.

Cleage, Pearl. *Deals with the Devil and Other Reasons to Riot*. New York: Ballantine, 1993, pp. 36–43.

Cole, Bill. *Miles Davis: A Musical Biography*. New York: Morrow, 1974.

Collier, Graham. *Jazz*. London: Cambridge U. Press, 1975, pp. 49–50, 52–59.

Coryell, Julie and Laura Friedman. *Jazz-Rock Fusion: The People, the Music*. New York: Delta, 1978, pp. 37–41.

Crawford, Marc. "Miles Davis: Evil Genius of Jazz," *Ebony*, January 16, 1961.

———. "Memories of Miles," *Daily Challenge*, October 21, 1991.

Crouch, Stanley, "Play the Right Thing," *The New Republic*, February 12, 1990.

———. "Miles in the Sky: The 60s," *Village Voice*, August 1986 jazz supplement.

Davis, Francis. *Bebop and Nothingness*. New York: Schirmer, 1996, pp. 71–83.

———. *Outcats*. New York: Oxford U. Press, 1990, pp. 89–93.

———. *In the Moment*. New York: Oxford U. Press, 1986, pp. 248–251.

Davis, Miles. "Self-Portrait," *Down Beat*, March 6, 1958.

——— and Quincy Troupe. *Miles: The Autobiography*. New York: Simon and Schuster, 1989.

Davis, Stephen. "Interview with Miles Davis," *The Real Paper*, March 21, 1973.

DeMichael, Don. "Miles Davis," *Rolling Stone*, December 11, 1969.

Dorham, Kenny. "Review of E.S.P.," *Down Beat*, December 12, 1965.

Evans, Bill. "Improvisation in Jazz": Liner notes to *Kind of Blue*.

Feather, Leonard. "Blindfold Test: Miles Davis," reprinted in Feather and Ira Gitler, *Encyclopedia of Jazz in the Seventies*, New York: Horizon, 1976.

————. *From Satchmo to Miles.* New York: Stein & Day, 1972, pp. 225–258.

————. "Miles Davis' Miraculous Recovery From Stroke," *Ebony,* December 1982.

Giddins, Gary. "The Danish Connection," *Village Voice,* November 14, 1989.

————. *Rhythm-a-Ning: Jazz Tradition and Innovation in the 80s.* New York: Oxford U. Press, 1985, pp. 78–85, 152–156.

————. "Chicago Fire," *Village Voice,* October 3, 1995.

————. "Miles to Go, Promises to Keep," *Village Voice,* October 15, 1991.

Gitler, Ira. *Jazz Masters of the Forties.* New York: Macmillan, 1966.

Gleason, Ralph J. "Miles Davis," *Rolling Stone,* December 13, 1969.

————. Liner notes to *Miles Davis in Europe.*

————. *Celebrating the Duke . . . and Other Heroes.* Boston: Little, Brown, 1975, pp. 131–147.

Goldberg, Joe. *Jazz Masters of the Fifties.* New York: Macmillan, 1965, pp. 62–86.

Golson, Benny. "Review of *Milestones,*" *The Jazz Review,* January 1959.

Goodman, George, Jr. "I Just Pick Up My Horn and Play," *The New York Times,* June 28, 1981.

Gordon, Max. *Live at the Village Vanguard.* New York: St. Martin's, 1980, pp. 98–102.

Green, Benny. *Drums in My Ear.* New York: Horizon, 1973, pp. 155–158.

Gridley, Mark C. *Jazz Styles: History and Analysis.* Englewood Cliffs, NJ: Prentice-Hall, 1988, pp. 205–225.

Haley, Alex. "Interview with Miles Davis." *Playboy,* September 1962.

Harris, Pat. "Nothing But Bop? 'Stupid,' Says Miles," *Down Beat,* January 27, 1950.

Harrison, Max. *A Jazz Retrospect.* Boston: Crescendo, 1976, pp. 161–166.

Hentoff, Nat. Liner notes to *Sketches of Spain.*

————. "Miles," *Down Beat,* November 2, 1955.

————. *The Jazz Life.* New York: Dial, 1961, pp. 205–213, 218–221.

————. "An Afternoon with Miles Davis," *The Jazz Review,* December 1958.

————. "Miles Davis," *International Musician,* February 1961.

Hodeir, Andre. *Jazz: Its Evolution and Essence.* New York: Grove Press, 1956, pp. 116–136.

————. Liner notes to *Miles Ahead.*

James, Michael. *Miles Davis.* London: Cassell, 1961.

Katz, Dick. "Miles Davis," reprinted in Martin Williams, ed., *Jazz Panorama,* New York: Collier, 1964.

Kernfeld, Barry. *Adderley, Coltrane and Davis at the Twilight of Bop: The Search for Melodic Coherence (1958–1959).* Ph.D. dissertation, 1981.

Korteweg, Simon. Liner notes to *The Complete Birth of the Cool.*

Litweiler, John. *The Freedom Principle: Jazz after 1958,* New York: Morrow, 1984, pp. 105–128.

Lohmann, Jan. *Miles Davis: The Discography.* Copenhagen: Jazz Media, ca. 1992.

————. Liner notes to *Miles Davis and Sonny Stitt Live in Stockholm 1960.*

McRae, Barry. *Miles Davis.* London: Apollo, 1988.

Meadows, Eddie. "The Miles Davis–Wayne Shorter Connection," *Jazzforschung,* 1988.

Mellers, Wilfrid. *Music in a New Found Land.* New York: Knopf, 1964, pp. 351–356.

Mingus, Charles. "An Open Letter," *Down Beat,* November 30, 1955.

Morgan, Alun and Raymond Horricks. *Modern Jazz.* London: Gollancz, 1956, pp. 94–108.

Morgenstern, Dan. "Miles in Motion," *Down Beat,* September 3, 1970.

————. Liner notes for *Miles Davis Chronicle: The Complete Prestige Recordings,* 1980.

Mulligan, Gerry. "Liner notes to The Complete Birth of the Cool," in Korteweg.

Nisenson, Eric. *'Round About Midnight: A Portrait of Miles Davis.* New York: Da Capo, 1996.

Owens, Thomas. *Bebop: The Music and Its Players.* New York: Oxford U. Press, 1995, pp. 113–127.

Pareles, Jon. "Miles Davis: The Alchemist and the Terrorist," *The New York Times,* October 6, 1991.

Porter, Lewis and Michael Ullman. *Jazz.* Englewood Cliffs, NJ: Prentice-Hall, 1993, pp. 281–299.

Ramsey, Doug. *Jazz Matters: Reflections on the Music and Some of Its Makers.* Fayetteville: U. of Arkansas, 1989, pp. 47–55.

Santoro, Gene. *Dancing in Your Head.* New York: Oxford U. Press, 1994, pp. 150–160, 163–172.

Saunders, Jimmy. "Interview with Miles Davis," *Playboy,* April 1975.

Schwendener, Peter. "Miles Davis: The Loss of Lyricism," *TriQuarterly,* Winter 1987.

Sidran, Ben. "Interview with Miles Davis," from *Talking Jazz,* San Francisco: Pomegrate, 1992, pp. 5–8.

Smith, Charles Edward. Liner notes to *Porgy and Bess.*

Tate, Greg. "The Electric Miles: Part I," *Down Beat,* July, 1983.

———. "The Electric Miles: Part II," *Down Beat,* August, 1983.

———. "Miles Behind," *Village Voice,* July 6, 1982.

———. "Silence, Exile, and Cunning," *Village Voice,* October 15, 1991.

Taylor, Arthur. *Notes and Tones.* New York: Perigee, 1982, pp. 11–18.

Tomlinson, Gary. "Cultural Dialogics and Jazz: A White Historian Signifies," *Black Music Research Journal,* Fall, 1991.

Vian, Boris. *'Round About Close to Midnight.* London: Quartet, 1988, pp. 76–77.

Williams, Martin. *The Jazz Tradition.* New York: Oxford U. Press, 1983, pp. 202–213.

Williams, Richard. *The Man in the Green Shirt.* Oxford: Bloomsbury, 1993.

Zwerin, Michael. "Miles Davis: A Most Curious Friendship," *Down Beat,* March 10, 1966.

Selected Discography

This is an alphabetical list of Miles Davis recordings that are cited by the various authors in this anthology. Such a list, by definition, cannot include every item in a musician's recorded oeuvre. Nevertheless, this discography does manage to cover much ground, and should prove useful to those who are attempting to build their own Davis collection. To use this listing as a buying guide, simply ask, or search the bins, for the appropriate titles. Most Davis recordings have remained in print since their original release and titles have stayed pretty much the same. American CD issue numbers have been included where known; note that "Columbia" and "Sony" are the same label, with Sony reissuing earlier Columbia releases.

To sort out discographical details, and for data on personnel, tune titles, recording dates, alternate takes, and the like, please consult the Schwann and Bielefelder record guides, as well as Jan Lohmann's *The Sound of Miles Davis,* the most complete Davis discography yet compiled.

Agharta (Columbia CZK 467897)
Amandla (Warner Brothers 225 873)
At Carnegie Hall (Columbia 40609)
At Philharmonic Hall (Sony SRCS 5722-3)
At the Paris International Jazz Festival (Sony SRCS 5659)
Aura (Columbia CK 45332)
Big Fun (Sony SRCS 57133-4)
Birth of the Cool (Capitol CDP 792862)
Bitches Brew (Columbia G2K 40577)
The Charlie Parker Memorial Volume 1 (Savoy SV-0101)
The Charlie Parker Memorial Volume 2 (Savoy SV-0103)
The Charlie Parker Story (Savoy SV-0105)

Chronicle: The Complete Prestige Recordings (Prestige 12)
The Complete Charlie Parker Dial Sessions (Stash STCD 567/68/69/70)
The Complete Live at the Plugged Nickel (Sony CXK 66955)
Decoy (Columbia CK 38991)
E.S.P. (Columbia CK 46863)
Filles de Kilimanjaro (Columbia CK 46116)
Four and More (Columbia C2K 48821)
Friday Night at the Blackhawk (Columbia CK 44257)
Get Up With It (Sony SRCS 57267)
In a Silent Way (Columbia CK 40580)
Kind of Blue (Columbia CK 40579)
L'Ascenseur pour L'Echafaud [Elevator to the Scaffold] (Philips 836305)
The Man With the Horn (Columbia CK 36790)
Miles Ahead (Columbia CK 53225)
Miles Davis at Fillmore (Sony SRCS 5717-8)
Miles Davis in Europe (CBS 462960 2)
Miles Davis in Person (Columbia CK 36649)
Miles Davis Volume 1 (Blue Note CDP 7815012)
Miles Davis Volume 2 (Blue Note CDP 78150122)
Miles in Berlin (Sony 80871)
Miles in the Sky (Columbia CK 48954)
Miles Smiles (Columbia CK 48859)
Milestones (Columbia CK 40837)
Music from Siesta (Warner Brothers 225 655)
My Funny Valentine (Columbia C2K 48821)
Nefertiti (Columbia CK 46113)
On the Corner (Columbia CK 53579)
Pangaea (Columbia C2K 46115)
Porgy and Bess (Columbia CK 40647)
Quiet Nights (Sony 36652)
'Round About Midnight (Columbia CK 40610)
Saturday Night at the Blackhawk (Columbia CK 44425)
Seven Steps to Heaven (Columbia CK 48827)
Sketches of Spain (Columbia CK 40578)
Sorcerer (Columbia CK 52974)
Star People (Columbia CK 80875)
A Tribute to Jack Johnson (Columbia CK 47036)
Tutu (Warner Brothers 225 490)
Water Babies (Columbia CK 80877)
You're Under Arrest (Columbia CK 40023)

Chronology

1926	Miles Dewey Davis III is born in Alton, Illinois, on May 26.
1929	Vernon Davis, Miles's brother, is born, probably in East St. Louis, Illinois.
1937	Davis begins his trumpet studies with Elwood Buchanan at the Crispus Attucks School in East St. Louis.
1938	Davis continues his studies with Elwood Buchanan at Lincoln Junior High School in East St. Louis.
1939	Davis receives a trumpet from his father on his thirteenth birthday.
1942	Tiny Bradshaw offers Davis a job with his touring band after his saxophonist, Sonny Stitt, hears Davis at the Rhumboogie Club with Eddie Randall's Blue Devils. Davis declines the offer because his mother wouldn't let him leave town until he finished high school.
1944	Davis's parents separate. Davis graduates from Lincoln High School in East St. Louis in January and gets his diploma in June. Davis allegedly records a private recording with a St. Louis R&B band that summer. In July, Davis plays third trumpet in the Billy Eckstine Band for a two-week gig at the Riviera Club in St. Louis. A pregnant Irene Birth moves in with Davis's family and Miles Davis's daughter, Cheryl, is born. Davis leaves East St. Louis for New York to study at the Juilliard School in September and find Charlie Parker. After searching for a month, he finds Parker at the Heatwave in Harlem.
1945	Davis makes his first commercial recording in April with tenor saxophonist Herbie Fields. Davis sits in with Coleman Hawkins at New York's Down Beat club, and with Eddie "Lockjaw" Davis and

Rudy Williams at the Spotlite. Davis joins Charlie Parker's group at the Three Deuces in the fall. In November, Davis records with Parker for Savoy, soloing on "Billie's Bounce" and "Now's the Time."

1946	Davis plays with Charles Mingus's group, and with Benny Carter's Orchestra (with J. J. Johnson) in Los Angeles. He records in March with Parker's group for Dial. In September, after Parker's breakdown, Davis joins Eckstine's band (with Stitt, Art Blakey, and Gene Ammons) and records with the band. Ammons first introduces Davis to heroin.
1947	Davis works with Eckstine's big band until it is dissolved in the spring. Davis freelances in Chicago, working at Jumptown with Stitt and Gene Ammons. Davis returns to New York and works the Spotlite with Illinois Jacquet. Davis rejoins Parker's group (with Max Roach). Parker's group records for Savoy and Dial. Davis records "Half Nelson" and "Milestones" on his first date as a leader in August for Savoy, with Parker on tenor sax and pianist John Lewis. Davis's son Gregory is born.
1948	Davis continues his work with Parker, recording again for Savoy. Davis leads his own group, with Parker, Alan Eager, and Kai Winding, at the Royal Roost. He wins the *Esquire* New Star Award. Davis brings his nonet to the Roost in September for two weeks opposite Count Basie.
1949	Davis's nonet records for Capitol in January and April. Davis coleads a quintet with Tadd Dameron (including James Moody and Kenny Clarke) at the Paris Jazz Festival in May. He becomes a heroin addict that summer. Davis plays Carnegie Hall with Bud Powell, Max Roach, and Serge Chaloff in December.
1950	Davis's nonet plays a week at the Clique Club and records for Capitol in March. Davis and Art Blakey are arrested at the Los Angeles airport and jailed for suspected drug use. Davis and Dexter Gordon work at Wolf's in Oakland. Davis works at Soldier Meyer's in Brooklyn and for a month at the Hi-Hat. He records with Sarah Vaughan in May and plays a jam session at Birdland with J. J. Johnson, Tadd Dameron, Fats Navarro, Charlie Parker, and Art Blakey. Davis works at the Onyx with Bud Powell and Wardell Gray. *Metronome*'s readers elect Davis to their magazine's All-Star Band. Davis separates from Irene Birth.
1951	Davis records his first dates as a leader (with Sonny Rollins) for Prestige in January.

1952	Davis plays Birdland in the spring and records for Blue Note with J. J. Johnson, Oscar Pettiford, and Kenny Clarke. Davis's father has his son jailed in East St. Louis for a few days hoping to induce him to quit heroin.
1953	On April 20 Davis records for Blue Note "Tempus Fugit" and "Kelo" with J. J. Johnson.
1954	In January or February Davis kicks his heroin habit in Detroit. He records five sessions for Prestige (including "Bag's Groove" and "Walkin'") and one for Blue Note. Davis first uses a stemless, Harmon mute.
1955	Red Garland joins Davis's band. Davis is jailed at Rikers Island for non-support of Irene. Davis records in June with Garland, John Coltrane, Paul Chambers, and Philly Joe Jones. His July performance with Thelonious Monk at the Newport Jazz Festival is acclaimed. Davis signs with Columbia Records and records for them on October 27. Birdland signs Davis to a twenty-week-a-year contract. His fall touring band includes Sonny Rollins. Davis's group plays on the "Tonight Show" (NBC-TV) on November 18 with Coltrane.
1956	Nodes are removed from Davis's vocal chords in February or March; his voice is permanently damaged following the operation, and is reduced to a husky whisper. Davis records his last dates for Prestige. In November, Davis freelances in France (with Lester Young), Germany, and Switzerland.
1957	Davis disbands his quintet in March and leaves for Europe. *Miles Ahead* is recorded in May, Davis's first recording on flügelhorn. *'Round Midnight* is released. Cannonball Adderley joins Davis's group in October. In December Davis records the soundtrack to Louis Malle's *L'Ascenseur pour L'Echafaud* in Paris and freelances in Holland and Germany.
1958	*Time* magazine does an article on Davis. Davis plays on Adderley's date for Blue Note. Coltrane rejoins Davis's group. Davis records *Milestones* and *Porgy and Bess*. Davis's sextet performs at the Newport Jazz Festival. Bill Evans and Jimmy Cobb replace Garland and Jones. On September 9 the sextet is recorded live at the Plaza Hotel.
1959	Davis records *Kind of Blue* with Evans and Wynton Kelly. In August Davis is assaulted by two New York City policemen in front of Birdland and arrested. Davis sues the City of New York for $1 million. Adderley and Evans leave the band, Wynton Kelly

	joins. In April Davis's group, augmented with a big band, play Gil Evans charts on CBS-TVs "Robert Herridge Theater."
1960	*Sketches of Spain* is released. In March and April Davis's group tours France, Sweden, Denmark, Germany, Switzerland, and Holland. Coltrane leaves the band and is replaced in February by Buddy Montgomery, later by Sonny Stitt. J. J. Johnson augments the group briefly. Davis buys a five-story former Russian Orthodox church at 312 West 77th Street in Manhattan. Davis's father gets hit by a train at an unguarded crossing in St. Louis. In September Davis's group tours England, France, and Sweden. Hank Mobley replaces Stitt. Davis marries dancer Frances Taylor on December 21.
1961	In March Davis records *Someday My Prince Will Come* with Coltrane and Mobley. In April Davis's band is recorded live at the Blackhawk in San Francisco. Davis learns he has sickle-cell anemia. On May 19 Davis's group, expanded to an orchestra, plays Gil Evans charts at Carnegie Hall. Mobley leaves the band and is replaced by Rocky Boyd.
1962	Davis's father is buried in May. In August Davis records a Christmas album with Wayne Shorter and Bob Dorough. An interview with Alex Haley is published in *Playboy* in September. J. J. Johnson and Sonny Rollins work sporadically with Davis. Jimmy Heath joins Davis in December. Kelly and Chambers quit.
1963	Ron Carter, George Coleman, Frank Strozier, and Harold Mabern join Davis's group. For an April session in Los Angeles, Victor Feldman and Frank Butler join the group and record "Seven Steps to Heaven." Mabern and Cobb leave. Herbie Hancock and Tony Williams join Davis's group in New York. Davis tours France in July.
1964	On February 12 Davis's group is recorded at New York's Philharmonic (Avery Fisher) Hall. On February 28 Davis's mother dies in St. Louis. Coleman is replaced first by Sam Rivers for a July tour of Japan, then by Wayne Shorter. Davis's group plays the "Tonight Show" in September, then tours Germany (records in Berlin), France, Sweden, Denmark, and Italy.
1965	*E.S.P.* is recorded. Miles and Frances separate. Davis undergoes hip surgery in April and August. Davis's quintet, with Wayne Shorter, Herbie Hancock, Ron Carter, and Tony Williams, are recorded at Chicago's Plugged Nickel on December 22–23.
1966	From January to March Davis is ill with a liver infection. Davis group later plays Newport. Marc Crawford introduces Davis to James Baldwin. *Miles Smiles* is recorded in November.

1967	Joe Henderson joins Davis's band in January 1967, expanding the group (already with Wayne Shorter) to a sextet. Henderson plays gigs at the Village Vanguard and then does a 15-city tour through March. *Sorcerer* and *Nefertiti* are recorded. Davis's group plays Newport and tours Belgium, England (taped by BBC-TV), Holland (taped by AVRO-TV), Sweden (taped by Swedish Radio-TV), Denmark, Germany (taped by SWF-TV), and France. Hancock records on electric piano for the first time with Davis.
1968	George Benson records with Davis in January and Miles Davis is interviewed by Arthur Taylor on January 22. In February Miles and Frances divorce. Chick Corea and Dave Holland replace Hancock and Carter. *Filles de Kilimanjaro* is recorded. Davis plays Gil Evans arrangements for the play *Time of the Barracuda* at the Berkeley Jazz Festival. On September 30 Davis marries Betty Mabry in Gary, Indiana.
1969	*In a Silent Way* is released. Jack DeJohnette replaces Williams, Herbie Hancock rejoins, and Joe Zawinul and John McLaughlin join the band. Davis plays the Fillmore East. In July Davis's group tours France (taped on ORTF-TV). *Bitches Brew* is recorded in August with Benny Maupin and Larry Young, and released later in the year. In October Davis is shot in the legs while sitting in his Ferrari. In late October and November Davis's group tours Italy, Austria (taped by Austrian TV), England (taped by BBC-TV at Ronnie Scott's), France (taped by ORTF-TV), Denmark, Sweden, Germany, and Holland.
1970	Steven Grossman replaces Shorter, and Airto Moreira and Keith Jarrett join the group. Davis divorces Betty Mabry. Davis plays on the Grammy Awards telecast. Davis plays the Fillmore East in March and June, the Fillmore West in April and October, the "Dick Cavett Show" in July, the Isle of Wight (England) in August, and the "Tonight Show" in October. Michael Henderson and Gary Bartz replace Holland and Grossman. Chick Corea leaves the group.
1971	Mtume joins Davis's group. *Tribute to Jack Johnson* is recorded in March. ABC-TV films Davis's group at Avery Fisher Hall on March 16. Davis is interviewed by *Newsweek* magazine. Davis has gallstone surgery and breaks up with Marguerite Eskridge. In October and November Davis's group tours Italy (taped by RAI-TV), Switzerland, France (taped by ORTF-TV), Belgium (taped by BRT-TV), Holland, Yugoslavia (taped by national TV), Austria, Germany, Sweden, Denmark, Norway (taped by NRK-TV), England,

and Portugal. Leonard Feather interviews Davis in the fall.

1972   David Liebman, Reggie Lucas, Pete Cosey, Badal Roy, and Al Foster join Davis's band. *On the Corner* is recorded in June. In July Davis is arrested after arguing with his tenant. In October Davis falls asleep at the wheel on the West Side Highway in New York City, crashes his Lamborghini into a divider and breaks both ankles. Davis's girlfriend, Jackie Battle, leaves him.

1973   Davis is arrested on February 23 in front of his New York apartment for possession of cocaine and a loaded pistol. Stephen Davis interviews Miles Davis. On May 5, ABC-TV tapes Davis's group in Santa Monica, California. In June Davis's group tours Japan (taped in Tokyo by NHK-TV); in July Switzerland (taped by Channel West Schweitz TV), England, France, and Italy; in October and November Sweden (taped by SR-TV), Denmark, Germany (taped by RB-TV), Austria, Italy, Spain, France, and England.

1974   Davis performs in Toronto in January. Davis's group is recorded at Carnegie Hall in June and tours Brazil in May. Davis has nodes removed from his larynx and is treated for a bleeding ulcer. Sonny Fortune replaces Liebman in the summer. Bill Cole's book *Miles Davis: A Musical Biography* is published.

1975   Davis's group tours Japan in January and February, where they record *Agharta* and *Pangaea*. Sam Morrison replaces Fortune in May. Davis again undergoes hip surgery and, after a long hospital stay, decides to stop performing.

1978   Davis tapes several sessions at Larry Coryell's Connecticut home with the guitarist and Davis on piano. Marguerite Eskridge has Davis jailed for non-support of their son Erin.

1980   *Miles Davis Chronicle: The Complete Prestige Recordings* is released. Late in the year Davis begins to play the trumpet again. He plays privately with his nephew, Vincent Wilburn, in Wilburn's punk rock band. Davis learns he has diabetes.

1981   Miles records his "comeback" album, *The Man With the Horn*. Davis's band plays the Kool Jazz Festival. Davis's group (with Mike Stern, Al Foster, and saxophonist Bill Evans) tours Japan. Davis's group performs on "Saturday Night Live" (NBC-TV). On Thanksgiving Day Davis and actress Cicely Tyson marry at Bill Cosby's Massachusetts home. In December Davis's group plays in Toronto.

1982   Davis suffers a stroke in February. In April and May his group tours Sweden, Denmark (taped by DR-TV), Germany, England (taped by Channel 4 TV), Italy (taped by RAI-TV), Holland, France, and Belgium. Eric Nisenson's 'Round About Midnight: A Portrait of Miles Davis is published. On July 11 Davis's group performs at the Montreal Jazz Festival, and on July 28 in Vancouver. John Scofield replaces Stern in November. Ian Carr's Miles Davis: A Biography is published.

1983   Star People is released. In February Davis's group plays in Toronto and Ottawa. On February 23 his band appears on the NBC-TV Grammy Awards telecast. We Want Miles is awarded a Grammy. In March-May his group tours France, Italy, Belgium, England, and Japan. Darryl Jones joins the band. In July he performs at the Montreal Festival and in Toronto. Branford Marsalis records with Davis. In October he tours Poland (taped by national TV), Spain, Germany (taped by SFB-TV), and France. Jack Chambers's Milestones I: The Music and Times of Miles Davis to 1960 is published. In November Fisk University awards Davis an honorary doctorate. Davis has another hip operation, then contracts pneumonia and can't perform for six months.

1984   Bob Berg joins Davis's band. In June Bryant Gumbel interviews Davis on the "Today Show" (NBC-TV). Decoy wins a Grammy Award for best jazz album. In June and July Davis's band tours France, Italy (taped by RAI-TV), Austria, Switzerland (taped by Channel West TV), Germany, Finland (taped by national TV), Holland, England, Italy, and Norway (taped by NRK-TV). Davis receives the Sonning prize from the Danish government. In November he plays in France and Spain. In December Davis appears on the Baltimore talk show "City Line," then takes his band to Denmark, where he rehearses Palle Mikkelborg's Aura and is interviewed by Leonard Malone on Danish television.

1985   In January and February Davis records Aura in Copenhagen. Davis and Mikkelborg are interviewed on DR-TV. On April 26 Davis's band is filmed in New Orleans for the Mark Obenhaus documentary Miles Ahead. On June 19 the Davis band plays in Toronto; on June 21 Davis opens the Kool Jazz Festival; on June 28 the Montreal Jazz Festival (taped by Bravo-TV). In July and August Davis tours Austria, Italy (taped by RAI-TV), Spain, Holland, Switzerland, France, England, Norway, and Japan. In August Mike Stern replaces John Scofield. In September Davis acts on the television show "Miami Vice." In October Davis's group tours France, Sweden, Denmark, Belgium, Germany (taped by NDR-TV), Switzerland, Austria, and Italy. Jack Chambers's *Milestones II: The Music and Times of Miles Davis since 1960* is published.

1986   Davis is interviewed by Ben Sidran on January 30. In April Robben Ford replaces Stern. Davis receives an honorary doctorate from the New England Conservatory. In June Davis's group plays Giant Stadium in East Rutherford, New Jersey, and Great Woods Center in Mansfield, Massachusetts (both taped for TV), then Vancouver. In July Davis tours Italy, Holland, France, Switzerland (taped by DRS-TV), and Spain (taped by TVE-TV). His band tours Brazil in September, then Germany (interviewed by NDR-TV), and France (the band is taped by Europe 1 and Davis is interviewed for television by Mike Zwerin). Davis's band performs on "The Dick Cavett Show" (ABC-TV) and Davis is also interviewed (broadcasted on October 7). In October and November the group tours France, Germany, Belgium, Yugoslavia (taped by national TV), Austria, France, Spain, and England (interviewed for TV on November 17). Davis and pop star Prince record.

1987   On the occasion of Ray Charles receiving a Lifetime Achievement Award at the Kennedy Center in Washington, Miles Davis and Cicely Tyson have dinner with President and Mrs. Reagan and Secretary of State George Shultz. *Tutu* wins a Grammy Award. Davis fires his nephew, Vincent Wilburn, from his band and replaces him with Ricky Wellman. In June and July Davis's group with Kenny Garrett tours Israel, Austria, Canada, Denmark, England, France, Italy (taped by RAI-TV), Germany (taped by SAT-TV), Sweden, Finland, Holland, and Japan. In September sixteen of Davis's paintings are exhibited. Davis tours Canada, Belgium, Germany, Norway (interviewed by NRK-TV), Sweden, Denmark, Holland, Spain, and France in October and November. Davis appears on the "David Letterman Show" (NBC-TV) on December 11 and records with Prince on New Year's Eve.

1988   Quincy Troupe begins interviewing Davis for *Miles: The Autobiography*. Davis's band tours France and Italy in February. Davis fires Darryl Jones. Gil Evans dies on March 20. *Siesta* is released. Davis's band is taped for television at the San Francisco Opera House on April 19. In late April and May, Davis tours Australia and New Zealand, and is taped for television in Hawaii. On June 8 Davis receives the New York State Governor's

Arts Award. In July and August Davis's group plays the Montreal Jazz Festival, then tours France, Switzerland, Holland (taped for TV), Germany (taped by SDR-TV), Spain, France, Turkey, and Japan. In July an exhibition of his paintings opens in Munich. In October his band tours Denmark, Norway, Belgium, Poland (taped by RB-TV), Austria, Germany, and Spain. On November 13, Davis is inducted into the Knights of Malta at the Alhambra in Granada, Spain. *Amandla* is recorded.

1989   In April Davis's group tours Italy (taped by RAI-TV) and France. On July 14, Davis's group appears on the "Arsenio Hall Show" (Fox TV) in Los Angeles and Davis is also interviewed. Kenny Garrett is replaced by Rick Margitza for a July tour of France, Andorra (taped by national TV), England, Holland, Germany, and Switzerland. In August Davis's group plays in Hawaii (taped for TV), and Garrett replaces Margitza. In October Davis is interviewed by NBC-TV for the show "Night Music" (his band plays two tunes). In late October and November Davis tours Germany, Spain, France, and Austria. Davis's autobiography is published. Davis and Cicely Tyson divorce.

1990   Davis tours Canada in February, then appears on the Grammy Award telecast in Los Angeles. In July Davis's band tours England, Holland, Germany (taped by NDR-TV), France, and Switzerland. In October Davis's band tours Germany (taped by PR-TV), France, and Holland.

1991   In March and June Davis's group performs in Germany. On July 1 Davis's band performs in Austria. On July 8 in Montreux, Davis performs Gil Evans charts with Gil Evans's and George Gruntz's big bands combined, conducted by Quincy Jones. In Paris on July 10 Davis records for Warner Brothers with various all-star small groups including Steve Grossman, Wayne Shorter, Chick Corea, Joe Zawinul, Jackie McLean, John McLaughlin, Herbie Hancock, Al Foster, and Dave Holland. Davis's tour concludes in Holland and England. On July 18 the French government makes Davis a Chevalier in the Legion of Honor. Davis dies at St. John's Hospital and Health Center in Santa Monica, California on September 28. He is buried in Woodlawn Cemetery in New York City opposite Duke Ellington.

Permissions

Arthur Taylor, interview with Miles Davis, *Notes and Tones*, Perigee, 1982. Reprinted by arrangement with the Berkley Publishing Group. Copyright © 1982 by Arthur Taylor.

Richard Williams, "The Conception of the Cool," from *Miles Davis: The Man in the Green Shirt*, Bloomsbury, 1993. Copyright © 1993 by Richard Williams. Reprinted by permission of Bloomsbury Publishing plc (London) and Henry Holt and Co., Inc.

Contributors' Notes

Amiri Baraka (LeRoi Jones) is a poet, playright, and essayist, and teaches African Studies at the State University of New York at Stony Brook. He is the author of *Dutchman, Blues People, Black Music, Eulogies, Black People & Jesse Jackson: Essays 1972–1988,* and many books of poetry, among them *Wise/Why's/Y's* and *Transbluesency: Selected Poems.*

Valve trombonist and arranger *Bob Brookmeyer* has performed with Clark Terry, Bill Evans, Stan Getz, Gerry Mulligan, and the Thad Jones–Mel Lewis Orchestra. His first recording as a leader was recorded in 1958. His arrangements include "ABC Blues," "Willow Weep for Me," "Samba Con Getchu," "Skylark," "First Love Song," "El Co," and "American Express."

Elwood Buchanan is a retired trumpet instructor. He taught Miles Davis trumpet at the Crispus Attucks School, Lincoln Junior High School, and Lincoln High School in East St. Louis, Illinois from 1937–1944. Previously, he was a member of Andy Kirk's band.

Pearl Cleage is an Atlanta-based writer whose plays include *Flyin' West* and *Blues for an Alabama Sky.* She is the author of a book of essays, *Deals with the Devil and Other Reasons to Riot,* and the novel *Tunnels of Love.*

Marc Crawford was the U.S. jazz correspondent for *Swing Journal* and taught writing at New York University. He was Theatrical Editor of *Jet* magazine and in 1984 established the off-campus jazz appreciation course for the General Studies Program at NYU as a forum for name jazz musicians. Crawford died in 1996.

Stanley Crouch is a poet, novelist, and cultural critic. He is a columnist for *The New York Daily News* and a Contributing Editor to *The New Republic.* A MacArthur Award recipient, he is the author of *Notes of a Hanging Judge* and *The All-American Skin Game, or The Decoy of Race.*

Francis Davis is a contributing editor of the *Atlantic Monthly* and teaches jazz history at the University of Pennsylvania. He is the author of *In the Moment, Outcats, The History of the Blues,* and *Bebop and Nothingness.*

Stephen Davis is a novelist and biographer whose books include *Bob Marley, Hammer of the Gods,* and *Jajouka Rolling Stone.*

Leonard Feather was a freelance writer and columnist for the *Los Angeles Times.* The author of *Inside Bebop, The Encyclopedia of Jazz, From Satchmo to Miles, The Passion for Jazz,* and *The Jazz Years,* among other works, Feather died in 1994.

Jazz critic and filmmaker *Gary Giddins* is a columnist for *The Village Voice.* A Smithsonian and Guggenheim Fellow, he is the author of *Riding on a Blue Note, Rhythm-a-ning, Faces in the Crowd, Celebrating Bird,* and *Satchmo,* the last two of which derived from documentary films of the same name.

Writer *Ralph J. Gleason* founded the periodicals *Jazz Information* (1939) and *Jazz: A Quarterly of American Music* (1958), was a founding editor of *Rolling Stone* (1967), and established (with Jimmy Lyons) the Monterey Jazz Festival (1958). He was a columnist for the *San Francisco Chronicle* from 1950 until his death in 1975. Gleason hosted the television program "Jazz Casual" and was the author of *Jam Session* and *Celebrating the Duke.*

Saxophonist and arranger *Benny Golson* has played with Tadd Dameron, Dizzy Gillespie, Art Blakey, and Art Farmer. He recorded his first date as a leader in 1958. Since the late 1960s he has worked as a freelance arranger, often for film and television. His compositions include "I Remember Clifford," "Stablemates," "Whisper Not," "Along Came Betty," "Blues March," and "Are You Real?"

Max Gordon was the owner of the Village Vanguard for 54 years until his death in 1989. He also operated the Blue Angel, another New York City nightclub. His autobiography, *Live From the Village Vanguard,* was published in 1980.

Benny Green is a London-based writer and tenor saxophonist. His books include *The Reluctant Art* and *Drums in My Ear.*

Nat Hentoff is a columnist for the *Village Voice, Wall Street Journal,* and *Washington Post.* A former editor of the *Jazz Review,* he is the author of *Jazz Is, The Jazz Life, The Jazz Makers, Boston Boy, Hear Me Talkin' to Ya,* and *Listen to the Stories,* among other works.

Dan Morgenstern has been the Director of the Institute of Jazz Studies at Rutgers University (Newark) since 1976. A former editor of *Down Beat* and other jazz magazines, he is the author of *Jazz People* and has won six Grammy Awards for his album annotations.

Eric Nisenson is a freelance writer who has written about jazz since the early 1970s. He is a regular contributor to *Jazziz* and *Lip Service* and the author of *'Round About Midnight: A Portrait of Miles Davis* and *Ascension: John Coltrane and His Quest.*

Ben Sidran is a pianist, radio announcer, and record producer. He was the host of VH-1 TV's "New Vision Series" and National Public Radio's "Jazz Alive" and "Sidran on Record." He has produced recordings by Jon Hendricks, Mose Allison, and Diana Ross and has made over fifteen recordings as a leader. He is the author of *Black Talk* and *Talking Jazz.*

Greg Tate has written about jazz since the early 1980s. He is a staff writer for the *Village Voice* and has contributed articles to *Down Beat, Vibe,* and other publications.

Drummer *Arthur Taylor* performed with Coleman Hawkins, Howard McGhee, Buddy DeFranco, Bud Powell, Miles Davis, Donald Byrd and Pepper Adams, Thelonious Monk, and John Coltrane. Starting in 1968 Taylor began taping jazz interviews, 27 of which were collected in his book, *Notes and Tones.* In 1984 he hosted a live radio interview program for WKCR in New York. Taylor died in 1995.

Richard Williams is a London-based journalist who has written about music since 1969. He has contributed to *The Times* and *Independent* and is the author of *Dylan: A Man Called Alias.*

Index

McQuillen, Bobby, 169
McShann, Jay, 194
"Mademoiselle Mabry," 34
"Maids of Cadiz," 75
"Man I Love, The," 27
Man with the Horn, The, 44, 171, 205
Mann, Herbie, 65, 71
Manne, Shelly, 60
"Marmaduke," 24–25
Marsalis, Wynton, 30, 32, 192, 235
Marsh, Warne, 33, 102
Mazur, Marilyn, 199
"Meaning of the Blues, The," 75
Melody Maker (magazine), 134
Messiaen, Olivier, 199
Metcalfe, Louis, 4
Metronome (magazine), 5, 11
Michelangeli, Arturo Benedetti, 222–23
Migiani, Armand, 88
Mikkelborg, Palle, 198, 199–202, 206
Miles, Buddy, 138, 139, 153
Miles: The Autobiography, 35–39, 199,
        204, 207–209, 212, 218
"Miles Ahead," 75
Miles Ahead (album), 31, 48, 59, 74–76,
        114, 127, 133, 225
Miles Davis at Carnegie Hall, 127
Miles Davis at Fillmore, 130
*Miles Davis Chronicle: The Complete
        Prestige Recordings,* 3
Miles Davis in Concert, 151
Miles Davis in Person, 98, 99, 100
Miles in the Sky, 106, 130, 198, 200
"Milestones," 24, 78, 204
Milestones (album), 30–31, 36, 38–39,
        43, 47, 77–78
Miller, Marcus, 198, 200, 206
Mingus, Charles, 9, 30–31, 34, 101
    works of, 32, 58, 62, 63
"Mingus Fingers," 58, 63
Minton's (New York club), 37
Mobley, Hank, 42, 100, 171
Modern Jazz Quartet, 32, 53, 61, 81,
        86, 89–90, 223
Monk, Thelonious, 32, 36, 45, 67, 71,
        101, 173, 194
    influence on Davis, 7, 25, 92, 100, 224
    performances with Davis, 58
    recordings of, 27, 29, 31, 86, 91–92

and refusal to play Sunday matinees,
        94–95
    works of, 78, 92
Montgomery, Buddy, 248
Moody, James, 12, 32
"Moondreams," 57
More Than You Know
        (Mikkelborg/Gordon), 201
Moreira, Airto, 16, 112, 116
Morgan, Lee, 19, 30
Morrison, Sam, 166
Morton, Jelly Roll, 99
Motown, 33, 34, 139, 157
"Move," 11, 46, 52, 56
Movies, 108–109
Mtume. *See* Foreman, James Mtume
Mulligan, Gerry, 10, 11, 13, 52
    in Davis's nonet, 11, 45, 53, 55–56,
        60, 72, 119, 126, 226
    viewed by Davis, 62
Murphy, Eddie, 35, 39
"My Funny Valentine," 87, 91
My Funny Valentine (album), 32, 33, 98,
        99, 101
"My Man's Gone Now," 171
"My Old Flame," 24
"My Shop," 75

Nance, Ray, 19, 24, 159
"Nardis," 197
Navarro, Fats, 23, 24, 37, 192
Nefertiti, 33
"Neo," 100
"New Rhumba," 75
New York Dolls, 162
New York Times, The, 41
Newport Jazz Festival, 14, 58, 59, 70,
        128, 164
Newton, Francis, 65–66, 68
Newton, Huey, 35
Newton, James, 24
Nisenson, Eric, 172–84, 207
North, Alex, 58, 62
"Now's the Time," 8, 78, 86, 89

"Old Devil Moon," 26
Oliver, Jimmy, 90
On the Corner, 150–51, 152, 157, 160
Orchestra at Town Hall (Monk), 31